THE KILLING OF THE
COUNTRYSIDE

Graham Harvey

THE KILLING OF THE COUNTRYSIDE

VINTAGE

Published by Vintage 1998

2 4 6 8 10 9 7 5 3 1

First published in Great Britain by
Jonathan Cape 1997

Vintage
Random House, 20 Vauxhall Bridge Road,
London SW1V 2SA

Random House Australia (Pty) Limited
20 Alfred Street, Milsons Point, Sydney
New South Wales 2061, Australia

Random House New Zealand Limited
18 Poland Road, Glenfield,
Auckland 10, New Zealand

Random House South Africa (Pty) Limited
Endulini, 5A Jubilee Road, Parktown 2193,
South Africa

Random House UK Limited Reg. No. 954009

A CIP catalogue record for this book
is available from the British Library

ISBN 0 09 973661 6

Papers used by Random House UK Ltd are natural,
recyclable products made from wood grown in sustainable forests. The manufacturing processes conform to the
environmental regulations of the country of origin

Printed and bound in Great Britain by
Cox & Wyman, Reading, Berkshire

*For Peter and Rhonda Harvey
to whom such things mattered*

Far spread the moory ground, a level scene
Bespread with rush and one eternal green,
That never felt the rage of blundering plough,
Though centuries wreathed spring blossoms on its brow.
Autumn met plains that stretched them far away
In unchecked shadows of green, brown, and grey.
Unbounded freedom ruled the wandering scene;
No fence of ownership crept in between
To hide the prospect from the gazing eye;
Its only bondage was the circling sky.

John Clare, 'Enclosure'

CONTENTS

PREFACE

A few miles west of Cambridge, where the Bourn Brook meanders toward the River Cam, something very curious is happening to the countryside. Wildflowers have begun to appear in the wet meadowland which now lines, the stream banks – ox eye daisy, lady's bedstraw and birdsfoot trefoil. Nearby a grass field blazes with the flowers of meadowland, while a wheat crop is speckled with cornflower, corn cockle and the rare shepherd's needle.

The contrast with surrounding countryside could scarcely be greater. As in much of lowland Britain the farming landscape of Cambridgeshire is dominated by featureless blocks of chemically-manicured crops stretching away to the far horizon. They are neat, ordered and practically devoid of wildlife interest. Here beside the Bourn Brook the wild flowers are returning, and with them many of the indigenous birds and animals that once made up our glorious wildlife heritage.

Clouds of butterflies drift on summer breezes. Reed buntings, yellow wagtails and grasshopper warblers dart amongst the willows. Otters haunt the stream and banksides. While this small corner of England continues to be farmed, the wild species that have gone from so much of our countryside are, here at least, beginning to come back.

The renascence is the accomplishment of a group called the Countryside Restoration Trust. Founded in the early 1990s by writer and broadcaster Robin Page and artist Gordon Beningfield it set out to prove that profitable farming did not have to be destructive of the natural world. Carried out sensitively it might actually enrich our countryside, as indeed it had for many hundreds of years. Sadly this is a message that those who shape European farm policy refuse to hear.

When *The Killing of the Countryside* was first published in March 1997 it provoked howls of outrage from the agricultural establishment. The author must have been walking around with his eyes shut. Let him take a look at the countryside. Who but a charlatan could deny that it looked as beautiful as ever? So went the accusation. Yet behind the show of public indignation lay a fundamental deceipt.

Robin Page tells of taking a group of elderley people to see his restored Cambridgeshire hay meadow. The experience proved too much for one woman. As she gazed upon the meadow flowers that had been such a familiar part of her childhood she was moved to tears. It was a sensual delight she had not experienced for years but one which she had never forgotten. No one too young to have been a child in the 1940s or 50s could have any conception of it, nor of the appalling destruction wrought by the post-war obsession with agricultural efficiency.

Of course the countryside still looks attractive, especially when viewed from a distance, from a passing car or railway carriage window. Paradoxically the gentle undulations of much of the British Landscape give it an aesthetic appeal even when stripped of its trees, hedgerows and wildlife. It is the appeal of form, the appeal of the dead landscape in an art gallery. It may please the intellect but it cannot compare with the full sensual pleasure of a countryside rich in wildlife; a tangled, vibrant, untidy countryside filled with the noise, the colours, the sheer exuberance of life.

This is the experience that contemporary agriculture has robbed us of. It represents a loss which farming's apologists can neither deny nor justify. The great service rendered by the CRT and its imaginative renewal project is in revealing to generations under forty how magnificent the countryside used to be in their parents' and grand parents' time. More important it shows how magnificent the countryside might become again. It would not mean abandoning agriculture or consigning farmers to lives of penury. Instead they would be required to become genuine custodians of our land just as they used to be.

Since this book first appeared farming fortunes have taken a tumble. Currency fluctuations, changes on world commodity markets, plus the lingering affects of the BSE crisis, have together led to substantial falls in the prices of many of farming's major products. Boom has turned to something rather more sombre. Farmers are learning that the relentless drive for efficiency gives them no more long term security. Yet the policies which led to the ruthless exploitation of our land and its wildlife remain largely in place.

There was a time not so very long ago when farming enhanced the countryside and its wildlife. Now it threatens them. Habitats must be rescued from the clutches of agriculture for their very protection. Twenty years ago a classic TV documentary showed what happened to battery hens when they were released from their cages and given freedom to roam. Who could forget those images – the pathetic, featherless creatures, fresh from the battery shed, for the first time learning to scratch and peck at the dirt. And the fine birds they quickly became, strutting confidently in their new plumage.

This is what happens to our land when it is freed from the cage of intensive farming – the meadows bloom, the hedgerows swarm with birds, the countryside lives again. The Cambridgeshire experiment shows how. Now to apply the lesson through the length and breadth of Britain.

Graham Harvey. March 1998.

ACKNOWLEDGMENTS

Practically everyone I met as an agricultural journalist contributed in some way to this book. Like seeds in an old meadow the idea has lain dormant for a long time. But with its final emergence there are those who are owed special thanks. I am particularly grateful for the help and advice of many in the conservation movement. They include John Taylor and Jim Dixon of the Royal Society for the Protection of Birds, Nick Milton of the Wildlife Trusts, Gail Murray of the World Wide Fund for Nature, Roger Martin of the Somerset Wildlife Trust, Stella Jarman of the Warwickshire Wildlife Trust, Nick Carter of the British Trust for Ornithology, Paul Wynne of Landscape 2000 project and Miles King of Plantlife. All gave generously of their time and expertise, though of course they are not responsible for the opinions expressed.

I am also happy to acknowledge the support of those who have themselves written eloquently in this area. Sir Richard Body, author of a series of penetrating critiques of modern agriculture, was, as always, enthusiastic and encouraging. Our early meeting got me off to a better start than I could have hoped for. Michael Winter of Cheltenham and Gloucester College of Higher Education generously allowed me an advance sight of his own book, *Rural Politics*. This perceptive analysis proved invaluable in helping me to understand the development of farm policy. The writings of Howard Newby of Southampton University proved to be equally enlightening on the social consequences.

I am grateful to Tim Lang of Thames Valley University for helping me to navigate the complexities of the modern food system, and to Robin Grove-White of Lancaster University for providing an overview of contemporary rural issues. Mike Robinson of Harper Adams

Agricultural College guided me through the links between an industrial agriculture and a depopulated countryside. I am indebted to many in the organic movement, particularly to members of the Soil Association. Over the years they have become a repository of sane thinking in an industry deluged by commercial rhectoric. Two rather frenetic breakfast briefings with Patrick Holden in the all-day pub in Colston Street proved invaluable.

There are others who, without great knowledge of farming or the countryside, nevertheless helped me to focus on the issues that mattered. I am happy to acknowledge the advice and encouragement of my friend Malcolm Bole and of my brother Tony. I am grateful to friends at The Archers, especially my fellow writers who have had to listen to me banging on about these issues at numerous script meetings. Particular thanks are due to Vanessa Whitburn who unhesitatingly rearranged the writing schedule to allow me time to complete this book. Thanks are also owed to all at Jonathan Cape, especially Dan Franklin and Will Sulkin. Their enthusiastic response to an unsolicited proposal from the sticks is the reason for this story being told. The wise and intelligent editing of Pascal Cariss has made this a better book than it otherwise might have been.

Finally, it has become almost a cliché to acknowledge the support of one's spouse, but I have no intention of breaking with tradition. Annie, you've been great. I honestly couldn't have done it without you.

Graham Harvey
March 1997

LIST OF ABBREVIATIONS

ADAS Agricultural Development and Advisory Service
BAA   British Agrochemicals Association
BTO   British Trust for Ornithology
CAP   Common Agricultural Policy
CLA   Country Landowners' Association
CS   Countryside Stewardship
DoE   Department of the Environment
EN   English Nature
ESA   Environmentally Sensitive Area
EU   European Union
GATT General Agreement on Tariffs and Trade
HLCA Hill Livestock Compensatory Amount
ICM   Integrated Crop Management
IPU   Isoproturon
LEAF Linking Environment and Farming
MAFF Ministry of Agriculture, Fisheries and Food
MRL   Maximum Residue Level
NAAS National Agricultural Advisory Service
NCC   Nature Conservancy Council
NFU   National Farmers' Union
NRA   National Rivers Authority
NSA   Nitrate Sensitive Area
NVZ   Nitrate Vulnerable Zone
OP   Organophosphate
RSPB Royal Society for the Protection of Birds
SAPS Sheep Annual Premium Scheme
SSSI Site of Special Scientific Interest

1

THE GRIM REAPERS

On Salisbury Plain, close to where the holiday traffic thunders westward, the great Iron Age fortress of Yarnbury Castle stands sentinel over a rolling downland landscape. Scoured from the soil more than two millennia ago, its massive earth walls are now draped in chalk grassland, the tough mat of wild flowers, grasses and herbs that once formed the green mantle of all the chalk country. A summer haunt of bees and flickering butterflies, it is a living garment woven by centuries of grazing with sheep.

Beyond the earth walls there is precious little grassland left on the downs. The mantle of the chalk has all but disappeared along with the sheep flocks that produced it. Instead the landscape is engulfed in a tide of intensive wheat, dreary stands of identical plants stretching away to the far horizon. The flowers of the chalk survive only on the ancient earthwork where they are protected from the bite of the ploughshare. The fortress of a warrior people has become the refuge of a threatened and dwindling habitat.

For the farmers of the Plain have transformed this landscape on a scale that would have seemed unthinkable even a generation ago. Without public consultation they have obliterated a living heritage thousands of years old. Nor is the destruction confined to chalk downland. Across the length and breadth of Britain the countryside has been reconstructed in the sole interests of intensive agriculture. The very essence of a nation is drained away, yet it seems scarcely a voice is raised in protest.

For an urban people the British remain remarkably well disposed towards farmers. This is surprising since the only time most of us encounter them is in a traffic queue behind a crawling slurry wagon on the morning we are late for work. Even so we retain a sentimental attachment to them. We like to think of them as honest, well-

I

meaning folk, kind to their animals and responsible in their care of the countryside.

Admittedly the popular image took something of a battering following the BSE crisis. The revelation that dairy farmers had fed cattle carcasses back to cattle came as a shock to many. There had been other concerns too – the continuing destruction of hedgerows, the calf trucks which, until the European beef ban, lined the dockside, the seemingly constant recourse to pesticides. Still we cling doggedly to our faith in the farmer as guardian of our countryside and wildlife. We want desperately to believe in Dan Archer.

Sadly our fond perceptions fail to square with reality. Dramatic changes have been taking place on Britain's farmland, changes that reveal farmers to be anything but the good custodians we like to think them. The numbers of a wide range of wildlife species have fallen dramatically. The skylark, the lapwing and the corn bunting; the barn owl and the grey partridge – birds that were once an everyday part of the farming scene – are now in steep decline.

Wild flowers, too, are disappearing from our countryside; species like shepherd's needle, cornflower and the exquisite pheasant's eye, along with a host of farmland butterflies – the adonis blue, the marbled white, the chequered skipper and the pearl-bordered fritillary – and several dozen species of invertebrates, little known most of them, yet each with its own place in the intricate lattice-work of Britain's farmland ecology.

The landscape they have shared for centuries has at once become hostile. Modern, intensive farming will no longer tolerate them. They are victims of the sprays, the fertilisers, the giant machines and the monocultures; of the sheer relentless pressure to maximise output from every hedge bank and field corner. We fondly imagine that agriculture allows wild species to flourish, if only at the margins – on the odd patch of rough grass, or the marshy patch at the bottom of the meadow. But there are few marginal areas left any more. For this is the age of farm support.

In the hot-house climate of state subsidies every last acre of marsh and rough grazing must be mobilised in the great drive for production. Out in the vanguard are the 100-horsepower tractor and the 40-foot spray boom. Everything must be sacrificed to them: the hedges and woods, the meadowlands, the ponds and marshes, along with all the creatures that inhabit them. Since agriculture uses 80 per cent of the total land area, it's not just a part of our countryside that is affected. Farming doesn't merely shape the British countryside, it *is* the countryside. And with the industry gripped by a mania to produce regardless of the consequences, the outcome is inevitably a desert.

Despite the BSE crisis there seems little prospect of a change of heart by those inflicting the damage. British farming is currently being reinvented by a small group of business moguls with little interest in its history and distinctly global ambitions for its future. These rural modernists scorn the notion of an agriculture based, as it has been for thousands of years, on natural cycles. For them the chemical industry has made nature irrelevant. They favour a countryside devoted entirely to industrial-scale food production, with the products traded on world commodity markets in exactly the same way as coffee and copper. The only space for wildlife in this new, utilitarian landscape is within a scattering of nature reserves or in ersatz habitats bought at high price.

Since this 'progressive' view of farming is supported by big business and the City, it is the one most likely to prevail. If so the current losses of birds and flowers from our landscape will turn out to have been merely the first casualties in a long process of attrition. But for the beef crisis this new agricultural revolution might well have gone largely unchallenged. Now, at least, there is the chance that the public may be consulted, for, as always, it is they who will have to pay.

As a rule the British are zealously protective of their countryside. The threat of a by-pass through a stretch of ancient woodland is enough to bring out the middle classes in droves, setting them shoulder-to-shoulder with New Age eco warriors in a stand against the bulldozers. But the threat from agriculture is more insidious. Who is there to object when the sprayer moves across a flower-rich hedge bank or the plough buries a centuries-old meadow? There are no squadrons of earth-movers lining up to carve a swathe across a verdant hillside, no powerful images for the TV news crew. This enemy is within.

For those whose only view of the countryside is from a distance it's hard to appreciate just how much damage has already been done. The landscape still looks attractive enough. The hedges are neat and well-trimmed, the fields comfortingly green. Yet such things mean little. They tell us no more about the health of the countryside than a holiday brochure accurately portrays a foreign resort. To discover the reality it is necessary to take to the fields. Only then does it become apparent that this once 'living tapestry' is becoming a shroud.

Nowhere has the destruction been greater than on the chalk

downs, those gently contoured slopes that ebb and flow across the south of England like an ocean swell. At Yarnbury Castle the downs are traversed by one of the great arterial routes to the west, the A303 trunk road. Crossing the Plain it skirts Stonehenge before dropping down into the Wyle Valley. This is a land of prehistory, of tumuli, hill forts and iron-age encampments. On these same bare hills the early Neolithic peoples began turning the first sods, setting Britain on a course for its farming destiny.

Four thousand years later the nature writer Richard Jefferies lay on a thyme-filled pasture, amid the harebells and flickering butterflies, and here imagined the 'sleep-forgotten warriors' still haunting the downland. Here also the writer W. H. Hudson entered the world of shepherd Isaac Bawcombe whose life was spent walking the solitary sheep pastures of the high down. But there are sheep pastures no longer on the high down. This is arable country now. In the spring the slopes shine bright with young corn; in the summer they grow yellow with its ripening.

For the thousands of motorists who speed along the dual carriageway en route to their holiday destinations in the south-west, the transformation matters not one jot. This landscape of open skies and smooth-rounded peaks still has a lightness to lift the spirits. But for those choosing to strike out along one of the myriad droves or trackways there is no such refreshment for the soul. This is no living tapestry. It is a landscape of the dead.

The most striking feature is the silence. There is no sound in this rolling prairie land; no buzzing of bees, no rasping of crickets, no birdsong. Saddest of all, there is no joyous ripple from Shelley's 'blythe spirit', no 'silver chain of sound' from George Meredith's *Lark Ascending*. The skylarks have gone from this modern cornfield. Here the heavens are as devoid of life as the waving wheat beneath them.

Down below the ripening ears, on the bare earth, no bugs or insects are visible among the forest of stems. Nothing lives here; the pesticides have seen to that. Those that don't kill the insect predators directly destroy the smaller invertebrates on which they feed. They also wipe out the fungal life on which the smaller creatures feed in their turn. The end result is the same: a barren earth. And along with the invertebrates have gone the small mammals which lived on them. Finding a shrew or fieldmouse in this miserable monoculture is worth a letter to *The Times*. And because the ground is dead the skies are empty, too, save for the odd pigeon, or a sparrowhawk straying in from the roadside verges. Just as there is no food for the small mammals, there is none for the insect-eating birds. Shepherd Bawcombe would find neither corn bunting nor greenfinch were he to walk the lofty downland paths today.

This is no longer a farmed landscape. It has become an industrial site set in a rural location. Like a well-run factory, it is tidy and efficient. But in a landscape once vibrant, once teeming with life, its emergence is a catastrophe. And the greater tragedy is that it has all been unnecessary.

The farmers of the Wiltshire downland have taken a little less than a generation to sterilise their own small part of Britain. They have done it not because of some immutable law of progress, nor even because of the market. They have destroyed the living countryside because the government paid them to do so, and paid them using our money, taxpayers' money. There is no real demand for the wheat they pour out by the truck-load, or at least there wasn't until world prices took off unexpectedly in 1995. For twenty years much of this crop had had to be dumped at knockdown prices.

Some food analysts now argue that the world has entered a period of shortages, others that the surpluses will return. But shortage or surplus, the public hand-outs seem to go on for ever, offspring of the immutable Common Agricultural Policy. Big agribusiness must have its return no matter what the cost to the rest of us. And so, in good markets and in bad, the chalkland farmers from Sussex to the Dorset ridges maintain their deadly monoculture of wheat. Or, rather, most of them do.

On Salisbury Plain, just a mile or so from the A303 trunk road, there is one farm that grows no subsidised cereal crops. Despite the cash inducements of the EU, the 680 acres at Parsonage Down are still clothed in old grassland, some of it a remnant of the unimproved pasture that once covered the entire chalk downs. No chemical fertilisers are spread on this ancient grass. Instead it is fertilised with organic manure and grazed with cattle and sheep in the time-honoured way.

In spring, when the surrounding wheat crops look bright green, the fields of Parsonage Down appear dull. For the artificial nitrogen has lent a vivid, unnatural hue to the prairie wheat around them. But step onto the old downland pasture and you are aware of another, more striking difference. This land is alive. Chalkland flowers grow in abundance in the dense, herb-rich sward – cowslips, salad burnet and the sturdy devil's-bit scabious; rarer species, too, like toadflax, dwarf sedge and the green-winged orchid.

As the spring deepens into summer the sounds of this ancient landscape grow louder – grasshoppers, crickets, bees buzzing between the bright chalkland flowers. Butterflies, like the skipper and the common blue, drift over the short-cropped grasses as skylarks climb on the summer thermals. Chaffinches and willow warblers haunt the gorses and brambles, stone curlews call shrilly in the evening air. And badgers, hares and foxes play out their flawless roles in a drama as old as the earth.

The Neolithic hunter would have recognised this landscape, as Richard Jefferies reflected while dreaming on an ancient tumulus. 'Summer after summer the blue butterflies had visited the mound, the thyme had flowered, the wind had sighed in the grass.'[1] The thyme still flowers among the grasses at Parsonage Down. Our grandfathers would have known this landscape, too. For the rural child growing up in southern Britain as recently as the last war, the life and sounds of the chalk grasslands would have been as familiar as the shopping mall to the modern child. This landscape was a part of the popular experience. The politicians with their farm subsidies have turned it into a museum piece.

Parsonage Down Farm is now a National Nature Reserve, a permanent reminder to future generations of what has been taken from them. That it survives at all is thanks to the care and foresight of the former owner, the late Robert Wales. He had farmed Parsonage Down from the early 1920s, and like most of the chalkland farmers of his time he grazed it with livestock. This was considered the best way to manage these thin, drought-prone soils.

The grazing of herb-rich pastures with cattle and sheep is no soft option. It demands the skilled balancing of pasture and livestock so that both will thrive. Achieving this balance year in, year out is an art not easily learned; it requires an intimate knowledge of both the animal and the living sward. Robert Wales applied this art to his own small part of the countryside. Though it failed to make him rich, it helped him survive the great depression of the 1930s when many farmers were in trouble.

After the war he stuck to his pastoral farming system, even though government subsidies were by then inducing his neighbours to plough up the ancient grasslands and go for richer pickings from cereals. When he died in 1979, aged ninety-three, the switch to corn-growing was becoming a headlong rush. European subsidies under the CAP offered an even bigger cash bonanza to farmers who took the prairie option. Land prices soared to a record £3,000 an acre as City investors scrambled to buy up farms and get a slice of the action. Had Parsonage Down been sold on the open market it would almost certainly have made £2.5 million, perhaps more. The centuries-old pasture would have been ploughed up and its wildlife lost.

But Robert Wales had foreseen the danger. Under the terms of his will the farm was offered to the Nature Conservancy Council – now English Nature – at the knockdown price of just £0.5 million, barely 20 per cent of its market value. The deal was authorised by the then Environment Secretary, Michael Heseltine. But in line with the market philosophy of the new Thatcher government, he insisted the purchase price be repaid to the Treasury within one year. Thus, having acquired the farm for the nation, the NCC were obliged to sell off part of it on the open market. This land was immediately put under the plough by the new owners, much to the distress of Robert Wales's friends.

However, most of the old pasture remains, secure in public ownership, a living oasis in a sterile monoculture. Elsewhere the drive to convert farming into an extractive process continues unabated, and not just on the southern downland. Everywhere on these islands rich and beautiful habitats have been ploughed, bulldozed and sprayed out of existence, not as a result of need, but in response to farm subsidies.

More than 150,000 miles of hedgerow have been lost in England alone since the introduction of subsidies. And they are still disappearing at the rate of 10,000 miles a year. Water meadows, moorlands, marshes and wetlands – all with their own particular flora and fauna – have been sacrificed to the obsessive drive for production. When an important site is threatened, somewhere like the Lower Severn Valley or the Somerset Levels, government protection is usually provided. But there is no protection for the small local sites, the ones of little scientific value yet which are far more important to most of us: the local pond, the boggy patches in the field corners. Before the coming of subsidies they were hardly worth draining. Now, in the surreal world of the CAP, they have acquired a value. And in the real world a generation of children are denied the chance ever to discover a water forget-me-not, a yellow wagtail or a dragonfly.

The destruction of our wildlife and countryside has come about through a deliberate and sustained national policy, a policy which costs the British people £10 billion a year in taxes, both overt and hidden. Whatever the original aims of the policy, it is clearly not working. Nor can it, for it is based on a fundamental error – that if you inflate the price of food you will assist farmers, and then they, from the goodness of their hearts, will take care of the countryside. It is a fallacy that has had tragic consequences for the nation, but one which no government appears willing to confront.

The industrialisation of Britain's countryside began in 1947, the year of the great post-war Agriculture Act. Food remained under rationing. At the same time there was a desperate need to save foreign exchange. By providing farmers with a substantial degree of price security, the new Labour government hoped to encourage expansion and give agriculture a central role in the nation's economic reconstruction.

Besides, the popular sentiment towards farmers was one of gratitude in the immediate post-war years. Had they not helped feed a hungry nation by ploughing up grassland and putting it into arable crops? In the first year of war alone more than two million acres were converted from grass for ruminants to wheat and potatoes for direct human consumption. The fact that farmers had already been amply rewarded with record grain prices – indeed many had made small fortunes from the war – seems not to have dampened the widespread sense of appreciation for the farming community.

So for the first time in Britain's history comprehensive production subsidies were introduced for all the major farm products, including cereals, milk and beef. From now on farmers were to receive guaranteed prices for what they grew, irrespective of world market prices. Well-intentioned though it might have been, this one muddle-headed decision was to lead ultimately to the ruin of Britain's countryside. Public funding was to change for ever the look – and the life – of the British landscape. No longer would farming remain an essentially biological process based on natural cycles. Instead it was destined to become a factory operation, hardly different from the manufacture of ball-bearings, with raw materials going in at one end and the manufactured products coming out of the other.

Almost fifty years later farm subsidies are still with us. Indeed, as members of the European Union we are operating them at a higher level than ever before. In a society that has introduced market forces into almost every area of public life, the growers of our food are still deemed to need taxpayers' support for their continued survival. Yet produce markets are as old as civilisation itself. If there is one area of the economy that would flourish in a free market economy it is surely the food sector. After all, it deals in a product that everyone needs.

The fact that no government dare state such an obvious truth shows how deeply we have absorbed the rural lobby's familiar chant. We really do believe farmers need subsidies. Even farmers believe they need subsidies. The politicians have managed to create a dependency culture that none can now break. And so the emperor continues to flaunt his new clothes. And the driver of the 100-hp tractor continues to tear out the hedgerow.

In fact the misguided ministers of the post-war Attlee government learned precisely the wrong lessons from the wartime performance of British agriculture. Its quick response to a sudden change in the nation's food requirement revealed not an industry in need of public support, but one that was adaptable and intrinsically healthy despite years of recession. The threat of German U-boats in the Channel produced a sharp increase in food prices. Farmers responded by ploughing up their grazing pastures and sowing the land to wheat, admittedly with some goading from government. It was the classic response to a clear price signal: the 'cashing in' of twenty years' fertility built up under grass in order to achieve a rapid boost in output.

Having profited from the wartime price boom, farmers should have been allowed to readjust to the less frenetic price regime of the peace. Instead the government chose to *reward* them with subsidies. Not only was this decision to lead to untold damage to the countryside, it was to fail the very farmers it was designed to help. For the politicians had opted to support not farmers, but farm output. In doing so they were effectively consigning Britain's farmland to the City investor and the industrial tycoon.

At the start of the last war there were almost half a million farms in Britain including part-time holdings. The majority were small, mixed units of less than 50 acres, with cattle, sheep, pigs and poultry as well as some arable crops. Before the age of state protection farmers needed to grow a range of products for financial security. If the price of any one product collapsed, there were others to buffer them against ruin. Economically this mixed-farm structure was extremely stable. It also happened to produce a vigorous and attractive countryside, rich in wildlife and largely free of pollution.

At the same time almost one million workers were employed wholly or partly on British farms. Thus almost 1.5 million families were able to make part or all of their living from the land, while delivering environmental benefits as a 'free' extra. Never has the British countryside looked so good. Never has it supported a richer diversity of habitat and wild species. Yet it cost taxpayers nothing. If the politicians had truly understood agriculture they would have recognised the mixed-farm structure as a national treasure to be nurtured and prized. Instead they set farming on a calamitous dash for intensification that was to put three-quarters of those farmers out of business.

The first effect of subsidies was to inflate the price of land. Clearly when the state decides to underwrite the price of any product, regardless of demand, the means of producing that product acquire an additional value. Had the government chosen to guarantee the price of cars, the value of car factories would have risen in the same way. Anyone subsequently buying a car factory would have been obliged to pay the inflated price. They would then have had to work it harder to get their money back. So it is with land. Higher prices have saddled farmers with a heavier fixed cost, forcing them to push up output to cover the additional overhead. And with the government willing to buy whatever they produced regardless of need, the outcome was predictable.

Farmers were no longer prepared to tolerate the odd patch of marshy meadowland, the acre or two of rough grazing, the stretch of redundant hedgerow. It was as if British farming were suddenly put on a permanent war footing. From now on every square yard would be made to pay its way, with disastrous consequences for wildlife. For it was on those very marginal areas that our wildlife flourished.

The second damaging effect of subsidies was to free farmers from the need to practise mixed farming. Price guarantees meant there was no longer any necessity to maintain a range of enterprises as an insurance against market instability and the variability of the weather. Farmers could begin to specialise, in meat or milk or continuous wheat. And because the more they produced the more government money they picked up, higher output became the main aim. So out came the hedges; in went the fertiliser spinners and the pesticide sprayers; up went the numbers of cattle and sheep to the acre. The age of factory farming had been born.

Fifty years of farm subsidies have changed the culture of rural Britain as well as its countryside. Our farmland is now managed by a generation of farmers who no longer question their 'right' to produce. As they see it the sole purpose of the countryside is to turn out more and more food, whether or not it is needed, whether or not it has to be 'dumped' on world markets at the expense of the British taxpayer and poor farmers in the Third World. Output first and last, this is the orthodoxy of a sector that once prided itself on rugged self-reliance. And such is the influence of the landowning lobby, both inside and outside Parliament, that hardly anyone questions it, not even when it is clearly turning the British countryside into a desert.

Intensive cereal crops and a monoculture of perennial ryegrass have largely replaced the old, flower-rich hay meadows. Ryegrass was chosen because it responded best to artificial fertilisers supplied by chemical companies eager to relieve farmers of their subsidy cash. Any hare or corncrake managing to rear young in these lush, dense pastures was likely to see them chopped to pieces by the forage harvester as dairy farmers embraced the new wonder crop of silage, and indulged, at public expense, their passion for things mechanical.

Britain's accession to the EEC in the 1970s further entrenched the principle of farm support. Direct subsidies from the taxpayer were now to be augmented by a hidden tax on food. While the Community closed its borders to imports, the prices of home-produced foods were inflated by the removal of surpluses from the market: the notorious Intervention buying system. Prices soared and farmers put the last remnants of their meadowlands under the plough. Farm ministers urged still higher production, a plea readily endorsed by leaders of the National Farmers' Union and the Milk Marketing Board. The butter mountains grew. The grain mountains swelled. And Britain's farmland wildlife was further choked, crushed and poisoned into submission.

By the early 1980s it had become obvious even in Whitehall that something would have to be done to slow the senseless scramble for output. Milk was the critical commodity. The annual ritual of selling off expensively produced butter to the Soviet Union had become politically unsustainable. In another industry overproduction might have led to a fall in prices allowing demand and supply to establish a new equilibrium, but not in the world of subsidised agriculture. Such a rational solution would have been unacceptable to the powerful industry lobby. The problem for European agriculture ministers was how to cut milk production while maintaining the public largesse to farmers. The solution was inspired – quotas.

The advantage of quotas was that they allowed the EU Commission to control supply – the dream of every manufacturing mogul since the industrial revolution. For the first time it became possible to create an artificial shortage without filling the Intervention stores, thus keeping prices high to the benefit of producers while creating no embarrassing surpluses. Having complained bitterly when quotas were first introduced, farmers quickly learned to exploit the system. UK dairy farmers currently hold quota amounting to 80 per cent of the country's needs. This means they have the absolute right to supply four-fifths of Britain's milk and dairy products at a price that may be double the cost of production.

Imagine the British car industry or the coal industry being

guaranteed four-fifths of the domestic market, all at protected prices? This is the measure of security now afforded to milk producers. Quota is no more than a licence to profit from dairy farming. Not surprisingly it has acquired a capital value and is now traded speculatively both by farmers and entrepreneurs. Tragically it has also maintained the destructive onslaught on Britain's countryside. The emergence of European food surpluses should have reduced farming intensity, but thanks to the distortions of the quota system – now extended to sheep and beef production – the pressures on our dwindling wildlife habitats remain as severe as in the years of food rationing.

Everywhere the nation's flower-rich meadows have vanished. Unbelievably, 97 per cent of Britain's meadowland has perished in the Government-inspired dash for production. And the destruction has gone on all around the country. In Cornwall meadows are now described as 'exceptionally rare'. In Gloucestershire a single meadow is all that is left in the Forest of Dean, while only a handful survive in the Severn Vale and on the Cotswolds. Even these are declining at an alarming rate. Watership Down, the Hampshire chalk grassland made famous by Richard Adams, once occupied over 1,300 acres. Now only 40 acres of the flower-rich turf are left, split into a number of tiny fragments.

Only 20 acres of limestone meadow remain in the whole of Northamptonshire, while in Nottinghamshire 200 square miles of the Trent Valley contain just five hay meadows. In the Clee Hills of Shropshire 50 per cent of the remaining flower-rich meadows were wiped out in the 1980s alone, while in Lincolnshire the surviving meadows can be counted on the fingers of two hands. In Radnorshire what remains of the county's meadowland is disappearing at the rate of 11 per cent a year. In Ayrshire only 0.001 per cent of the county remains in meadowland.

The devastation in Cheshire has been particularly severe. For Cheshire is a grassland county – it carries more cows to the acre than almost anywhere in Britain. Drive across the Cheshire Plain in summer and you are unlikely to see a primrose. Get out of the car and you probably won't hear a skylark either, just the sound of a tractor and fertiliser spreader applying more nitrogen to the thick, lifeless ryegrass sward. This is a landscape created by the chemical giant ICI. From its Dairy House demonstration farm near Nantwich the company exhorted thousands of dairy farmers to spend their subsidy money on fertilisers, and in doing so played a key role in the desertification of Britain. Artificial fertilisers are as lethal to wild plants as the plough.

None of this could have happened without subsidies; at least, not on anything like this scale. Without the support of taxpayers, farm prices would have slipped as production exceeded market demand. The drive to produce ever greater surpluses would have tailed off, as would application rates of fertilisers and pesticides. The essential balance between farming and wildlife would have been restored. But the European farming lobby is too powerful to allow this to happen.

Agricultural support was estimated to have cost European consumers £48 billion in 1990, with taxpayers contributing an additional £27 billion.[2] Of these sums no less than £46 billion was transferred to farmers who then spent much of it on fertilisers, pesticides and the general destruction of the countryside. In the UK the CAP operates as a variable tariff, forcing consumers to pay more for their food than the world price, then passing part of this hidden tax to farmers. From 1979 to 1993 the food price surcharge varied between 31 and 49 per cent, although, exceptionally, it all but disappeared in 1995 when world prices surged.[3]

This covert form of subsidy is particularly pernicious since it places the greatest burden on the least well-off. Poor people spend a higher proportion of their income on food than the wealthy, so they are the hardest hit. In essence the CAP takes cash from the most disadvantaged members of the community and puts it into the pockets of the wealthiest.

Professor Patrick Minford estimates the cost of the CAP to UK consumers at £6.5 billion annually, net of gains to farmers.[4] To this must be added the country's budgetary contribution to the EU, currently amounting to £3.5 billion. Much of the Community budget is spent on farm support. Thus the cost of EU membership amounts to £10 billion, around 1.5 per cent of GDP. This is the price we pay for access to the single market. But there is another price, one that is less easy to measure – the ruination of the British countryside.

The transfer of money from taxpayers and consumers is not even a particularly efficient way of helping farmers. Price support simply pushes up the costs of inputs, including land, fertilisers and pesticides, so much of the cash ends up in the pockets of chemical manufacturers and land agents. At the same time the inflated costs lead to an ever greater intensity of farming with the inevitable consequences for the environment.

Not even the Conservatives remain in doubt about the damaging nature of farm subsidies. A special study set up by former Agriculture

Minister William Waldegrave before his move to the Treasury concluded that all EU member states were losers from the CAP – with the possible exception of Ireland.[5] Yet ministers declare themselves powerless to bring about real reform. They argue that there remains no great impetus for change among other EU member states, and the political price of unilateral withdrawal from the CAP would be too high. Such a move would spell the end of the single market, leading to a welter of competing national subsidy regimes.

While ministers have shown themselves willing to disrupt Community business on behalf of the beef industry, there is seemingly no appetite for confronting Brussels in defence of the British countryside. Instead government appears content with band-aid remedies to ameliorate the worst effects of price support. Most of these measures can be lumped together under the general heading of environmental land management schemes. Areas of countryside are identified as having exceptional wildlife or landscape value or as being at particular risk from intensive farming. These are given any one of a number of special designations – Environmentally Sensitive Area, Site of Special Scientific Interest, Nitrate Sensitive Area.

Alternatively particular habitat types may be singled out for protection under the Countryside Stewardship Scheme. By means of an impossibly bureaucratic process farmers are then able to claim compensation for adopting environmentally friendly measures such as cutting back pesticide sprays, looking after the hedgerows or maintaining the last remnants of flower-rich meadowland. In essence they are paid not to do what they wouldn't have considered doing anyway but for subsidies. Even William Waldegrave has acknowledged the absurdity of paying farmers not to use marginal but 'ecologically interesting' land for farming when it was often overpricing that persuaded them to do so in the first place.

Such schemes amount to little more than window dressing. They make wild species a matter of special designation, then relegate them to a reserve. No longer are our flora and fauna to be part of a balanced land-use policy. They are made museum pieces, a sideshow, while the real business of the countryside is the efficient, large-scale production of food in a sterile environment by largely industrial processes. Can this be an activity worth £10 billion a year in public support?

The government's remedy looks more like a public relations exercise than a genuine attempt to preserve and enhance a living landscape. Perhaps this is not surprising since the Conservatives have for many years pursued a somewhat different agenda – the promotion of a large-scale corporate agricultural industry in place of small family farms. A succession of agriculture ministers have portrayed themselves as reluctant adopters of an ill-conceived European farm policy over which they have little or no control. Yet it is they who have chosen to apply it in a way that does maximum harm to the rural community as well as to the British countryside.

The structure of UK farming is unlike that of other member states. Our farms are far bigger. Britain was the first country to enter the industrial age; it was also the most ruthless in forcing its rural population off the land and into the factories. As a result there are more large farms and fewer small farms in Britain than in other EU member states. Whatever its failings the CAP was devised to support small farmers, in Germany and France particularly. Yet throughout the period of Britain's membership, UK governments have chosen to direct European subsidies to the largest farmers. This is why the policy has been uniquely damaging to the British countryside.

Ask town-dwellers to describe their idea of a farmer and the chances are they will conjure up a picture of the kindly countryman leaning on the gate to eye up his cattle, a look of quiet contentment on his face – the caring husbandman labouring happily in some beautiful corner of the land. As a description of the typical recipient of farm subsidies it is well wide of the mark. In Britain less than 10 per cent of farms account for 50 per cent of farm output.

Their owners are neither shrewd stockmen nor horny-handed sons of the soil. Our taxes go to subsidise hard-headed businessmen; exploiters of resources rather than guardians of the landscape. They are more likely to be wearing Armani suits than overalls, and the closest they get to the fields is driving over them in the Range Rover. They are farming's middle managers, more concerned with gross margins and cash flows than with the countryside. For them managing a 'food factory' is hardly different from manufacturing plastic washers. These are the people we choose to shower with public money. The tragedy for the countryside is that they are so efficient at using it.

For they leave nothing to chance, these rural industrialists. The sprayers go at exactly the right time. The artificial fertilisers are applied precisely where they will have maximum effect. The fields are sown with the crop varieties that will fully utilise the chemical inputs. The workforce is pared to a bare minimum – very often it is purely contract labour. To further reduce labour costs giant machines are employed, with the trees and hedges stripped away for ease of operation. The landscape is reshaped to suit the technology. There is no room for nature here, except, perhaps, in a boundary hedge or in a field corner copse planted up for cosmetic reasons.

This is one of the ironies of subsidised agriculture. It doesn't merely strip wildlife from the land, it drives out the people, too. The billions of pounds in EU hand-outs, intended to aid small farms, are instead feeding a rampant agribusiness that is rapidly swallowing them up. The government considers this no bad thing, wedded as it is to the concept of free market efficiency. The European ideal would require it to hand over large sums of public money to what it perceives to be small, inefficient businesses. Not surprisingly it demurs, choosing instead to see the cash go to the biggest and, in its terms, the more efficient operators. In doing so it saddles the British people with the worst of all worlds – high food prices and a devastated countryside.

It is as if the Government decided to offer a subsidy to food retailers, then opted to make the hand-outs dependent on turnover. Clearly the lion's share would go to Tesco, Sainsbury's and the like, with the corner shops left at a greater disadvantage than ever. Yet this is how farm support is dispensed. No doubt the public would prefer to see its money used to subsidise people and wildlife rather than machinery, agrochemicals and the price of land. A better solution still might be to let the public keep its money and instead scrap the subsidies altogether. The market would do a better job of feeding people and providing a rich and diverse countryside.

In 1992 the then Agriculture Minister, John Gummer, returned from Brussels proclaiming a triumph for farmers and the nation. As part of planned CAP 'reforms' aimed at reducing the EU's food surpluses, the Commission had proposed limiting production subsidies to the first part of the output from every farm. Thus all farmers would pick up a subsidy on, say, the first hundred tons of wheat, or on the milk from the first fifty cows. After that it would be up to them to earn what they could from the market. This 'reform' would at least have had the advantage of concentrating public support on small farmers as the founding fathers of the Common Market had intended.

John Gummer successfully opposed the plan. He won the right for Britain to go on directing the public hand-outs to the biggest farmers, claiming this as a great national victory. In fact it was a national disaster. Giving the money to small farmers would merely have been to waste it. Handing it over to a voracious agribusiness was to condemn the countryside to another round of needless exploitation.

This decision reveals the intent of British agricultural policy – to support the big farmers together with their corporate backers: the banks, the investment houses and the multi-national feed and chemical companies. When a UK agriculture minister proclaims a victory for British farmers it is not the small farm on the Welsh hills he has in mind, but the high-tech lowland farm, probably owned by a pension fund. Increasingly, family-owned farms are being handed over to specialist farming companies to manage. These companies run them for maximum returns, then split the profits with the owner. But these days the profits come chiefly from public subsidies. Indeed, this is the aim of the exercise; to maximise the subsidy income. Unwittingly the British taxpayer is funding the concentration of farming into ever bigger units. Can this really be why we are taxing the poorest residents of our deprived inner-city areas: to maintain the income of a multi-million pound corporate farming structure? And who is to tell them that their money is contributing to the destruction of the British countryside?

In the boardrooms of many of today's big farming companies a new scenario is being worked out. The proposition is that soon the largest, most highly mechanised UK cereal farms will be in a position to compete successfully in world markets. Current subsidies, the land moguls argue, are a necessary stop-gap measure to help the industry re-structure before it has to face the inevitable blast of world competition. But even assuming our industrial-scale farm enterprises are one day able to sell at world prices, is this really what we want for a small, heavily populated island like Britain? Are we really prepared to strip away what's left of our hedges and woods, our wild birds and mammals, in order that a handful of farming companies can sell their wheat to China as cheaply as Kansas or Manitoba can?

Big business farming provides precious few jobs for country people these days. Mechanisation has seen to that. Nor does it contribute greatly to the rural economy. Most of its inputs come from foreign-owned multinationals. Are we taxpayers expected to go on spending billions of pounds a year in support to an industry that one day just might be able to earn a hundred million or so from grain sales? The government seems to consider the investment worthwhile. But the likelihood is the British people would prefer to keep their country-side, or what's left of it, for themselves and their grandchildren.

On the chalk downs of southern England, the land of Hardy and Hudson and Jefferies, a new habitat type has crept in among the oceans of waving wheat. Sadly it's not one likely to inspire great poetry. These fields appear almost like wastelands, a scrubby mixture of wheat stubble, coarse grasses and annual weeds. This is set-aside, the EU's newest attempt to support farmers while claiming 'reform' of the system. As part of the 1994 GATT deal on world trade, the European Community agreed to limit the tonnage of cheap surplus grain it dumped on world markets. So EU farm ministers extended the scheme under which cereal producers were paid not to grow a crop. Set-aside is a fitting monument to the folly of subsidised farming.

Describing the flowers in the 'living garment' of old chalk grassland, W. H. Hudson wrote: 'Commonest in spring . . . is the bird-foot trefoil . . . and the kidney vetch, with curious embossed or jewelled flower heads. Creeping rock rose with soft, silky petals, and clustered bell-flower, deep blue, looking like Canterbury bells . . . Crane's-bill and musky stork's-bill – mere specks of red; little round-leaved mint, a faint misty purple; and the scented plantain, its leaves like leaves cut out of green cloth, pressed flat and sewn upon the green fabric . . . Restharrow, very dark green on a light green turf, with minute pink and white butterfly blossoms. Woodruff, round and among the furze bushes, like powdery snow newly fallen on the green earth; and curiously named squinancy-wort, exceeding small and fragrant, blooming all over the turfy downs, here white, there rose-red, or deep red, or purple, so variable is it in colour. More abundant still, and more variable, is the minute milkwort . . . It is indeed blue in many places, as if a summer shower of blue rain had fallen from an unclouded sky, and the small stems were still beaded with the drops.'[6]

Hudson's living garment covers the chalk downs no longer. EU farm subsidies have robbed the people of this gem, along with a thousand other jewels of the farmed landscape. In its place the Ministry of Agriculture gives us monoculture, wasteland and scrub. Over the past fifty years farm ministers and their civil servants have appropriated the right to reconstruct the countryside. Without reference to the British people, they have reshaped it to suit the interests of their clients – the big farmers and their agribusiness associates. The time has come to reclaim it while some remnant still remains.

2

THE DESERT IN OUR MIDST

When artist Edith Holden walked the fields and lanes of her native Warwickshire in the early years of the century, she found plenty to put in her new nature diary. Cornfields strewn with yellow corn crowfoot, pink bindweed and bright red poppies; meadows filled with purple knapweed' and yellow hay-rattle, quickened by the flickering of butterflies and bees. In the hedgerows finches and warblers darted among the bryony and the dog roses. Edith Holden painted them all, adding her own observations and favourite poetry to mark the changing seasons.

Seventy years later the completed diary, or *Nature Notes* as she called it, was to provide a new generation with a glimpse of the British countryside as it had been – in an age of sunlight before the Flanders mud. Published in facsimile form in 1977, *The Country Diary of an Edwardian Lady* became a publishing phenomenon.[1] Running to thirteen editions, it sold more than 3 million copies around the world and appeared in the UK weekly best-seller lists no fewer than 183 times. It occupied the number one slot for a total of 66 weeks, and spawned a small industry of 'Country Diary' spin-offs, from tea towels to coffee mugs. Something about this talented young woman and her depiction of a countryside as yet unspoiled touched the book-buying public. It was the memory of innocence lost.

At the time the book appeared Britain's wildlife and countryside had already fallen into steep decline. More than thirty years of farm price protection had created a production juggernaut with a blind and seemingly insatiable urge to homogenise the landscape. Throughout lowland Britain hedges were being grubbed out, ponds and ditches filled in, marshes drained, meadows ploughed and woods and copses felled, all in the name of higher output. In the wake of the diggers and bulldozers came the sprayers and fertiliser spreaders to 'rationalise' the species content of the new prairie landscape.

In the space of a generation once common arable flowers like blue cornflower and yellow charlock had become rarities. Butterflies like the adonis blue, the marsh fritillary and the silver spotted skipper vanished from the farmland landscape. Those who loved the British countryside could only watch aghast. Why was the nation so bent on obliterating the finest features of its landscape for the sake of a few more tons of stolen wheat? It made no sense.

From the politicians who devised and drove the policy there came scarcely a murmur of concern. The official line seemed one of shrugging acceptance. Such changes were inevitable, the result of market forces and advancing technology. It was progress. Little wonder that bewildered lovers of the countryside should turn so eagerly to a publication that confirmed their sense of loss. Here was the proof, a reminder of that half-remembered landscape. *The Country Diary of an Edwardian Lady* provided a comfort blanket in a rural environment that had become at once alien and hostile.

In the very year the book appeared the government's own official wildlife agency was issuing dire warnings about countryside change. The Nature Conservancy Council (NCC) reported that most wildlife-rich habitats in the intensively farmed parts of Britain – on the fertile uplands as well as the lowlands – were declining in size, in quality or in both.[2] And the decline was serious, said the NCC. The rate and extent of change during the preceding thirty-five years had been greater than in any similar period in history.

The report described the remaining wildlife habitats as 'islands in an agricultural sea'. They would continue to dwindle in total area, the council forecast, and they would become increasingly fragmented. Their constituent wildlife populations would become smaller and more isolated and so more liable to accidental extinction and genetic isolation. As a result the national populations of most species would fall, while species extinction was likely to take place at an accelerating rate.

Despite the warnings farm production continued to surge ahead. Given the level of public cash inducements on offer it was hardly surprising. In 1973 the UK had become a member of the EEC, now the European Union. Direct subsidies from the taxpayer had been replaced by inflated and wholly artificial prices for farm products. Under the CAP farmers sold at a 'target price' protected from the generally lower world price by levies on imports. When the price of a product fell below its target price the EU would step in to buy it for

Intervention. This was the origin of the notorious food mountains. A barely hidden production subsidy, its value has been put at up to £2.5 billion in 1977, or around £6,000 per farmer; this at a time when Europe was virtually self-sufficient in all major food commodities.[3]

So the destruction continued, fuelled by the seemingly inexhaustible largesse of the public purse. Almost twenty years on, the dire predictions of the NCC now appear all too apposite. Scores of arable land species are currently under threat. Among the flowering plants corn gromwell, pheasant's eye, shepherd's needle and corn buttercup, while endangered bird species include the corncrake, stone curlew, Montagu's harrier, the cirl bunting and the grey partridge. Half a century of public funding has given farmers unprecedented power to re-design rural Britain. Their legacy to a new generation is a sterile and lifeless landscape. How could it have been allowed to happen?

In the popular imagination the British countryside was never so glorious as in the decades leading up to the First World War. A half-remembered idyll, it is viewed through faded sepia images of men and women posed unsmiling round a loaded hay cart, or the autumn ploughman turning his team at the end of a furrow. Almost always the backdrop is the same – a row of towering elms; a sprawling hedgerow of blackthorn, ash and hazel; a tangle of grasses and flowers at the field edge. No sterile factory floor this. Nature is always in the wings. The wild and unplanted is as much a part of the scene as the sown and the sower.

It is no accident that the Edwardian countryside should have been so rich in wildlife. For much of the first half of this century Britain followed a pattern of farming that not only allowed wild species to flourish, but positively nurtured them. It created diversity. At the time when Edith Holden was recording the natural history of her native Warwickshire, much of Britain's farmland still bore the imprint of the old Norfolk four-course rotation. This was one of the great triumphs of British agriculture. It was what gave farming its truly golden age.

Devised in the late eighteenth century, the four-course replaced the traditional third-year fallow of the earlier 'three-course' with a root crop of turnips or mangolds, while in the second of two cereal crops it inserted an undersown 'seeds' crop of grass and clover. These simple changes were to transform British farming and dominate cropping patterns for close on a century. From now on half the country's tillage area would be in grain crops for human consumption and half in fodder crops for cattle and sheep. Combined with a sizeable area of permanent grazing, the new system was to reinvigorate the farming economy, supporting an increased livestock population and greatly boosting the output of meat and milk.[4]

Despite many local adaptations, the basic four-course was applied over much of lowland Britain. Its main purpose was to control crop weeds and pests, and to help maintain soil fertility. It also proved hugely beneficial to wildlife. Before the age of agrochemicals, the mix of flora and fauna found in temperate cereal fields was essentially that of the steppe or prairie ecosystem. Although far from being a wholly natural vegetation type in Britain, the cereal field had evolved its own characteristic life forms over many thousands of years. It represented a rich, semi-natural wildlife habitat covering more than 10 million acres.

Through the highly productive Norfolk four-course, this ancient habitat was maintained in close proximity to livestock and the hedgerows that enclosed them. Across lowland Britain, the cereal field and the woodland edge – as represented by the hedge – were bound in intimate association, along with more localised habitats such as chalk grassland, coppice woodland, heaths and wetlands. A small-scale patchwork of distinct plant and animal communities mirrored the small-scale patchwork of fields and copses that made up the lowland landscape. This was the glory of the British countryside: an extravagance of nature created as the by-product of a rational farming system. It was the glory Edith Holden captured so poignantly in her famous nature notes.

This basic pattern of farming lasted almost unaltered until the Second World War. As Oliver Rackham observes in his classic *History of the Countryside,* much of England in 1945 would have been instantly recognisable to Sir Thomas More, and some even to Emperor Claudius.[5] Apart from the effect of urban expansion, almost every hedge, wood, heath and fen on the large-scale Ordnance Survey maps of the 1870s appeared on Luftwaffe aerial photographs taken in 1940. The countryside destruction which had taken place in those seventy years was less than in any five-year period since. For it was then, at the start of World War Two, that the government took control of farming.

One of the lesser known episodes in the war against Hitler's armies was the secret testing of a new chemical weapon. In conditions of security to match those of the bouncing bomb, special development teams were sent out to 300 trial sites throughout Britain. The operation had been authorised by the chief scientist of the Ministry of Agriculture. In the field it was aided by the 'War Ags', the War

Agricultural Executive Committees which controlled the way farms were run. For this was not a weapon of war. It was to be used exclusively on the home front, in the production of food. Its name was 4-chloro-2-methylphenoxyacetic acid, later shortened to MCPA. When dusted on broad-leaved weeds it caused them to twist, contort and die. The age of pesticide farming had dawned.

One of the research team was later to recall that every member had been excited by the novelty of the project.[6] They had shared the satisfaction of 'taking part in a great agricultural adventure'. It was an adventure orchestrated jointly by the Ministry of Agriculture and Fisheries and the chemical company ICI. Early in the war ICI's agricultural adviser, Sir William Gavin, had been made chief agricultural adviser to the Ministry. Government money had largely financed the development of Britain's first hormone weedkiller. The change from biological to agrochemical farming had become official policy.

At the end of the war MCPA dust was marketed to UK farmers as Methoxone or 'cornland cleaner'. Had farm prices been allowed to return to free market levels its uptake might not have been great. But having taken control of farming, the politicians were not about to let go. The 1947 Agriculture Act introduced the subsidies that guaranteed farmers a profit whatever their costs. That same year ICI began working on the development of a cheap prototype boom sprayer. By 1948 it was carrying out field trials of a new liquid formulation of MCPA. Before long hormone weedkillers were being applied to virtually every cereal crop in the UK.

The farming system that emerged was not merely an up-dated version of what had gone before – a streamlined form of the Norfolk four-course. Under the protection of public support, farmers and the Ministry of Agriculture and Fisheries – later to incorporate food – had between them changed the nature of agriculture, and in doing so had recast the landscape. No longer was farming to be an essentially biological process, tried and tested by a thousand years of crop rotation and sound husbandry. It was to be a factory process that merely happened to use land. Without public debate Britain had embarked on a vast experiment in food production, one in which the long-term consequences could only be guessed at.

The first damaging effects were not long in coming. By the early 1960s severe environmental damage had become apparent as a result of the widespread use of organochlorine insecticides like DDT. An attempt to eliminate gnats from Clear Lake, California, had instead succeeded in wiping out a colony of fish-eating grebes.[7] In Britain research by the Nature Conservancy (later the NCC) showed how the pesticide caused a thinning in the egg shells of the peregrine falcon leading to its population collapse. Despite a stout defence of the chemical by MAFF, the phasing out of DDT was finally begun in 1969.

The damage caused by specific pesticide groups like the organochlorines is not the only hazard of chemical farming. Many of the most worrying effects are insidious, long-term and unpredictable. An apparently insignificant change in an ecosystem can appear years later as a sudden and catastrophic collapse. Yet such is the understanding of agriculture in Whitehall that until recently few would even acknowledge farmland to be an ecosystem, or more accurately a series of ecosystems. Now at last MAFF thinking has begun to change. The silent fields have seen to that.

Each year 300 volunteer bird-watchers take to the fields and woods of Britain as part of the annual bird census organised by the British Trust for Ornithology. Between March and mid-July the observers make ten visits to farms throughout the UK, plotting bird sitings on large-scale maps. At the end of the season registrations for each species are combined onto species maps. Clusters of sitings mark the locations of territories, so the results provide a detailed picture of the distribution of common farmland birds.

The census has revealed a dramatic fall in population numbers for a whole range of farmland species over the past twenty-five years – the tree sparrow down 89 per cent; the bullfinch down 76 per cent; the song thrush down 73 per cent; the spotted flycatcher down 73 per cent; lapwings down 62 per cent; skylarks down 58 per cent; linnets down 52 per cent. Population numbers of the corn bunting are now too low to be routinely monitored.

Of the 28 species classified as farmland birds, the distributions of 24 contracted during the 1970s and 80s.[8] Of the 18 farmland species for which it is possible to assess populations, 15 are less abundant in the 1990s than in 1970, and seven species are estimated to have suffered population falls of more than half.

Some of the reasons are all too apparent. Hedges, rough grazings and patches of scrub make up important nesting sites for many farmland birds. Yet in aggregate huge areas of these small, localised habitats have been swept away in the drive to maximise profits from cereals. There has also been a relentless shift from spring-sown cereals to autumn sowing. So fewer weed-rich autumn stubble fields are available for the seed-eating birds which account for most of the farmland species now in decline. But as well as these obvious physical changes to the landscape there are more subtle and potentially more damaging forces at work.

It would be hard to describe the weed knotgrass, *Polygonum aviculare,* as one of the more attractive plants of the cereal field – hardly to be compared with pheasant's eye or corn cockle or even fumitory. A 'straggling and usually prostrate annual',[9] it carries up to six tiny, pink flowers on small spikes. Once it was classified as a common farmland .weed, but not any longer. Its population has collapsed. Too many of the dozens of herbicides listed in *The UK Pesticide Guide* cause it to twist and die.

There are few figures to record its decline. When cereal-growers rushed to drench their crops in the new hormone weedkillers, there was no official monitoring of how the new products were used or of their effects on the wider environment. Circumstantial evidence on the decline in knotgrass numbers is contained in the contamination figures for grain samples sent to the Cambridge seed testing station for registration. Throughout the 1940s and 50s knotgrass seed was a common contaminant of cereal seed. Then from the mid-1960s it began to disappear.

No one mourned the plant's passing. Scarcely anyone really noticed. But for one former resident of cereal fields its loss was of critical importance. The leaf beetle *Gastrophysa polygoni* is one of dozens commonly found in cereal fields, or at least it used to be. In the colourful world of leaf beetles, the Chrysomelidae, there is nothing remarkable about *G. polygoni*, recognisable chiefly by the reddish-yellow colour of its pronotum, the upper foreplate of the thorax. It just happens to be totally dependent on knotgrass.

Also known as the knotgrass beetle, it feeds almost exclusively on the weed.[10] Although on occasion it is known to eat the closely related weed black bindweed, its strong preference is for *Polygonum aviculare.* In the absence of the species it cannot survive. Thus as hormone weedkillers have eliminated the weed from cereal fields, the beetle has gone into decline, too. Again there are no survey figures, but routine reports from entomologists of the Ministry of Agriculture's development agency, ADAS (scheduled to be privatised at the time of writing), suggest that the main population collapse took place in the 1960s, just when the use of herbicide sprays had become universal. *G. polygoni* featured strongly in reports dating back to the 1950s, but by the 1970s the beetle's distribution had become localised. Indeed it had all but disappeared from many cereal fields. As with the plant it fed on, the beetle's loss went largely unnoticed.

Yet its larvae had been an important food source for game chicks like the partridge, as well as for many wild birds. Thus the destruction of a weed had indirectly affected the bird population on farmland. Such knock-on damage along the food chain is certain to have affected dozens of species as the industrialisation of farming gained momentum. *G. polygoni* is far from unique in having particular dietary requirements. Almost two-thirds of the food insects preferred by partridge chicks are known to be phytophagous – they feed on broad-leaved weeds. And for the past forty years farmers have been busy spraying them out.

Nowadays most cereal growers spray their crops with herbicides – weedkillers – at least twice, sometimes more, a practice that has decimated many once-common weed species. So even when these chemicals are not directly toxic to insects, they can wipe out large numbers simply by removing their food source. Arable fields are not merely fields with crops in them. They make up a complex ecosystem with dozens, perhaps hundreds, of species interacting within the crop and in the soil that sustains it. The adoption of chemical farming was certain to have unexpected side effects; the destruction of our farmland birds, for example. The only surprise is that anyone should be surprised.

When in the late 1960s the young zoologist Dick Potts went in search of a job studying farmland ecology he didn't receive too many offers. Farmland was for crops, he was told, not for wildlife. For his doctorate he had studied the way the organochlorine insecticide dieldrin, used in sheep dips, had polluted watercourses then moved up the food chain through fish and seabirds. Now he wanted to look at similar pesticide effects on farmland ecosystems. Unfortunately few scientists viewed farms in this way. Fields were not nature reserves, they reminded him.

The offer, when it came, was from a surprising direction. The Game Conservancy Trust is an independent research charity operating from a rambling manor house on the banks of the Hampshire Avon. Its finance comes chiefly from landowners with an interest in shooting and fishing, and by the late 1960s the members were getting very worried about their partridges. Population numbers had been falling. Changes to agriculture were suspected. Dick Potts was taken on to investigate the causes. So began a unique and pioneering study of how farming methods determine the health of wildlife and the countryside.

While concerned primarily with game birds, the Trust's farmland ecology project has shed new light on the decline of wild bird populations on farmland. It was Dick Potts's colleague Nick Sotherton who in the late 1970s confirmed the close dependence of the leaf beetle *G. polygoni* on knotgrass. Now the work, spanning more than twenty-eight years, has begun to show how industrial farming methods are linked to the loss of wildlife in the countryside.

From its base at Fordingbridge the Game Conservancy Trust has been monitoring partridge numbers since the 1930s. The grey partridge, *Perdix perdix,* is a native species predominantly associated with cereal crops. The study has shown that chick survival is one of the key factors determining the size of the breeding population, and this in turn is linked to the availability of food insects. High on the list of preferred species are beetles – including leaf beetles, ground beetles and weevils – along with the larvae of moths and sawflies. Many such invertebrates are abundant at the edges of cereal crops where gamebird chicks do their foraging. Or at least they used to be.

Game Conservancy Trust monitoring has revealed a worrying fall in partridge breeding densities dating back to the 1950s. Numbers declined throughout the 60s and 70s and by the late 1980s were down to just 4 pairs to 250 acres. Back in the 1950s average breeding densities were five times as high.[11] The initial collapse coincided with a steep rise in the use of pesticides, and suspicion immediately fell on the highly toxic compounds then in use, such as the insecticide dieldrin.

However, the more noxious materials were gradually replaced by less toxic products, many of them applied at lower dose rates. Even so partridge numbers continued to fall. Clearly a more elusive mechanism than direct poisoning was in play, and there was every likelihood that it was having an impact on other farmland bird species.

It is now known that at least 10 farmland bird species have suffered population declines of 50 per cent or more during the past twenty-five years.[12] Few birds live exclusively in cereal fields – perhaps only the skylark and the corn bunting can exist there permanently. However, many common birds of grassland, hedge and woodland edge feed in cereal fields from time to time. Dick Potts, now the Game Conservancy Trust's director general, estimates that at least 78 bird species could be affected by the ecological condition of cereal crops.

By 1970 the Fordingbridge research team had established a long-term monitoring system for plants and insects in cereal fields spread across the Sussex Downs. They wanted to find out whether the population collapse in grey partridges could be attributed to fluctuations in the numbers of prey insects. Following more than two decades of detailed observations a picture is emerging of the way industrial agriculture is destroying British wildlife. It does so by disrupting the food chain.

The area chosen for the study lies between the river Arun in the west and the river Adur in the east. This is the downland of the writer W. H. Hudson – a land of 'wild nature and a wide prospect'.[13] The wide prospect still remains, though sadly little is left of wild nature. By 1990 Game Conservancy Trust scientists had recorded a steady drop in numbers for more than 70 per cent of the invertebrate groups found in the study area.[14] The steepest fall was among the family known as rove beetles, Staphylinidae, noted by entomologists for their flying ability. Overall their numbers went down by more than two-thirds, with those of the genus *Tachyporus* contracting by 9 per cent a year.

Tachyporus species, many of which are fungus-feeding, began to fall in number following the widespread introduction of fungicide sprays during the 1970s, though no direct link has been proven. Cereal growers now use an average of three fungicide applications a year in their battle against crop disease. In doing so they appear to be knocking out the food source of an entire family of insects, which are then no longer available to the food chain. Such is the complexity of ecosystems.

There seems little doubt that the collapse in wildlife numbers over much of lowland Britain is due, at least in part, to the effects of chemical sprays. Agrochemical use has soared during the past thirty years. In 1994 every acre of winter wheat grown in Britain received an average of eight pesticide sprays, including three applications of fungicide.[15]

While the overall volume of pesticides has fallen back since its peak in the late 1980s, upwards of 11,000 tons of active ingredient – the raw chemical compound – are still being poured over British cereal crops each year. The total for all farm crops is 21,000 tons. With hundreds of individual products officially cleared for use, it is impossible to predict the long-term impact on arable ecosystems of either an individual chemical or the pesticide cocktail.

At the time agrochemical use began to take off in the 1950s, no official monitoring programme was in place. Routine checks are now carried out by MAFF's Pesticide Usage Survey Group, based at the Central Science Laboratory in Harpenden. But the group concentrates on direct toxic effects, and in any case did not begin its work until 1970, more than a decade after the major expansion in herbicide sprays had taken place. Whatever the damage done in those early years, it is now clear that their overall impact on the plant life of lowland Britain has been catastrophic.

Some species once considered problem weeds are now among the rarest plants in the country. The corn buttercup, *Ranunculus arvensis*, though widespread until the 1960s, now occurs in fewer than 25 sites.[16] Lamb's succory and thorow-wax have become extinct. The sharp decline of many more species – among them cornflower, broad-leaved spurge, red hemp-nettle, shepherd's needle and the almost extinct corn parsley – is at least partly due to herbicides.[17] Other factors may have played a role: new seed cleaning methods, changes in crop rotation and high fertiliser inputs have all been implicated in the de-flowering of Britain's farmland. But none can have matched the killing efficiency of the spray boom.

Cereal crop monitoring by the Game Conservancy Trust also began in the 1970s. In the Sussex study some plants – like cornflower and pheasant's eye – were already extinct locally, while many more were in steep decline. In the intervening quarter century little has changed for the better. Of 131 flowering plant species recorded on the site, all but one – cleavers – have continued to dwindle in number. Some species like corn gromwell and narrow-fruited corn salad, once abundant in most fields, now survive in just a handful of field edges. Corn parsley survives in a single field corner. All three are likely to disappear.

The mass destruction of so many familiar field plants has contributed in no small measure to the growing cynicism of the public. Who can relate to a drilled monoculture of identical wheat plants that will not tolerate even a few poppies or corn marigolds? Before the coming of the sprayer something like 17 per cent of all British flowering plants were found in cereal fields. With them came the invertebrates – ground beetles and butterflies – together with the seed-eating birds like yellowhammer and cirl bunting. The invertebrates brought in the insect-eaters – the fieldfare and skylark; also the small mammals: the voles, the mice and the shrews. The mammals in their turn attracted those larger hunters – the owl and the kestrel. Thus it was the arable weeds that brought life into our cereal fields. Now it is their destruction that drapes the fields in silence.

Could any of this have happened without subsidies? Price support greases the cogs that drive the great engine of destruction through our countryside. Cereal growers currently spend around £50 an acre on chemical sprays. Chemical fertilisers cost them as much again. But in 1996 they received subsidy cheques to the value of £108 an acre under the arable aid scheme operated by the CAP. Thus the public unwittingly finances the destruction of its own wildlife.

Subsidies and agrochemicals belong together; they are the twin buttresses that prop up industrial agriculture. Without pesticides farmers would not have dared abandon their rotations. Without public support they could not have afforded to, at least not on the present scale. Nor would they have obliterated Britain's hay meadows. For the silence that has fallen on our crop fields now hangs over our grasslands too.

Britain is a nation of grass; its hues clothe our hillsides and carpet the valley floors. More than half the UK's 30 million acres of farmland is occupied by grass; this in addition to the 15 million acres or so of unenclosed 'rough grazings', a category which includes large areas of coarse mountain and moorland grass.[18]

Like the cereal crop, a grass field is an ecosystem. In its semi-natural state the sward is made up of a mixture of grasses and flowering plants, the precise botanical composition being determined by such factors as climate, soil type, rainfall and the way the grass is managed. Each plant species is associated with its own characteristic fauna, and generally the more botanically diverse the sward the greater its wildlife interest.

An ancient chalk downland turf, for example, may contain a dozen or more grass species together with a number of chalkland flowers such as cowslip, dropwort and devil's bit scabious. There may be a number of rarer plants too: burnt orchid, dwarf sedge or clustered bellflower. On lower land a classic hay meadow could well contain more than a hundred species, including flowering plants like meadow buttercup, black knapweed, hay rattle, cowslip and wild daffodil.

Britain's most botanically rich grasslands are valuable as examples of ecosystem types.[19] Their floral diversity is often matched by the variety of invertebrates that inhabit them. Many of these associated fauna have specific food plant requirements: both the adonis and chalk hill butterflies are dependent on the horseshoe vetch. Species-rich grasslands also act as reservoirs of plants that are elsewhere becoming rare; culinary herbs like marjoram, thyme and basil, or the early ancestors of some of our forage crops and vegetables such as sainfoin and cabbage. Thus grasslands can represent an important gene pool from which to breed new varieties.

Yet this unique resource is rapidly being obliterated from the landscape. Under the inducements of guaranteed prices and an artificial market, UK farmers have spent the past half century 'improving' their grasslands to the point where the vast majority of them are now scientifically and culturally worthless. Like our arable lands, much of our grassland has been reduced to a lifeless monoculture. The aim of our production-fixated livestock industry is simple – to fill the green fields of Britain with a single species, the fast-growing perennial ryegrass.

Perennial ryegrass is the cuckoo of the pasture. In a fertile, well-drained soil it crowds out other species and soon dominates the sward. This gives the species distinct farmer appeal in a system that rewards the biggest producers with the highest subsidies. It is why the plough has been devouring old pastures at an unprecedented rate, making space for the grass that will put a few extra litres of milk in the bulk tank and fatten the bullocks a week or two earlier. But there is another weapon in use against Britain's flower-rich pastures, one that has done even more damage than the plough. Like the pesticides of the cereal fields, it is a gift from the chemical industry.

In 1856, at the height of farming's 'golden age', pioneering crop researcher John Bennet Lawes and his collaborator Joseph Henry Gilbert laid down a grassland experiment in one of the fields of Rothamsted Manor in Hertfordshire. At that time the Park Grass field had been in grassland for several hundred years and was managed by grazing or mowing for hay. Like the rest of Britain's farmland it was fertilised solely with organic manures, chiefly farmyard manure. Lawes and Gilbert wanted to discover how different levels of mineral fertilisers as well as organic manures affected the productivity of permanent pasture.

In the event the treatments produced such startling changes to the species composition of the sward that the Victorian pioneers concluded the results would be of greater interest to the botanist than to the farmer.[20] The experiment showed that fertilisers lead not only to higher yields, but to the wholesale loss of species. The greater the increase in production, the lower the species diversity of the pasture. In other words chemical fertilisers knock out wild flowers. Yet a century later Britain was offering its farmers cash inducements to apply fertilisers to flower-rich meadows over the length and breadth of the country.

Between the mid-60s and the mid-80s the application rate of nitrogen fertiliser to permanent grassland went up by 380 per cent and the area treated rose by more than 100 per cent. Today 85 per cent of all grassland in England and Wales is treated with nitrogen fertiliser. The average rate is around 100 units an acre, although short-term grass leys receive higher amounts than permanent grass.

As with the development of herbicides, the rapid expansion of intensive grassland began during the last war. And once more the chemical company ICI played a major part in the change. At the start of the war the company was well placed to make its influence felt in the corridors of power. Its former agricultural adviser was now chief adviser to the Minister of Agriculture, while several of its senior scientists sat on Ministry technical committees. Following vigorous lobbying, MAFF was persuaded to embark on a massive campaign to promote silage, a winter fodder crop better suited to monoculture and high fertiliser inputs than traditional hay.

The campaign was run by the 'War Ags', with advisers being sent on training courses organised by ICI. The company was also pushing the concept of 'ley farming', the production of livestock from heavily fertilised, short-term grassland in place of old, highly fertile pastures with a range of species. After the war the company continued to work closely with MAFF in the promulgation of intensive grassland. Indeed, farming advisers from ICI and the government's own advisory service, NAAS, were almost indistinguishable in their urging of farmers to use more nitrogen fertiliser.

When it comes to safeguarding meadow flowers there is no 'safe' level of nitrogen. Experiments in a flower-rich Somerset hay meadow have shown that rates as low as 20 units an acre annually, a tiny amount by modern standards, are enough to knock out the less competitive meadow flowers.[21] As in the cereal ecosystem, when plant species disappear the invertebrates go too. An unimproved grassland may contain up to 50 species of flowering plant and 20 species of butterfly; an improved ryegrass sward will contain only one plant with no associated butterflies. The impoverishment even extends to the soil. Fertilisers have been shown to reduce the soil populations of such fauna as earthworms, millepedes and springtails. Though the intensive livestock areas of western Britain may look green enough, they are no less wildlife deserts than the arable 'prairies' of the east.

Such complexities are of little concern to the dairy farmer with a profitable quota to fill. Nitrogen fertiliser from the bag is the cheapest way to produce more milk. As a result unimproved species-rich grassland is now a rare and threatened habitat. According to the UK Biodiversity Steering Group the total national reserve is currently estimated at less than 40,000 acres, and a number of characteristic species, like green-winged orchid, snake's head fritillary and adder's-tongue fern, have become extremely scarce.

The total destruction of semi-natural lowland grassland since

1930, estimated at 97 per cent, is on a scale that is scarcely comprehensible. Even in the Yorkshire Dales, an area with more upland meadows than most, less than 5 per cent is now considered species-rich. In Worcestershire, another supposed 'stronghold', barely 1,200 acres survive – remnants, only, of a habitat that once clothed much of lowland Britain.

At Rothamsted Experimental Station Lawes and Gilbert's early experiment on grassland manuring is maintained to this day, one of a number of classical experiments which have run continuously for more than a century. The control plots receiving no fertiliser still contain more than 60 species, just as they did in 1856. In the unlimed plots receiving heavy applications of the nitrogen compound ammonium sulphate there remains just one species in the sward, the grass Yorkshire Fog.

For a century now we have known that artificial fertilisers despoil the environment. Yet Britain's farmers have felt it necessary to demonstrate the fact afresh in every corner of the land. There is no way of recovering what has been lost. After three decades or more of fertilisers there are precious few seeds left in the soil 'seed bank' but those of ryegrass. Wildflower seeds 'imported' from elsewhere may produce an imitation meadow, but they will never re-create what was there before. Britain's glorious meadowlands have gone for ever, victims of the drive to produce more surplus butter. Now there is evidence that their destruction may not even have delivered a real increase in productivity.

In the *Origin of Species* Charles Darwin wrote: 'It has been experimentally proved, if a plot of ground be sown with one species of grass, and a similar plot be sown with several distinct genera of grasses, a greater number of plants and dry herbage can be raised in the latter than in the former case.'[22] New research from the American prairies supports Darwin's view. It shows that the greater the diversity of species the better the utilisation of soil nitrogen.[23] As an ecosystem the species-rich meadow is more productive. The apparently higher output of the grass monoculture is sustained only by heavy inputs of chemical fertiliser, much of which is lost to the ecosystem and ends up polluting the local stream or river.

If Edith Holden were to compile her *Nature Notes* today she would find precious little to fill the pages. Warwickshire has weathered the industrialisation of farming no better than any other lowland county. Sites of wildlife interest now occupy just 5 per cent of the total land area, yet still the destruction continues. Over the past decade no fewer than one in five of its remaining flower-rich meadows have been lost to intensive agriculture. There are now less than 60 such meadows in the entire county.[24] After landfill – chiefly the development of former mineral workings – agriculture is the single greatest cause of habitat loss. At the turn of the century farmers were responsible for creating the countryside that Edith Holden so loved. As the century nears its end today's farmers have all but dismantled it. And many of them now have even greater ambitions.

3

THE NEW INHERITORS

Long before the BSE crisis erupted, the National Farmers' Union was aware that its members' image was in need of a shine. What with pesticide scares and daily demonstrations over calf exports, they had been getting a bad press. The union's response was to publish a glossy publicity brochure showing the caring side of the industry. Called *Farming – Take a Fresh Look,* it had on its front cover a photograph aimed straight at the public's comfort zone.

The location is a family farm in one of Britain's hill areas. On a bright spring day the breeze snatches a wisp of smoke from the chimney of a mellow stone farmhouse nestling beneath a wooded hillside. In the foreground the farmer and his dog move a small bunch of ewes and lambs across a meadow not yet wakened from its winter dormancy. Yellow daffodils speckle the grassy bank which borders the farmhouse garden, while on the trees the first dusting of leaves is visible.

This is the farming we all want to believe in, farming on a human scale, as warm and reassuring as log fires in winter and the smell of fresh-baked bread. But there is another view of farming in the late 1990s, one whose images fill the pages of the farming press. It is a world of vast fields and regimented crops in rows stretching into the far distance; a world of giant, self-propelled spray machines and featureless landscapes where nothing lives but what is planted.

This is the face the image-builders would rather we did not see – agriculture as a purely exploitive activity, ruthless, acquisitive and coldly rational. In public relations terms it is a disaster. Sensibly the NFU turns for its propaganda material to family farms, particularly those in the hills and uplands. These are the farms we are happy to support. Yet in economic terms they are irrelevant. Nowadays it is the large agribusiness enterprises which account for the vast bulk of

UK output. The publishers of farming papers know this only too well. While the public may warm to pictures of cosy farmhouses in the hills, the images farmers expect are those illustrating production on a big scale.

British agriculture is currently going through an unprecedented process of restructuring. Following three years of soaring profits arable farmers, in particular, are scrambling for extra acres to take advantage of economies of scale. At the same time many more are handing over their farms to professional management companies to run on their behalf. The purpose is the same – to improve efficiency and lift profits, to squeeze still more from the subsidy system.

The result has been a dramatic fall in both the number of farms producing the bulk of our food and the number of people running them. British agriculture is fast adopting a corporate structure dominated by relatively few large farming companies. The family farm is becoming marginalised.

Already the process is well advanced. When Rural Affairs Minister Tim Boswell published guidelines on how to conserve dwindling populations of farmland birds, he sent them to just 11,000 arable farmers. The rest he considered too small to be worth bothering with. As few as 9,000 specialists are estimated to account for 60 per cent of the UK's entire cereal production.[1] A similar concentration has taken place in other farming sectors. In dairying, for example, 9,500 farmers produce 60 per cent of all milk, while 11,500 livestock farmers account for 60 per cent of the country's beef and sheep.

With 2,000 acres of arable crops in Cambridgeshire, farmer and broadcaster Oliver Walston is likely to be among those 9,000 cereal specialists. Early in 1995 he started to get hate mail. There were threatening letters, mostly anonymous, warning of the dreadful fate that was to befall him. There were phone calls, too, or rather menacing messages left on the answering machine. The general thrust of their argument was that someone ought to see to him.

The threats were not from irate taxpayers. They were from fellow farmers. His 'crime', the single act which had aroused the anger of his former colleagues, was to reveal to the public the size of his subsidy cheque.

It used to be simple to obscure the truth of EU arable subsidies. They were safely hidden in inflated market prices and export aids. But following the 'reforms' of 1992 they have become rather more visible. Through the changes introduced by Agriculture Commissioner Ray MacSharry, price support was to be progressively reduced, allowing farm prices to edge toward market levels. At the same time there was to be compulsory set-aside under which part of the arable area on every farm would come out of production.

However, crop farmers were to be 'compensated' for this loss of support. From now on they would get a new form of subsidy, the arable area payment, which would be posted direct to the farm. The rates for 1995 were set at £109 per acre for wheat and £193 per acre for oilseed rape. In addition there would be a fixed payment of £138 an acre on land in set-aside. Under the reforms Oliver Walston was sent a cheque for nearly £200,000 courtesy of MAFF and the EU Commission. He promptly wrote an article for the *Sunday Times* thanking taxpayers for their generosity and suggesting they needed their heads examining.

'My Bumper Crop From Brussels' ran the headline alongside a picture of a laughing Walston standing in his subsidised wheat crop. 'I am a happy man. Not just because the harvest has been easy this year, not because prices are higher than last year, but because by Christmas I will receive a little brown envelope. The postmark will be Guildford but the cheque inside, for almost £200,000, will come from Brussels. It is my share of the CAP.'

This gentle piece of satire brought the ire of the landed sector crashing through his letter box. His fellow farmers were outraged. They had had their fig leaf snatched away, and by one of their own kind too. They accused him of treachery and of 'letting the side down'. An Essex farmer, with nearly 8,000 acres and an annual subsidy cheque amounting to nearly £1 million, warned him about the dangers of discussing in public issues that were 'too complex for the average person to comprehend'. These were matters farmers should reveal only to intimates – their accountants, for example.

The Ministry of Agriculture is equally diffident about revealing who gets what under the new scheme. In a House of Commons Written Answer, Minister of State Michael Jack released figures covering combined payments under arable and livestock schemes. These showed that in 1994 almost 11,000 farmers each received at least £30,000, more than 7,000 received at least £40,000, and 5,000 received more than £50,000.[2]

A handful are thought to have collected lottery-style pay-outs under CAP reform. A dozen are believed to have banked government cheques worth more than £1 million each, while four received more than £5 million. Despite years of overproduction, farmers continue to be paid as if their products were in short supply. In 1993/94 UK farm support, including both direct payments from the taxpayer and market support, made up 50 per cent of total gross output for cereals.[3]

Then in 1995 the unimaginable happened. With global wheat stocks at their lowest level for twenty years, the world price of grain actually rose above the EU Intervention price. This was almost unprecedented. For the first time in decades the EU could begin exporting wheat without the support of huge export subsidies. Cereal growers whose area payment cheques were supposed, in part, to compensate them for reduced prices, found they could sell their grain at higher prices than ever.

The falling value of sterling added to the general euphoria. In the three years following Britain's withdrawal from the European exchange rate mechanism the value of the pound slipped by 30 per cent. Through the convoluted mechanisms of European green currencies this was translated into higher support payments for the UK, a fortuitous convergence of events which made British grain growers feel the war had started again. They had not seen a surge in prices like this since there had been U-boats in the Channel.

In autumn 1996 chartered accountants Deloitte and Touche Agriculture reported farmers in England as having closed the books on their most profitable year ever thanks to a combination of high produce prices, world shortages and EU aid payments.[4] Clients with accounting year ends up to June 1996 had recorded an average net farm income 29 per cent higher than a year earlier, though the accountants warned that with volatile markets farmers should plan for leaner times to come.

Even so by 1995 the net income of cereal farms had risen in real terms by 138 per cent over just four years. *Farmers Weekly* roared in defence of its readers. 'Why should farmers alone be ashamed of making good profits? A good dry harvest is nothing more than farmers deserve.'[5] Unfortunately when farmers find themselves flush with cash they rarely think of rushing out to buy a new Jag or BMW. They are far more likely to set their sights on the odd parcel of land that comes up for sale next door. Usually it is worth more to them than to other buyers, since by adding it to their main holding they can spread their overheads and bring down the costs per ton of grain. Thus the established farmer is invariably able to outbid the would-be new entrant.

In the years following CAP reform farmland prices have climbed almost as steeply as farm incomes, bid up chiefly by arable farmers with big profits to spend. In the three years from 1992 to 1995 farmland prices rose by 67 per cent, with the price of prime arable land leaping by an unprecedented 92 per cent.[6] This was at a time when the residential property market remained firmly in the doldrums. Not surprisingly, 1995 was described by land agents Savills as 'a splendid year for farmland investors'. Despite the BSE crisis the land price boom continued into 1996.[7]

Farmers enjoy spending their profits on land. They see it as a tangible sign of success – expanding the empire, building bigger businesses to pass on to their offspring. In economic terms their incomes are said to be capitalised into land values. But with a large part of those incomes coming from subsidies, it is the taxpayer who fuels land price inflation.[8] According to the Royal Institution of Chartered Surveyors the strongest demand in 1995 was for arable land eligible for the area aid subsidy scheme.[9]

The taxpayer's reward for enhancing the capital worth of landowners is the further impoverishment of the countryside. Inflated land values spur farm intensification as the new owner works the land harder to get his money back. Agricultural suppliers want a slice of the action, too. When farm incomes rise so does the cost of inputs: the sprays, fertilisers, animal feeds and machinery farmers have come to rely on. In the year following the 1995 cereal bonanza fertiliser costs went up 25 per cent, agrochemicals by 8 per cent, seed by 20 per cent and machinery by 9 per cent.[10] This was predictable. It has been established that half the gross margin increase generated by any support programme gets swallowed up in input costs.[11]

This is the paradox of state support for agriculture. While it may increase asset values, it puts little or no cash in the pockets of the majority of farmers. Instead it traps them in a spiral of inflation, pushing up rents, which are linked to land values, and raising the cost of their inputs. The penalty for losing yield to pests and disease becomes ever more costly.

In the summer of 1994 cereal growers in many parts of England faced a late-season threat to their wheat. Under particular conditions of warmth and humidity the orange wheat blossom midge can attack crops in large numbers, laying its eggs at the flowering stage of the plant's growth cycle. The resulting larvae feed on the surface of young grains at the 'milky ripe' stage. Mould growth in the resulting cavities can lead to discolouration and the loss of market value.

In June 1994 the fly began appearing in wheat crops. A few brave farmers withheld sprays in the belief that larvae-feeding insects like ladybirds and rove beetles would mop-up the pest naturally. But with so much already invested in the crop – the rent and bank borrowings on the land plus the cost of inputs like seed and fertiliser – most farmers were not prepared to take the risk. Instead they sprayed with insecticides, and in particular the organophosphate compounds chlorpyrifos and triazophos. In the single month of June a total of 750,000 acres were sprayed. As a result the midge infestation was brought under control, but the damage done to wildlife was incalculable.

Broad-spectrum insecticides like chlorpyrifos and triazophos do not merely kill the target pest, they are likely to wipe out thousands of other insects in the crop. This means the birds feeding on these insects will be reduced as well. The wide-scale use of insecticides in the summer of 1994 is thought to have caused more ecological damage than in any previous year.[12] Yet the following summer farmers were again out spraying with insecticides, this time against cereal aphids. The combined effect of high profits and rising costs made them less willing than ever to risk yield losses.

When inflation threatens their margins farmers have three main responses open to them. First they can try to reduce their costs. This usually means shedding staff and relying on bigger machines to get the job done. It is no coincidence that the sales of larger tractors have boomed in recent years. At the end of 1995 *Farmers Weekly* announced triumphantly that the average output of new tractors sold that year had broken through the 100hp barrier for the first time.[13] Ominously, a clutch of truly giant American tractors – 350hp or more – are currently attracting a lot of attention at UK agricultural shows.

As an alternative to cost-cutting farmers can try to raise their output, to push for still higher yields. By increasing output they can spread their overhead costs over a larger volume of product, and so reduce unit costs. However, on the highly mechanised farm any such increase is likely to mean even heavier chemical inputs – more fertilisers and pesticide sprays. These will damage still further the fragile farmland ecosystem. But for many farmers the pressures of rising costs and diminished margins have made a third option attractive. They are handing their businesses over to farm management companies to run on their behalf.

Contract farming is a major growth sector in post-reform agriculture. Companies, large and small, are getting in on the act. In return for a fee and a substantial share of the profits they will take on the entire management and running of a farm, supplying when necessary all the labour, machinery and inputs. Contract farming is one of the forces behind the massive restructuring now taking place in the industry. Although farmland may remain in the nominal ownership of a large number of people, it is increasingly under the control of very few. Vincent Hedley Lewis, senior farming partner with accountants Deloitte and Touche Agriculture has forecast that by the turn of the century 80 per cent of agricultural production will be in the hands of just 12,000 decision-makers.[14] Whether or not they own land, these will be the people who determine the fate of our countryside and the quality, or otherwise, of our food.

Four big players dominate the contract farming business. One of the first in the field was the Herefordshire-based company Velcourt, whose clients include some of the big landowning institutions, insurance companies and pension funds, as well as private farmers and landowners. What they all share is the desire to see their land farmed more profitably, and they have decided a specialist farming company is more likely to deliver. Velcourt's corporate blurb sums up the reasoning. 'As the financial pressures intensify, it is often best to separate land ownership from its operation, leaving the latter to experts who can reap the full rewards of economies of scale and specialist business management.'

In 1994 Velcourt farmed almost 60,000 acres on behalf of landowning clients. The other big players in contract farming are Sentry Farming, Booker Agriculture and CWS Agriculture, the Co-op's farming division, which farms 50,000 acres on its own account as well as managing farms for other landowners. Beneath the big four, dozens of smaller companies and individual contractors fight it out for a share of a fast-growing market. The more ruthless of them do little more than mine the soil and exploit rural workers.

Contractors seldom feel any long-term commitment either to the land or to the local community. The first thing they are likely to do on taking over a farm is to sack the staff. Some may be re-hired on a self-employed basis, but the more unscrupulous firms will merely take on people at busy times, at harvest for example, then lay them off immediately afterwards. Much of the day-to-day work will be done by a small core of peripatetic workers.

The main routine job will be spraying. Contractors have no incentive to withhold pesticides for the sake of the environment. On the contrary, they are likely to have a profit share to protect. Whenever there is the merest chance of a crop disease they will spray, just to be on the safe side, particularly with the cheaper broad-spectrum chemicals which are usually the most environmentally damaging.

Some of the hungrier companies are reported to offer landowners a guaranteed £150 an acre annually in return for contracts to run their farms over a three-year or five-year period, this in addition to providing owners with a share of the profits.[15] At these prices the contractor has no option but to exploit the land for all it is worth knowing that after the term of the agreement he can walk away.

The well-established farming companies take a rather more responsible attitude. Velcourt's publicity pledges 'a positive attitude towards management of the countryside', one which is 'sensitive to the needs of local flora and fauna'. Sentry Farming goes further. It offers a 'Green Guarantee'. The company says it will not use agrochemicals or fertilisers at levels 'which could cause undue damage to wildlife and the environment', though the word 'undue' might be open to interpretation. The company also undertakes, *where possible,* to 'preserve trees and hedges as habitats for wildlife'.

Such statements are not wholly a matter of public relations. Farmland subject to environmental management agreements now attracts a premium in the market, as does land eligible for arable area payments. There are subsidies in hedges nowadays, and a contractor ripping one out unnecessarily is not likely to hang onto his contract for long. Nevertheless a farming company is almost certain to drive the land hard.

Whatever their green credentials, the contract companies have one overriding objective – to make high profits. How else would they persuade owners to entrust their farms to them? A cut in labour is almost inevitable. Jobs are lost, and those that remain are filled by the company's own staff. The local manager may be a young graduate brought in from the other end of the country. The link with the local community is broken.

Partly because of their minimal use of labour, most farm management companies are heavily reliant on pesticides. Many view agrochemicals as the surest way to achieve high yields and maximum profits. Comparative cereal-growing trials carried out by Velcourt linked the highest margins to a pesticide programme which included no less than four treatments with insecticide, one of which was the broad-spectrum organophosphorus compound dimethoate.[16] Yet evidence is accumulating that similar margins can be obtained from lower-yielding crops receiving far fewer pesticides.

In a flag-waving exercise at the 1995 Royal Show, Velcourt set up a demonstration crop of Hereward winter wheat grown on a high-input system. There for the admiring farmers stood the perfect crop, with not a weed, not a blemish; and alongside it a signboard giving technical details of the sprays and chemicals used. These included a weed grass herbicide, three doses of insecticide – two in the autumn and a third in spring – four fungicide sprays and three applications of chemical growth regulator. Total input cost up to mid-June – £117 an acre.

On a nearby plot a similar demonstration crop of winter wheat had been grown by a team from Long Ashton Research Station near Bristol. Their aim was rather different. They wanted to show that crops grown with low levels of pesticide could be equally profitable. The input cost of this crop was less than half that of the Velcourt system, yet the profits were expected to be similar. If cereal-growing were not supported by large subsidies, farmers would have no option but to follow such low-input methods. But as things are, the generosity of taxpayers makes it worthwhile to chase peak yields with ever higher doses of pesticide.

The farming companies claim to use chemicals responsibly. They apply only those products needed to deal with specific threats from weeds, pests and diseases. At the same time they are clinically efficient in their pursuit of maximum profit. In its own publicity material Velcourt boasts of achieving yields and profits which consistently outperform those of the top 10 per cent of farmers in the Cambridge University Farm Business Survey. While this may delight Velcourt's clients, its methods inevitably subject arable ecosystems to a severe chemical pasting.

The big farm management companies are applying their profit-orientated methods across vast swathes of the British countryside. And they are able to pick up all the subsidies for doing so. Thanks to the UK government's stout defence of large farmers, land farmed by a contract firm operating on 50,000 acres or more is as eligible for arable support payments as the small farmer with just 50 acres. In 1995 area payments, the EU's direct subsidies to arable farmers, amounted to £109 an acre for cereals, almost enough to cover Velcourt's chemical bill.

The land farmed with such ruthless efficiency retains little wildlife, although the farming companies may choose to dig a pond or plant the odd copse or hedge for cosmetic reasons. Nor are there any gains for rural communities. Corporate farming destroys local jobs and buys its machinery and chemicals globally. This is capitalism in its purest form, cold, rational. Yet we continue to shower it with vast amounts of money from public funds, while the NFU lobbyists maintain the fiction that somehow this benefits the fabric of the countryside.

The annual Cereals Event held in June is a specialist show for business-minded arable farmers, a chance to inspect demonstration plots of the latest crop varieties together with the machinery and sprays that produced them. Host farm for the 1996 event was the 2,690-acre estate of the Nevile family at Aubourn in Lincolnshire. The land is chiefly devoted to arable crops, details of which were set out in the event's official guide. Under the arable area scheme they are eligible for a direct public subsidy of around £270,000.

On the Nevile estate EU largesse supports a chemical operation that runs with the precision of a motor assembly plant. A demonstration plot of the winter wheat variety Brigadier gave visitors to the 1996 event an insight into the process. Sown in September, the crop was sprayed twice in the autumn, once with an insecticide and later with a combined treatment of insecticide and weedkiller. In April and May the following year it received no less than six separate fungicide treatments. In addition there were applications of growth regulators and trace elements.

In terms of sheer technical efficiency the system is impressive. It is also applied with considerable care for the environment. The management team follows the principles of Integrated Crop Management (ICM), which aims to balance economic production with positive environmental management. For example, a half-metre unsown strip is left around most fields partly to provide feeding and hunting grounds for insects, birds and small mammals.

Even so, farming systems based on continuous arable cropping and heavily reliant on agrochemicals inevitably reduce the overall biodiversity of the landscape. Their support with public money means they are applied over a far wider area than if left to market forces alone. The Nevile estate is farmed by a management company, Aubourn Farming, which was set up in the mid-1980s by the estate manager. Now part of land agents Savills, the company provides management and advisory services to farmers and landowners occupying 50,000 acres, chiefly in Lincolnshire, Yorkshire and Nottinghamshire. Thus the efficiencies of industrial agriculture are spread across the British countryside.

The NFU may consider it politic to put a family hill farm on the cover of its publicity brochure, but this is not where the bulk of public support goes. Most ends up with large farmers or with the contract farming companies who manage an ever increasing part of the British countryside. Any one of the major companies running 50,000 to 60,000 acres on behalf of private landowners or City investors may be sharing in an annual windfall of £5 million or so from the taxpayer. Payments to farmers and landowners under the arable area scheme are added to the output side of the balance sheet.

This will provide the contract company's fee and also the profit to be shared with the client at the end of the season. In this way taxpayers continue to fund the concentration of British farming.

Writing in *Farmers Weekly* Vincent Hedley Lewis, who himself farms 1,700 acres of arable land in Lincolnshire, warned politicians against capping support payments to large farmers. Such a decision would be folly, he wrote. Large farming businesses were the ones with the resources to compete in the 1990s and beyond. An upper limit on arable area payments would put an end to rationalisation which was vital to the future prosperity of UK agriculture and the rural economy.

It seems Mr Lewis is equally opposed to any attempt to control inputs such as fertilisers and agrochemicals. At the 1995 Oxford Farming Conference he warned that 'artificial input controls' would discriminate against 'efficient' farmers.[17] They would be prevented from making the cuts in unit production costs necessary if they are to compete without public support.

Thus chemical sprays and large farms are claimed to be crucial for the industry's survival in a free-trading global food market. It is a view endorsed by Julia Walsh, chief executive of ADAS. 'The critical focus over the coming years will be upon competitiveness. This will require strict attention to reducing unit costs.'[18] An annual injection of £6.5 billion or so in public funds to make British agriculture more competitive is therefore construed as a worthwhile national investment. The argument has a long pedigree.

In December 1968 the *Daily Telegraph* ran a story under the headline: 'British Hedgerows Fall to Advance of Machines'.[19] Alongside a picture of a flat, featureless landscape, the article tells of thousands of miles of hedgerow being torn up to make way for giant farm machines. A Lincolnshire farmer, who admits to having removed sixty miles of hedgerow from his 3,000-acre farm, defends the action. 'If the farmer doesn't organise his land to produce cheap food he will not be able to compete with stuff dumped from abroad.' Thirty years ago the countryside was being impoverished to make agriculture competitive; and then, as now, it was being carried out with a huge injection of public money.

At the time that Lincolnshire farmer was stoutly defending the degradation of the British landscape, he and his fellows were being supported with £2.2 billion from the taxpayer, measured at today's values. Far from being exposed to a competitive world market, they were enjoying a degree of protection afforded to few other industries. The hedges of East Anglia were not ripped out in spite of subsidies, they were ripped out because of subsidies. And still the support system remains in place to plunder the British countryside.

A drive through Lincolnshire today provides a glimpse of the landscape of competitive agriculture. Here are the massive, hedgeless fields and the dreary monocultures to take on the farmers of Calgary and Kansas. We have created a prairie to out-compete the prairies, destroyed our heritage for the chance to sell cheap grain on world markets. Now we are to transplant this landscape across the length and breadth of lowland Britain.

For all their apparent devotion to a featureless countryside, the farmers of eastern England do their best to blot it out at home. Many of the farmhouses set amid bleak and empty fieldscapes are screened by trees and shrub-filled gardens; small oases in the deserts their owners have created. It is as if the farmers were trying to forget the world they have made. Out there is the factory, a place of function and utility, no more a place to linger and feel comfortable. Though they dare not admit it, they know they have created a wasteland. The tragedy is it need never have happened.

A study carried out at London University's Wye College has looked at how much land Britain would need to feed itself by the turn of the century.[20] The model incorporates forecasts of farm production, population size and food demand. Based on the most conservative extrapolations it suggests that 2.5 million acres of land could be surplus to the country's food production needs by the year 2000. Assuming current levels of self-sufficiency and production increases in line with those of recent years, the surplus could be as high as 15 million acres.

Studies for Europe as a whole are equally startling. One scientific group suggests that of 315 million acres of farmland in Europe, at least 125 million could be taken out of food production. Under some scenarios as many as 250 million acres might be removed; thus Europe could feed itself on just 20 per cent of its present land area. Annual fertiliser nitrogen use could be reduced from 11 million to just 3 million tons, and pesticide use from 400,000 to 100,000 kilograms.

Such projections open up seemingly limitless possibilities for the future of rural Britain. Far from being bound to the present damaging treadmill of production to stave off mass hunger, we have an opportunity to return to a more diverse and varied countryside, to an agriculture that again allows space for wild species. But the nation's new agri-industrialists have their eyes on a bigger game.

Unlimited price support may be on the way out; academics may forecast the return of surpluses, but riding to the rescue in a cloud of prairie dust come the new tiger economies of Asia and the Pacific rim. As their incomes power ahead so does their demand for grain. Richer countries eat more meat, and meat is produced from grain. Thus world prices are bound to rise in the longer term. That, at least, is what the big farmers and farming companies are counting on.

Certainly international food markets are changing fast. In South Korea, for example, per capita meat consumption has almost trebled over the past fifteen years, while its wheat and coarse grain consumption has doubled to 289kg a head. Population growth combined with higher living standards are projected to increase world grain requirements by 32 million tons a year, an annual increase of 1.8 per cent.[21] This is good news for arable farmers. After a decade or more of watching their grain dumped on world markets with the aid of substantial export subsidies, they now see a real prospect of selling it to people who actually want to buy it. The coffee-time talk at farming conferences is no longer about the price of fertiliser, but the economic advance of the Chinese middle class.

Lester Brown's disturbing book *Who Will Feed China?* fuelled the euphoria with its projected rise in industrialisation and fall in cropping area.[22] It held out the prospect of a grain deficit to dwarf even the combined export potential of the major producers. This is the revolution on which the big UK cereal growers are pinning their hopes. When the subsidies finally dry up they aim to be out there pursuing new markets in Asia and the Far East, helping to feed the hungry and earn export revenue for Britain.

The steep rise in world grain prices from the end of 1995 seemed to presage the new post-subsidy era. World cereal consumption had exceeded production for the third consecutive year, and global stocks were at a twenty-year low. Here was the way to survive when the public took away the price support.

Thus the current aim of the country's leading arable farmers – that inner corps of decision-makers who account for two-thirds of all output – is to bring down their unit costs. The years of subsidised dumping by the EU have left Britain with a range of sophisticated grain-handling equipment at its east- and south-coast ports. But to make use of them in a free-trading environment, UK growers have somehow to reduce their costs and become competitive. This is what lies behind the dramatic restructuring of British agriculture.

Some industry analysts forecast that the average UK cereal grower will need at least 800 acres to remain profitable. This is eight times the present average cereal area on British farms. Hence the scramble to buy land. Large farmers become larger by swallowing up their neighbours' land, while others stay in the race by handing over their farms to contract farming companies. Either way the consequences for the countryside are dire: bigger areas of cereals monoculture, fewer staff, heavier machines, a greater reliance on pesticides.

Thanks to subsidies this 'rationalisation' of lowland Britain is being carried out largely at public expense. Having financed the industrialisation of farming, taxpayers are now unwittingly paying for its globalisation. They are being required to turn yet more of the countryside into a featureless desert so that farmers can compete on world markets with the prairie producers of the USA and Canada.

And if the hoped-for world grain bonanza fails to materialise there is the possibility of getting into something really novel. Britain's industrial farmers no longer see themselves as growers of food but as suppliers of raw materials. While today's crops are still mainly processed into edible products, a range of alternative, non-food crops are currently under development. These include genetically modified oilseed and starch crops, producing materials for use in cosmetics, detergents, lubricating oils, pharmaceuticals and polymers.

Then there are the short-rotation coppices grown for fuel energy. Many in the industry see such biomass crops as an ideal way to fill empty acres no longer needed for food. The use of oilseed rape in the manufacture of fuels like biodiesel and bioethanol is also well developed, particularly in France. This is how the UK arable industry sees its future in a global market – as a low-cost producer of commodities to be shipped to processing markets around the world. And increasingly the lowland landscape is being stripped of its wildlife in preparation for the brave new era.

Outlining a ten-year plan for European agriculture Chris Bourchier, head of agricultural development at ADAS, identified 'global convergence' as the most likely policy option for the future.[23] Based on 'liberalised trading conditions and competitive pricing', it would utilise surplus land for 'real economic benefit', such as the growing of non-food crops on set-aside land.

Whether UK farmers can ever become substantial players in world commodity markets must remain questionable. Set against the potential of such land-rich states as the US, Canada, even France, the possibilities for Britain seem limited. They rest largely on assumptions that the recent tight world supply position will continue, but following good harvests in 1996 this is by no means certain. Given the EU's vast over-capacity for feeding itself – even without the accession of the former 'granary countries' of central and eastern

Europe – it may be that surpluses will reappear. Even the NFU has forecast that rising stocks are likely to present the EU with new difficulties by the end of the decade.

Structural changes in response to a world food shortage might be justified, but the current transformation of lowland agriculture is not the result of market signals. It is taking place on the back of public support. From the shelter of a protected market the industry is gearing itself up to meet an anticipated global demand that may or may not materialise in the future. The nation with the biggest farms in Europe is setting out to make them even bigger. The price for the countryside is likely to be high.

4

THE COUNTRYSIDE IN RANSOM

The marshy meadowlands of Somerset were witness to the last great battle on English soil. In 1685 the army of King James put down the Duke of Monmouth's ill-fated rebellion at Sedgemoor. Almost three hundred years later another uprising was fermenting on those same low-lying meadows. Farmers were demanding the 'right' to produce more subsidised food crops for the EU even though this would have destroyed a wetland wildlife site of international importance.

This time it was a government minister who was sent to sort out the Somerset rebellion. However, instead of confronting the rebels as the king's army had done, he bought them off, and in doing so put the entire countryside in jeopardy. The message was clear. No matter that Europe was in structural surplus for all major commodities, farm incomes and farmland values were to be maintained whatever the cost to the country and the countryside.

If there had been any doubts about the continuing strength of the farming lobby these were now dispelled. Without question it was the short-term financial advantage of agriculture that drove rural policy. Where this threatened politically sensitive wildlife areas they were to be protected at the margins as best they could, but nothing would be allowed to slow the inexorable advance of the agribusiness. It was a defining moment in post-war rural politics, for it marked the final separation of the British people from the land.

Most of the population had long been removed from it physically, of course. But this was, if anything, a more profound loss. From now on the public was to have no say as of right over what happened in the countryside. If people wanted wildlife they would have to pay for it, for every bird and every wild flower. At Sedgemoor the British public effectively lost the spiritual possession of their own land.

The Somerset Levels and Moors are an unlikely place for a

conflict. Bounded by the Mendip Hills to the north and the Blackdown and Quantocks to the south and south-west, the Levels make up the flood plains of eight rivers as they meander towards the Bristol Channel. This is a quiet, unspectacular landscape of rectangular meadows separated by a network of ditches or rhynes, many of which are lined with pollarded willows. It is also of immeasurable wildlife value.

The Somerset Levels support some of the largest blocks of species-rich wet meadows in the UK, along with half the nation's resource of lowland wet grassland.[1] The ditch systems themselves teem with plants and invertebrates, while the bird life is unsurpassed almost anywhere in the country. In the early 1980s the Levels carried one of the largest populations of breeding waders in lowland Britain. Lapwing, snipe, curlew and redshank were all present in large numbers. Yet not even this incomparable site could escape predation by an insatiable agribusiness.

With the lowest land below the level of spring high water, only a complex system of drainage channels, embanked rivers and pumps prevents large parts of the Levels reverting to open water. The traditional farming patterns reflect their propensity for flooding. Low-intensity livestock farms predominate, with the marshy fields grazed or cut for hay. It is this system which maintains the wild flowers in the meadows and provides breeding conditions for wading birds.

Enticed by inflated farm prices and generous drainage grants, an increasing number of farmers have abandoned their traditional methods and converted to the intensive systems they had read about in *Farmers Weekly*. If there was money to be made filling European Intervention stores with surplus butter, they wanted a share of it. Thus throughout the 1970s and early 80s drainage and agricultural intensification took place over much of the Levels.

Yet when a couple of farmers applied to MAFF for grants to fund a pump-drainage scheme on West Sedgemoor it was clear the improvers had gone a ditch too far. In wildlife terms West Sedgemoor was the finest of the Levels, providing a refuge for many of the species driven from other areas by drainage. To protect the threatened habitat, the Nature Conservancy Council declared it was to have 16,000 acres of the Levels designated as Sites of Special Scientific Interest, SSSIs. All future applications for drainage grants would first have to be referred to the NCC for approval.

Local farmers were incensed. They saw the move as an unwarranted interference in their right to manage the land as they chose.

Were they not entitled to the same European grants and subsidies as farmers anywhere else in Britain? There followed an angry stand-off between the farmers and conservationists. Matters came to a head when the NCC wrote to the farmers of West Sedgemoor advising them on how their activities were to be controlled in the first 2,400-acre SSSI. The response was immediate and hostile. In a managed media event NCC officials and local conservationists were burnt in effigy for the benefit of local TV crews. That is when Tom King, local MP and Secretary of State for the Environment, was dispatched to Somerset to sort out the trouble.

The Thatcher government of the early 1980s had its own reasons for wanting to end highly visible conflicts between farming interests and conservationists. Growing disquiet about the pace of countryside destruction had suddenly found a focus with the publication of Marion Shoard's scathing indictment of intensive agriculture, *The Theft of the Countryside*.[2] Though 'establishment conservationists' dismissed her prescription of planning controls for agriculture, she exposed both the scale of the damage wrought by farming and the huge level of public subsidy it received.

At the same time the NCC released data from a comprehensive study of habitat loss which it had begun in 1980. These showed that of the country's stock of key wildlife sites, the 3,500 SSSIs, no less than 13 per cent were being damaged or destroyed each year.[3] The public was outraged. MPs' postbags were full of angry letters demanding action to halt the destruction. The government's response was to highlight the new Wildlife and Countryside Act. Here was the way to protect the countryside and put an end to conflict. It would provide conservation by consent.

The Bill's passage through Parliament had been a difficult one, chiefly because the government tried throughout to protect farming and landowning interests. Lobbying by the National Farmers' Union and the Country Landowners' Association had been intense, and the government was determined to uphold the voluntary principle. Amendments that would have compelled landowners to protect wildlife sites were thrown out.

Instead the Ministry of Agriculture was merely required to take account of conservation matters when considering grant applications for improvements in SSSIs and national parks. And when an application was turned down on the grounds that the improvement might lead to damage to a wildlife site, the farmer would be entitled to compensation. In fact the farmer couldn't lose. State grants and subsidies were to be his birthright. When these were denied, public money would be forthcoming in some other form.

This was the message Tom King took to the revolting farmers of Somerset. At a meeting in Burrowbridge village hall, a mile from West Sedgemoor, he urged them to give the Wildlife Act a chance to work. There were forces in society, he warned, that would see the Act destroyed, not out of concern for the farmer but because they desired compulsion, confiscation rights and planning controls. Tom King added portentously: 'If we in Somerset fail to make this Act work, we run the risk of letting in something very much worse.'

Of course the farmers did make it work. They trooped off home and waited for the compensation cheques to arrive – the compensation for not intensifying at public expense and for not adding more costly surpluses to the groaning Intervention stores. As economists John Bowers and Paul Cheshire observe in their penetrating critique of rural policy, we had arrived at the absurd situation where farmers were offered large sums of money as inducements not to plough simply because equally large inducements were on offer to do just that.[4] Since most farm income comes by one route or another from support, compensation for profit forgone is, in effect, compensation for the loss of that support.

In this way the cost of conservation is made unnecessarily high. Through farm subsidies the public are obliged to bid up the cost of protecting their own countryside, their heritage. This was the 'deal' that Tom King sold to the farmers on the Somerset Levels. It is a principle now enshrined in virtually all countryside policies. Since the early 1980s a plethora of new schemes have been introduced to protect special habitats or particular parts of the countryside. All work in the same way. Farmers are paid to manage their farms in specified ways to maintain wildlife and habitats.

Yet the artificial inducements to intensify – the production subsidies – are still largely in place, so the cost of maintaining protected sites is constantly inflated. As farm subsidies rise so does the price of paying farmers not to take them up. Meanwhile in the wider countryside, those areas with no special designation for conservation, the obsessive drive to industrialise the landscape continues unabated.

In the flower-rich meadows of West Sedgemoor the conflicts of the 1980s now seem a distant memory. Snipe and lapwing nest in the tussocky grasses, while sedge warblers skitter through the rushes which line the ditches. In the air swifts dive on the waves of winged insects rising from the summer grassland, while far off a pair of hobbys tumble and soar in the still air. On this section of the Levels at least, the bird life appears as abundant as ever.

In the winter of 1995/96 the Royal Society for the Protection of Birds reported record numbers of over-wintering teal and widgeon on its West Sedgemoor reserve. Wintering wader populations were up too, with the number of lapwings being counted in their tens of thousands. No longer is the wildlife of West Sedgemoor under threat. But it is a sanctuary that has been bought at a price.

By the end of 1995 about 5,700 acres of the 140,000 acres that make up the Somerset Levels and Moors had been designated as SSSIs and were protected by management agreements. For 190 such agreements then in place farmers were paid a total of £370,000 a year for farming in the traditional way and not intensifying their land use. Most payments are calculated on the basis of 'profits forgone' – the farmer receives the annual sum as compensation for the extra profit he would have made had he been free to intensify his farming.

When the owners of listed buildings or commercial premises are denied permission to develop their properties, they are seldom entitled to compensation. But under the Wildlife and Countryside Act compensation payments are enshrined in the system. Oliver Rackham put it succinctly: 'One man, refused permission to drain a marsh, is able *in perpetuo* to draw public money to match both the hypothetical produce and the subsidies forgone; while another, forbidden (under a different statute) to build a factory in his garden, gets nothing.'[5]

The 'voluntary principle' turns out to be nothing less than a bribe. A farmer on a designated SSSI has only to threaten a change in his farming methods to receive guaranteed levels of compensation. The 'robbers' must be paid to go away, even though the stick they threaten us with is subsidised by the taxpayer.

The nation's stock of SSSIs comprises the last precious remnant of its once-glorious countryside. These are the glittering jewels in a battered and tarnished crown. Britain currently has more than 6,000 designated SSSIs occupying about 8 per cent of the land area. Under the official guidelines for their selection each site is intended to represent 'a significant fragment of the much-depleted resource of wild nature now remaining in this country'.[6] The overall network is supposed to ensure the survival of a 'necessary minimum' of Britain's wildlife and physical features.

This is the mechanism chosen by government to protect the country's heritage from a rapacious agribusiness; instead of controlling the predator it isolates the prey. Big farming is allowed to continue its work of homogenising the landscape at large while the vestigial remains of once-extensive habitats are concentrated into scattered islands and secured only by the payment of annual tributes. It is conservation by isolation. No longer does wild nature have a place in the countryside. Instead it is stored away in a secure rural recess. Even this has failed to protect it.

A report commissioned by Wildlife Link, which represents all the major voluntary organisations concerned with habitat protection, showed the SSSI system to be severely flawed.[7] The report revealed that about 5 per cent of all sites were damaged each year. A 1990 survey carried out on one-third of English SSSIs indicated that as many as 40 per cent of sites were deteriorating or had been damaged. Over-grazing was identified as one of the chief causes of chronic damage. Even on these supposed jewels of our wildlife heritage a bloated agribusiness was exerting its influence.

Management agreements covering these irreplaceable remnants of habitat cost taxpayers more than £7 million a year, chiefly in payments for profits forgone. Owners can also claim compensation for any fall in land value following notification of a site as an SSSI, an opportunity that has led to some spectacular pay-outs to landowners. In 1991 sheep farmer and former Scotrail chairman John Cameron was awarded £568,294 because he was prevented from claiming grants for tree planting and agricultural improvement on an SSSI at his Glen Lochay estate in Scotland.

Wildlife conservation law makes support payments the entitlement of every farmer and landowner. Though subsidies are financed from taxation, they cannot be withheld where a farmer happens to have an exquisite hay meadow or wetland site on his land. Taxpayers must fund the destruction of their heritage or come up with sufficient cash to induce a change of heart. There is always the possibility that farmers will threaten intensification even when they have no intention of carrying it out. They are merely 'working the system'. Yet despite its obvious shortcomings, the 'voluntary principle' remains central to the government's entire conservation strategy.

In 1987 Agriculture Minister Michael Jopling announced a new scheme to extend countryside protection beyond the relatively few wildlife strongholds represented by the SSSIs. It followed an earlier row over the threatened drainage and ploughing up of the Halvergate Marshes, the one sizeable stretch of open grazing marsh remaining in eastern England. As always, sweeteners were the government's chosen remedy. Farmers were offered subsidies for environmentally friendly farming as an alternative to their subsidies for growing wheat.

The arrangement gave rise to Michael Jopling's new conservation initiative, the Environmentally Sensitive Areas (ESA) scheme. This scheme differed from SSSI protection in that it was funded, in part, by the European Commission. However, the sacred voluntary principle was retained. Farmers continued to have a right to production subsidies. They could be dissuaded from claiming them only through the provision of cash. Many were more than happy to take it.

Since 1987 no fewer than 43 ESAs have been established in the UK, including the Pennine Dales, the Test Valley, the Cotswolds and Dartmoor. Together they occupy more than 8 million acres and cover a range of habitat types from lowland wet grassland to heather moorland. Under the EU agri-environment regulation introduced as part of the 1992 CAP reforms, a plethora of similar schemes have followed. These include a Moorland Scheme and a Habitat Scheme together with Countryside Stewardship and a Nitrate Sensitive Areas scheme in England and Tir Cymen in Wales.

In 1995 MAFF budgeted £52 million for its various agri-environment schemes, just 1.8 per cent of overall public spending on agriculture. Expenditure under the Arable Area Payments Scheme alone amounted to £1.3 billion. Not surprisingly, actual spending under the agri-environment schemes fell well short of the budgeted sum. Most farmers were doing so well from production subsidies they had no intention of signing up to anything that would restrict their freedom to apply pesticides and artificial fertiliser.

An example was provided by the Wildlife Trusts in evidence to the House of Commons Agriculture Committee.[8] Farmers in the Suffolk River Valley ESA scheme were being offered £97 an acre for converting intensive arable land to extensive grazing pasture. Yet under the Arable Area Payments scheme they were able to claim £138 an acre for set-aside, £109 an acre for cereals and £192 an acre for oilseed rape. Taking account of land values and crop prices, the profit forgone by converting to grassland could be as much as £263 an acre. Understandably, Suffolk farmers showed no great eagerness to make the switch. Of more than 80,000 acres eligible for the scheme, just 800 acres had been entered for conversion by the summer of 1996. State supported production continues to price conservation out of the market.

The Somerset Levels were included in the ESA scheme from its inception in 1987. Having defused one rebellion by the local farming community, the government was anxious to consolidate the new spirit of co-operation by extending the environmental incentives beyond the SSSIs. Thus across most of the Levels and Moors farmers were offered special payments for withholding herbicides, reducing fertiliser rates and generally farming in the way their forebears had for generations. And there were yet more generous hand-outs still to come.

Despite the new conservation incentives the wildlife value of the most ecologically interesting areas of the Levels continued to decline. Routine monitoring by the Royal Society for the Protection of Birds and the Somerset Wildlife Trust showed a steep fall in the numbers of wading birds, together with serious damage to important groups of plants and animals. The main reason for these losses was the long-established practice of setting the water levels in the rhynes and ditches to benefit agricultural production rather than the wildlife. Despite its ESA status this unique wetland habitat was slowly drying out.

The Somerset Levels have been subject to drainage work for centuries. The first people to improve the rivers and construct sea embankments on a large scale were the abbots of Glastonbury and the bishops of Bath and Wells in the eleventh century. The current network of rhynes is what has made the area such an important wildlife site; it is, after all, a land reclaimed from marsh. During the post-war drive for agricultural production, however, millions of pounds' worth of new pumped drainage schemes were installed, chiefly with the aid of generous grants from MAFF. The overall water levels in the drains and ditches are under the control of autonomous flood defence committees, funded by and answerable to MAFF. These curious bodies are strongly representative of farming and landowning interests. They have but a single mission – to raise the output of subsidised winter wheat from this fragile wetland ecosystem.

In 1991 the RSPB published its report analysing the causes of wildlife loss on the Levels.[9] Since the remorseless drying out of the land was identified as the principal cause, the simplest and most cost-effective remedy would have been to raise the winter water levels in the drains and ditches – literally to stop working the pumps so hard. But to do so would have been to remove the farmer's absolute right to maximise his output of subsidised food. Instead the government embarked on a bizarre scheme to create, at public expense, a series of wet 'islands' in a landscape already being drained at public expense for farm production.

Following the RSPB report, MAFF introduced an additional tier of payments into its Somerset Levels ESA scheme. From now on it would make special payments of £170 an acre to farmers offering blocks of species-rich grassland which could be maintained at high water table, thus providing suitable conditions for wading birds and wetland plants. At the same time the National Rivers' Authority – now the Environment Agency – began implementing a programme of 'patchwork rehydration', installing the dykes and pumps needed to maintain areas of high water level alongside drier areas.

In conservation terms the scheme has been highly successful. Widgeon, teal and shovelers are returning to the raised water level sites in great numbers. But the cost to the public is enormous. In 1995 management agreements in the Somerset Levels ESA were running at £2.2 million; and this was in addition to the £370,000 paid out as compensation to farmers in the SSSI. These costs looked certain to rise substantially since MAFF was less than halfway to its target of 6,000 acres under high water level management.

The water-management infrastructure for maintaining these 'wet' areas acts as another drain on the public purse. Although the water engineering is hardly sophisticated, the Environment Agency allocates £100,000 a year to the scheme for the capital costs alone. It seems likely that the annual cost of maintaining the wetland habitat on just a small fraction of the total acreage in SSSIs will far exceed £3 million. Yet until the coming of farm subsidies the nation gained the benefits of this huge natural resource for free.

A more rational solution to environmental degradation might be to reduce both production subsidies and drainage spending, while allowing water levels to rise at the pumphouse. Wetland conditions would return over a far wider area, and along with the patterns of low-intensity livestock farming that are adapted to it. Although poorer drainage would reduce the incomes of individual farmers, it would unquestionably serve the country's interest.[10] Why should the farmer complain? There will always be natural disadvantages to farming on a wetland, just as there are to farming on the slopes of Mount Snowdon. Is it the duty of urban taxpayers to provide the wetland farmer with the same income-earning opportunity as the farmer on prime Lincolnshire arable land?

Unfortunately such a rational solution to habitat loss would be unthinkable to the government for it would mean abandoning one of the great canons of post-war policy – that of the untouchability of farm subsidies. Nor would it be possible under current EU structures. Through the Common Agricultural Policy Britain is effectively locked into a federal farming state of Europe as it has been for more than twenty years.

This is the deceit underlying all the government's countryside schemes. They come as minor bolt-on appendages to an overpowered support system which is the real engine of destruction in the British countryside. The CAP dispenses almost £3 billion a year in support of UK food production while providing just £34 million for 'agri-environment' measures to help wildlife and the environment. The juggernaut has to be stopped. Applying green camouflage cannot save what remnants of the countryside still remain.

Conservative ministers are all too aware of this. William Waldegrave's CAP review group reported that the removal of production support would make environmental schemes more cost-effective.[11] But his government has also ruled out early action to end the damage. Lasting reform will only come through concerted European action, and, while the EU Commission hints at a greening of agricultural policy, there seems little chance of radical reform in time to save the British countryside.

At the 1996 Oxford Farming Conference debate the proposer of the motion that the public purse should not subsidise agricultural production was none other than Environment Secretary John Gummer. But like the farmers who voted it through, he knew that real reform was many years away. 'Neither British agriculture nor our environment can be properly safeguarded except within a strong European Union,' he argued. In other words the rescue of the British countryside must await the agreement of states whose own smaller farm structures protect them from the most damaging effects of the CAP. As Europe deliberates Britain becomes a wasteland.

With the real remedy postponed, the UK government pursues palliatives in the form of its various countryside schemes, euphemistically known as environmental land management. Their true object is to entice farmers away from intensive, subsidised production. In England MAFF has made Countryside Stewardship (CS) its new flagship scheme, following a successful trial by the Countryside Commission. Unlike the ESA scheme, Countryside Stewardship is open to farmers anywhere in the country, not just those in designated areas like the Somerset Levels and Moors. Instead it is targeted at specific habitat types or landscape features.

Thus farmers can pick up annual payments of £100 an acre for re-creating old grassland, £53 an acre for making hay on small upland meadows or £111 an acre for re-creating heathland. Capital payments are available, too. The rate for laying a metre of hedge is

£2, while hedge planting is worth £1.75 a metre. In effect farmers are being paid to replace and restore the features they have spent fifty years destroying. And still the generous production subsidies remain in place.

Farming has boomed in the 1990s. Between 1992 and 1995 farm incomes doubled to £4 billion. Little wonder that farmers are reluctant to commit themselves to conservation schemes. Why should they while the public continues to throw money at them for growing cereals? A 1994 study of payments under the Countryside Steward-ship scheme showed that the incentive to switch from cereals to grassland was at best small even for the farmer making average margins.[12] For the top performing arable farms it was scarcely worth thinking about, and since 1994 cereal farm incomes have gone up by nearly one-third. The dilemma for conservation agencies is whether to spend more of their meagre resources on trying to match the subsidy-driven rise in farm profits.

This auction of the countryside makes a mockery of the very concept of 'stewardship'. The word itself implies service, custodian-ship, looking after land on behalf of others. To an earlier generation it was a fundamental tenet of farming. They felt a clear duty to take care of the land, to hand it on in better shape than they had found it. Now their successors expect to be paid for everything they do.

For twenty years the Farming and Wildlife Advisory Group has urged farmers to take a few simple measures for the benefit of wildlife – keeping fertilisers and pesticides out of the hedge bottoms and trimming hedges every second or third year instead of annually. Far from adding to their costs, such measures would actually save them money. While responsible farmers adopt them enthusiastically, most continue to ignore the advice. Until there is cash on offer, wildlife conservation is not their concern. Government and EU policies have brought farmland management firmly into the market place. Farmers and landowners are encouraged to exploit it for whatever it will earn, to 'sell' to the highest bidder. At the moment the highest bidder is the EU Commission, though international grain traders have begun competing hard.

In purely market terms the Countryside Stewardship scheme has been a considerable success, bringing 230,000 acres under environ-mental management in 5,200 separate agreements. MAFF is to increase its funding from £12 million in 1996/97 to £17 million by 1997/98. Yet, ironically, the true stewards of the countryside are among those least likely to benefit. To collect a grant for restoring a meadow or planting a new hedge you need first to have destroyed the originals. The farmers making most from environmental payments are those who did the greatest damage during the frenzied years of all-out production.

It is these former 'rationalisers' of the landscape who are often the most active planters of trees and diggers of ponds.[13] Unfortunately such visible indicators of environmental concern are poor recompense for the rich habitats they replaced. The sad fact is that many farmers with a genuine concern for the countryside were driven out of business years ago. For half a century UK governments have pursued a policy of handing over large sums of public money to the biggest farmers, whether or not they showed any respect for the environment. It is a policy which rewarded the expanders, the exploiters and the grubbers-up while disadvantaging those who preferred to farm in a kinder way.

In effect, post-war farming policy has applied a form of natural selection to the countryside, favouring the industrialisers of the landscape and eliminating the custodians. So it is hardly a surprise that those who thrived in this cash-driven culture should now demand payment for putting the hedgerows back. Given the devastation that has taken place, the country is probably left with no alternative. But where is the sense in paying over the odds by continuing to support farm production?

Some in the industry argue that the 1992 MacSharry 'reforms' of the CAP have already put farm policy on the right track. After all, they have succeeded in levelling the EU grain mountain which had reached Everest proportions by 1993. And as EU Farm Commissioner Franz Fischler told the 1996 Oxford Farming Conference, they have introduced into price policy the idea of environmental responsibility. In return for area payments farmers are obliged to put part of their arable acreage into set-aside.

In reality the reforms have done little to help Britain's beleaguered wildlife. Although the arable area scheme was intended to 'decouple' support by paying farmers on an acreage basis rather than on yield, it remains indirectly linked to output. Cereal growers are still paid a substantial subsidy in proportion to the size of their crop. The artificial stimulus to production continues. Set-aside may have brought some small benefits for birds, but only where it is actively managed for conservation. If anything it adds to intensification by pushing up market prices. Like quotas it is designed to keep prices high by restricting production.

Most set-aside land is part of a rotation. Although the land is technically 'out of production', farmers are still allowed to spray it with herbicides. Any insecticides used on the preceding crops will have wiped out much of the insect life, so its value to birds is limited. Leaving 5 per cent or so of arable land lying fallow for a few months does not in itself provide a thriving and diverse ecosystem. To be of any value it must be managed for wildlife, and little of it is.

At the same time the mere fact of having to put land into set-aside makes many farmers resist the idea of devoting any more land 'to conservation'. So they are less willing to take up habitat improvement schemes like Countryside Stewardship. Thus the so-called 'reform' of the CAP has led to the further impoverishment of the landscape. Far from offering a solution to the crisis in the countryside, set-aside has become part of the problem. Support remains as high as before. The difference is that more of the cost is now transferred from the consumer to the taxpayer.

The incentive to produce is undiminished. Land values continue to inflate – they have doubled since the introduction of 'reforms'. The pressure to drive every acre for high yields remains. Many farmers respond to set-aside by applying even more pesticides and fertilisers to the rest of the arable land in their bid to maximise the returns.

Agricultural support continues to make wildlife too expensive for most farmers. Some may be prepared to plant up the odd field corner in the cause of good public relations. Others manage a few field boundaries for wildlife, picking up an annual grant of up to £100 a metre for doing so. But to most the business of farming is about maximising returns by exploiting the subsidy system. This is why they have been bidding up the price of land to record levels.

A change in land ownership is always a threat to wildlife. The transfer is usually from a smaller, traditional farmer to the larger 'expansionist' next door. The odds are the new owner will have a very different approach to farming. He will absorb the additional acreage into his 'core' operation, and almost inevitably landscape features will be removed. For example, the rate at which grassland is lost from land changing hands is twice that of land remaining in the same ownership.[14] The current scramble for farmland highlights the continuing threat to the British countryside. It also points up the abject failure of rural policy.

Two or three times each year MAFF gets together representatives of the leading conservation organisations to discuss the performance of its various agri-environment schemes. Groups including the Wildlife Trusts and Royal Society for the Protection of Birds are invited to comment on such matters as the uptake of environmental schemes, their funding and their success in meeting wildlife targets.

But the bloated subsidy system that makes them necessary in the first place remains firmly off the agenda. Conservationists are allowed to comment on the cosmetics but not the cause of environmental damage.

Like the victim of a street mugging, the British countryside lies haemorrhaging from wounds inflicted by a brutal agricultural system. The well-meaning bystanders are invited to suggest tonics and remedies for the patient's pallor, but they must ignore the knife that still protrudes from his chest. Thus the champions of wildlife are drawn into supporting the fiction that there is nothing amiss which cannot be corrected by fine tuning of the agri-environment schemes.

The latest piece of tweaking is aimed at halting the loss of farmland birds. The Game Conservancy Trust's twenty-nine-year study of the cereal field ecosystem in Sussex has highlighted the importance of the traditional undersown ley in maintaining bird populations.[15] Undersowing was an essential part of the old Norfolk four-course rotation. A cereal crop – usually spring-sown barley – was used as a nurse crop for a grass ley which was sown into it. A typical ley mixture might contain the grasses timothy and perennial ryegrass along with the deep-rooting cocksfoot as an insurance against drought. In addition there was likely to be a clutch of clover varieties like white clover, alsike and trefoil.

The combination of grasses and clovers encouraged a number of invertebrates including sawfly larvae, leaf weevils, butterflies and leaf hoppers. These in turn attracted insect-eating birds. After harvest the undersown ley provided an ideal weedy stubble for birds to feed on through the winter months. However, with the introduction of subsidies and the decline of mixed farming the practice of undersowing virtually died out. Farmers are more concerned to maximise yields from winter-sown cereals supported by heavy inputs of fertiliser and agrochemicals.

Stung by criticism over falling bird populations, government is now attempting to re-introduce the practice through the Countryside Stewardship scheme. In autumn 1996 MAFF commissioned proposals for a special acreage payment to arable farmers who agreed to introduce undersown cereals, though how much money the Treasury might be persuaded to put into such a scheme remained uncertain. Whatever the sum it was certain to be dwarfed by more than £1 billion paid each year to cereal growers alone. The pressure on farmers to specialise and intensify their production remains irresistible.

UK conservation policy rests on our trying to buy up whatever remnants of wildlife habitat the agribusiness chooses to sell. We then tuck them away in fortified enclaves, safe from the main activity of the countryside. This is no nature policy. It is conservation by designation, habitat by franchise. Our wild species are assessed, surveyed, monitored and apportioned, but never allowed to thrive because we will not challenge the prerogative of farmers to decide the shape and content of our countryside. Until they begin to serve the national interest, any spending on land management schemes can be no more than a holding operation.

We need a dramatic reduction in farm subsidies, at least in those that continue to encourage production. There is no logic for product subsidies; the market will deliver the food we need. The support we provide farmers, both in direct payments and through inflated prices, merely prompts them to 'reclaim' more habitat and drive more wildlife from the land. The NFU will argue that we cannot have an attractive countryside without a prosperous farming community – without farm profits there is dereliction; without farmers to manage the land there is wilderness, so goes the familiar refrain.

Yet the visitor to the lifeless prairie lands of Lincolnshire or the green deserts of Cheshire could be forgiven for thinking that a little more dereliction might be no bad thing. The NFU's argument begs a deeper question. It presupposes that farming is *per se* 'a good thing', that any one farmer is as good as any other. From the point of view of wildlife and the countryside this is clearly untrue.

The farmer with a sense of custodianship for the land is unquestionably better for the country than the farmer whose chief concern is to exploit the land for short-term gain. Unfortunately we have spent the past fifty years applying a subsidy system that rewards the latter and disadvantages the former. And the landscape we have inherited reflects our choice. To change the landscape we now have to change the culture of agriculture.

Our system of farming is over-capitalised and too heavily dependent on inputs. We are locked into a high-input, high-output cycle chiefly because the price of land is inflated. The rise in land prices during the 1990s is analogous to the property boom of the late 80s. It is driven by unrealistic expectations, and, as in the property market, there must finally come a day of reckoning. The land-price boom is fuelled by high cereal prices, which are, at least in part, dependent on subsidies. When subsidies go land values will fall.

The impact of such necessary readjustment will be lessened by a strong world grain market. Should wheat prices remain buoyant the change may be relatively pain-free. But a return to the price levels of the 1980s would undoubtedly cause difficulties for farm businesses that are over-extended. However, it is a step that must be taken if the cycle of countryside destruction is ever to be ended.

Though bankruptcy is a tragedy for individuals, farm bankruptcies are no tragedy for the nation. The land will not be abandoned. It will be farmed by someone else at lower cost and at lower intensity, to the benefit of the countryside and national economy. While a number of today's farmers and landowners will inevitably lose out, the lives of vastly more people – both rural and town dwellers – will be much improved.

5

NO FIGURES IN THE LANDSCAPE

There is a popular mantra, much repeated by the National Farmers'
Union, to the effect that farming is the cornerstone of rural society.
The theory is that farmers create jobs in the countryside, use local
suppliers and spend their profits in village shops and pubs. In short,
agriculture powers the rural economy. Thus when farmers are doing
well everyone else benefits. It is a persuasive argument. Indeed for
fifty years it has been one of the main justifications for continuing to
spend public money on farm subsidies. It is also severely flawed.

On the rich, fertile grassland of the West Midlands a young family
has taken a step that few others would dare to in modern Britain.
Without inherited land or wealth they have become farmers. It may
have taken every penny they could save and borrow, but they have
taken over the tenancy of a county council-owned smallholding.

From a strictly economic point of view their move makes little
sense. The farm is only a fifth of the size of the average full-time
holding as defined by MAFF.[1] In any case, Agricultural Minister
Douglas Hogg thinks county councils ought to sell off their farms.
They were intended to act as starter units for new entrants to the
industry. And since, according to the Minister, they no longer
perform that function, they ought to go. But for one couple, at least,
the chance to rent their first forty acres or so is the fulfilment of a
long-cherished dream.

For years they have worked as part-time farmers, buying draft ewes
from the Welsh mountains and lambing them on rented land near
their home. As well as holding down jobs and bringing up a young
family they have also managed to work their way through agricultural college, studying hard through the evenings. So when the
opportunity comes to rent a council farm they don't spend a lot of
time thinking about it. They sell the sheep, put their house on the

market and borrow heavily from the bank to finance the "in-goings". Soon they are milking their own cows through the vintage milking shed.

The couple might have stepped straight from an NFU publicity brochure. Hard-working, concerned for their animals and with a genuine love of the countryside, they represent the humane side of dairy farming. Technically their first enterprise is a great success. Both have plenty of experience with livestock, so they know how to take care of the cows and get the very best out of them.

Yields are good and the quality of their milk superb. The hygienic standards they achieve would be a match for almost any dairy farm in Europe. At the same time their costs are low. There is no money wasted on expensive tractors or machinery, little capital locked up in elaborate buildings or acres of concrete. Even with a small herd of forty-odd cows the profits should be rolling in. Yet the couple admit they are barely managing to "hang on by their fingertips". Even after their move to a second, slightly bigger county council holding, their future in farming remains precarious.

The frenzied world of subsidised farming is as hostile to people as it is to wildlife. Fifty years of price support has destroyed communities and thrown families off the land as fast as it has uprooted the hedges and woods. Subsidies discriminate against the small and humane, protecting the established farmer and barring the entry of newcomers. For young families whose aim is to start in dairy farming, the obstacles are the most formidable of all. And the biggest by a long way is the milk quota.

Milk quotas were introduced as a panic measure in 1984. After years of procrastination the EU needed to take decisive action to halt the seemingly unstoppable tide of milk production, which was by then outstripping consumption by over 20 per cent. Spurred on by inflated prices and generous investment grants, Britain's dairy farmers had been happily riding the bonanza. Cold-stores were stuffed to the rafters with surplus butter, and each year thousands of tons were sold off at knock-down prices to the Soviet Union. The broadsheet leader columns were scathing. Something had to be done.

The conventional remedy for overproduction is, of course, a price reduction. As always, this was unthinkable to Brussels. There remained only one practical alternative – supply control. Quotas are a way of controlling milk output by limiting the amount each farmer is allowed to produce. Quite simply, a quota is a licence to produce milk. In 1984 every dairy farmer in Europe was given one, the size of each allocation being set in proportion to the farm's 'base year' production in 1981.

So incensed were farmers when the scheme was introduced that the National Farmers' Union's public relations department went into overdrive. In market towns across the country cows were paraded in High Streets and shopping malls under the banner – 'Quotas kill cows'. However, it soon became apparent that, far from being a threat, the quota might be a valuable asset. After all, it gave the holder an absolute right to produce milk at a guaranteed and inflated price. What's more, the price was likely to stay high since the EU now had an effective way to engineer a milk shortage throughout the Community. The quota could be seen as a licence to profit.

In Britain the rules as implemented by MAFF allow farmers to buy and sell quota, or to lease it out. So the net benefits become capitalised into the price. In 1995 the purchase price of quota averaged 60p a litre, while the cost of leasing it worked out at 12p a litre. By the autumn of 1996 the purchase price had risen to 70p and the leasing price to 17p, in part because the BSE crisis had led to a backlog of cull cows on farms.

Thus a farmer who had the good fortune to be milking 100 or so cows in the early 1980s might now find himself in possession of a capital asset worth £400,000 or more. He could give up milking cows and live quite comfortably on the rental – as indeed many dairy farmers do. Quota is traded and speculated upon by land agents, farming companies and City investors. Farmers of retirement age use it as a tax-free retirement fund. Arable farmers invest their subsidies in it. Milk quota is an £8 billion lottery hoard funded by a hidden tax on consumers. The losers – apart from long-suffering shoppers – are the outsiders who want to be farmers.

In the 1930s dairy farming offered a promising start in the industry for youngsters with ambition. They could rent a few acres, buy half a dozen cows plus some second-hand milking equipment and they were in business. Many of today's biggest dairying empires were begun in just this way. But not any more. Even before quotas were introduced, farm rents and livestock prices were being inflated by price subsidies. Now the new entrant faces an added obstacle – the cost of leasing quota. At 17p a litre it is like having to pay an extra 'rent' of £1,000 or so on every cow before he or she even starts paying other costs. Quota is worth more than cows, more than the land itself.

Each year dairy farmers spend about £500 million buying and leasing enough quota to keep them in business. Ultimately it is consumers who pay, of course. The quota lottery adds 2.25p to the price of every pint of milk bought in Britain. The proceeds are not distributed evenly through the industry but are concentrated on larger producers. These are the farmers who can afford to bid most for scarce quota. As with land, they are able to spread the cost over a greater volume of output. Dairy farming has become a club for the wealthy.

Our new-entrant family in the West Midlands must spend about £14,000 a year on buying and leasing quota for their small dairy herd. This is twice as much as they pay in rent on their 50-acre farm. It is a burden they may not be able to carry much longer. Yet if they are forced to give up it will be a tragedy for the nation as well as for themselves. Their system of farming is far better attuned to public concerns about animal welfare and the environment than those of the intensive farmers who have come to dominate the industry.

Their herd is small so they can ensure each one of their cows gets individual attention. All the cattle are bedded on straw, the cows in cubicles and the younger stock loose in pens. Mastitis, which is rife in many herds, is virtually unknown here. Slurry use is minimal. Instead of polluting the ditches and streams, the couple prefer to spread traditional farmyard manure, a waste material that is environmentally benign. On the face of it these are just the kind of farmers Britain should be encouraging, particularly as they also happen to be highly efficient producers of milk.

This is contrary to the conventional wisdom. Small farmers are believed to be inefficient, and certainly if their working hours were fully costed the profit margin might appear modest.

But the labour is supplied almost entirely by the family – the couple themselves with help from their two elder daughters. They choose to work long hours for the independence and life-style farming gives them. But on other measures of efficiency – on their use of land and capital – there are few large farms to touch them.

Their costs, unlike those of intensive producers, are low, and because they have the time to give their animals individual attention, their yields of quality milk are high. With a small herd they inevitably lose out on economies of scale, but this is more than offset by the extra output produced by their caring form of management.

In a free market their humane style of dairy farming would be extremely competitive. With their low cost-base they could make a profit at a milk price far below that currently charged to consumers. But what they and other new entrants cannot do is meet the capital costs of getting started when these in-goings are massively distorted by subsidies. Through price support the British public bars some of its brightest and most able youngsters from the land. Instead it chooses to build up the capital assets of the country's biggest and most intensive producers.

Even in urban Britain of the 1990s there is a continuous stream of young men and women who want to get into farming. It was ever thus. In the past these first-generation farmers have done much to invigorate the industry with fresh ideas and enthusiasm. But price support has slammed the door on them. The only people who can start in farming nowadays are lottery winners and the chairmen of former nationalised industries. For the first time in Britain's history a generation of young citizens is denied access to the land – not by the laws of the market, but by deliberate public policy.

The absurdity of that policy was summed up in an impassioned speech during the 1996 Oxford Farming Conference debate. William Dunn, an aspiring young farmer from Devon, brought the debate to life with a vigorous attack on the CAP. All it did, he argued, was hand over the lion's share of subsidies to the nation's biggest farmers while driving young people from the land. The contribution earned him warm applause from an audience which included a fair number of the nation's biggest farmers. It seems unlikely that many of them went home to lobby their MPs for change.

Price support for dairy farmers is one of the country's best-kept secrets. Indeed many milk producers even deny that they get it simply because, unlike arable farmers, they do not receive direct subsidy cheques in the post. But just how much their businesses are propped up by consumers is revealed in a comparison of world prices. In the United States, where farmers receive some level of price support, farmers were paid 17p a litre for their milk in 1994. In New Zealand, where all farm support was abolished in the 1980s, dairy farmers were paid 12p a litre. In the UK the farmgate price was 23p a litre.

This is why British dairy farmers are prepared to pay through the nose to lease or buy quota. It gives them access to a market in which the price has been maintained 6p a litre or more above the true world price. Support for UK dairy farmers is estimated to have been worth £1.7 billion in 1993/94.[2] The bulk of it went to the biggest farmers. Since 9,500 dairy farmers now account for 60 per cent of all UK milk production,[3] it follows that on average each of them must have been more than £100,000 better off thanks to public support.

It would be a mistake to think that the structure of UK dairying has been frozen since the introduction of quotas. In 1970 more than 100,000 farmers made a living out of milk. The number fell by a third in the decade leading up to quotas, and a third in the decade afterwards. In the 1990s the drop-out rate has accelerated further as producers cash in on the surging value of quota. By 1996 there were fewer than 27,000 dairy farmers left in England and Wales, and their numbers were falling at the rate of 100 a month.

Far from providing opportunities for aspiring new entrants to farming, the quota released by outgoers was being snapped up by large producers strong enough to outbid the competition. The big were getting bigger while the small were getting out. In 1993 ADAS forecast that more than 20 per cent of producers would leave the industry over the coming five years.[4]

Under the protection of an inflated price the big cats of the industry are fighting for quota and market share. John Sumner, ADAS head of dairy development, has written that the primary objective for any dairy business is 'to increase profitability and enhance competitiveness' – this in an industry supported by £1.7 billion in public support. As in the arable sector, subsidies are funding the restructuring of dairy farming into a largely corporate enterprise.

The stories in *Farmers Weekly* say it all. 'Rotary Brings a Revolution' ran the headline above the story of the Lancashire farmer who installed a rotating parlour capable of milking 400 cows in two hours.[5] Another featured a Dorset farming company which had concentrated its dairy operation onto five units milking between them more than 1,000 cows.[6] One of the units enabled one person to manage 250 cows and had a parlour capable of milking 500 three times a day on a shift system.

Farmers Weekly editor, Stephen Howe, extolled what he called the 'dairy farmer's dream': the world's first commercial robot milker.[7] Such are the fruits of Britain's massive public investment in dairy farming – high capital costs with minimal labour. Along with them come all the other trappings of intensive milk production: the monoculture of ryegrass, the giant silage machines, the maize harvest which dumps half the topsoil in the lane. This is the landscape of publicly protected agriculture, the landscape of high capital. Sadly it is a landscape with little room for people.

One of the great ironies of post-war agriculture is that a policy designed to help farmers has been such a dismal failure at keeping them in business. For the mechanised rural 'food factory' of the 1990s has grown up on the land vacated by a dozen family farms that failed to survive. In the early 1950s there were about 454,000 farms in the UK.[8] Now there are half that number, and of these just

23,000 produce half of all the food we grow. In a period of unprecedented public support for agriculture almost a quarter of a million farms have gone out of business.

The reduction in jobs on farms has been even more dramatic. At the end of the war UK farms employed nearly a million people. By the mid-1960s there were half a million regular staff. But by 1994 the number of farm jobs had fallen to 120,000, of which one-third were part-time. Today the fields of rural Britain are lonely workplaces. The harvest and hay-making gangs of sepia imagery have long vanished. If there is anyone at work at all in the new open landscape of wheat and ryegrass it is likely to be a solitary worker cocooned within a giant tractor.

In place of the small family farms comes corporate agriculture, the big company farms employing minimal labour and run by techno-crats with their eye on the budget and balance sheet. It is a transformation that has not come about by chance, but through public policy. This is not to deny the reality of scale economies. No doubt concentration was bound to occur in a fragmented industry. Yet the fact remains that the change has taken place largely as the result of political decisions. We have allowed our taxes to subsidise machines and price out people.

The mechanics of change have been investigated by Bruce Traill, who looked at the effects of rising price support levels on UK farm employment, earnings and investment.[9] He concluded that a 1 per cent rise in farm prices produced a sharp increase in investment, peaking at £12 million in the second year and reaching a cumulative total of £44 million. The most favoured investments were in plant and machinery.

By contrast farm employment, although rising initially, fell to about 1 per cent below its original level. Thus higher support prices increase capital intensity and, in the long run, reduce the demand for hired staff. Farmworkers lose their jobs while farm machinery manufacturers make a killing. Most of the income benefit to farmers becomes capitalised into higher land prices. Hardly a rational use of public funds, particularly at times of high unemployment.

As Gale Johnson of Chicago University has observed, no social objective is met by a policy in which the primary beneficiaries are the owners of land. 'Since farmers in the industrial countries, on average, hold more wealth than non farmers, it is not obvious that policy should be used to increase their wealth even further relative to the rest of the population.'[10]

Supply controls are another policy instrument which discriminates against paid staff. They include measures like set-aside and quotas, designed to limit farm output. With milk production restricted by quotas it is no surprise that the price to farmers rose continuously through the late 1980s and 90s. The winding up of the 60-year-old Milk Marketing Scheme in 1994 gave it a further boost, replacing a statutory monopoly buyer with a near-monopoly private buyer. The former Milk Marketing Board – now called Milk Marque – controls 60 per cent of supplies, selling on to an undersupplied market by setting initial bidding prices.

This 'deregulation' of milk led to a further 10 per cent rise in the UK farm price, pushing it to almost double that at which unsubsidised New Zealand farmers sell on to world markets. In this way the big dairy farmers find the cash they need to put in expensive rotating parlours and robotic milkers, enabling them to shed staff and cut labour costs. Throughout the 1990s farmworkers' jobs have been disappearing at an average rate of 12 per cent a year. Like the youngsters barred from entry to agriculture, Britain's herdsmen and herdswomen have little to thank subsidies for.

Supply controls in the arable sector have had an even more immediate impact on jobs. In return for arable area payments on crops like cereals and oilseeds – worth £1.1 billion in 1995/96 – farmers have to agree to put a percentage of their land into set-aside. This means leaving it fallow and not growing a crop on it. There are extra payments for farmers who opt to put additional land into set-aside over and above the obligatory area. The total UK set-aside budget for 1995/96 came to £215 million, this in addition to the arable area payments.

But while fallowing land may produce rich rewards for farmers, it is decidedly bad news for their staff. A Reading University survey suggested that, on average, for every 320 acres of arable land in set-aside one full-time farm job is lost.[11] And for those staff who keep their jobs the reduced workload is likely to lead to a drop in earnings. Thus part of the price for supporting the incomes of farmers is being paid by their staff.

A survey published in the summer of 1996 showed that the ambition of many farmers was to farm more land with fewer staff.[12] Across the range of farm sizes respondents reported a cut in staff numbers during the past five years. Many intended to shed more labour in the next five years even though they expected to be farming as much or more land.

Job losses are only a part of the transformation now taking place in the farm labour market. With subsidies driving up land prices and spurring the replacement of labour with capital, farmers are looking for more creative ways to trim wage costs. From industry, they have borrowed the concept of the flexible workforce, which makes more use of casual and contract workers. Seasonal or contract staff have always been important in agriculture, particularly for such jobs as potato planting and sugar beet harvesting. There is evidence that they are now playing a more central role in even the larger farm sectors of cereals and milk.

Andrew Errington has analysed the changing structure of the agricultural workforce.[13] On arable farms the drive to cut fixed costs has already led to a quarter of full-time staff being made redundant. Instead a greater reliance is placed on contractors or self-employed, casual workers. Alternatively, the farming system may be simplified by eliminating an entire enterprise with its associated staff. Dairy farmers are also making more use of contractors for operations like silage-making and, increasingly, routine stock tasks such as foot-trimming are being contracted out.

Applying the concept of the flexible firm to agriculture, Andrew Errington and Ruth Gasson identify core jobs, which are held by the farmer and farm family members, by salaried partners and by key workers such as the head herdsman or arable foreman.[14] In a less secure position are peripheral staff working on permanent contracts. They are likely to have skills which are less specific to the farm business, skills which might include milking or tractor driving. These staff are not indispensable. Their training can be provided outside the firm and, at a time of sharply falling employment in the industry, they can be readily replaced. Their bargaining position is weak and they enjoy no real job security or promotion prospects.

The model includes a second group of peripheral staff. These are the casual workers, the reserve troops, hired and fired to meet seasonal peaks in labour demand. They are employed to perform a narrow range of tasks over a finite period and, since they need no particular skills, they are easily recruited from the external labour market. They are also easily replaced. Not surprisingly their pay and conditions fall well short of those of permanent employees.

Such is the new reality of working the land. What was traditionally a poorly paid but secure job has now become even worse paid and considerably less secure. Public policies aimed at improving the incomes of one rural group have succeeded in driving down the wealth and conditions of another. Of course, there are those for whom a more flexible work pattern is an advantage. Seasonal work appeals to people with commitments at other times of the year; for example, mothers who need to be at home during school holidays. Others see it as a way of testing the job market or gaining work experience. But to many it remains second-best. The ideal is a secure, full-time job.

For most townspeople the image of the farmworker has its roots in the great characters of literature, like Thomas Hardy's Gabriel Oak, reliable, a little unworldly but of enduring strength. Or W. H. Hudson's shepherd of the downs; the naturalist and stockman with the quiet authority of those who are masters of their trade. More recently there is A. G. Street's dairyman, George Simons, who, of all those associated with the land, had given the most and received the least.

These are archetypes of the noble labourer, indelibly associated with the countryside. Their like could still be found in rural Britain, even as late as the 1950s and 60s. Now they are gone. For one effect of the new agricultural revolution has been the de-skilling of farmworkers.

Before the coming of agribusiness their accumulated experience of land and livestock was highly valued by employers. Though the shepherd or farm foreman seldom received the pay of his industrial equivalent, his skills were widely respected. A local knowledge of soil types or of the best way to manage a pasture could determine the profitability of a farm. Now such subtleties of husbandry are irrelevant. A standard technology exists for every crop, a blueprint devised by technical specialists and marketed by the agrochemical companies. The new skill lies in devising the appropriate pesticide cocktail.

In the world of intensive agriculture the skilled staff are those who operate machines; the unskilled are those who mind them. The farm manager's chief preoccupations are with the timing of inputs and the control of costs. Traditional farming concerns for soil, plant and animal are given a lower order of priority. The prevailing culture is no longer one of good husbandry but of sound business management. And its primary objective is to remove people from the land.

This is the landscape that public policy has created; a landscape fashioned for the efficient production of renewable commodities. A bland, featureless landscape in which half our food is produced on 20,000 'land factories' under the control of just 12,000 people. A landscape in which human skills are devalued and where the frenzied drive for production leaves no room for creativity or concern. It is a landscape that MAFF designed and the people paid for. Fortunately it does not yet cover the entire British countryside.

The annual June census of agriculture shows that two-thirds of all registered UK farms, 160,000 in total, fall outside the bleak landscape of agribusiness. These are the part-timers, the people whose farming activities make up only part of their working lives. In terms of their output they are economically insignificant. Largely ignored by MAFF, they receive virtually no subsidies. In 1994 just 3 per cent of the £5.6 billion spent on farm support ended up with the 45 per cent smallest farms.

The very expression 'part-timer' is often used as a term of disparagement, implying a less than professional approach to the job, even hobby farming. Yet the fact that someone chooses to spend part of their time working as a bricklayer or telephonist does not in itself make them less effective in the job of running a farm. Indeed it could be argued that they are the truly efficient farmers since they survive without the help of subsidies. It is the specialist cereal grower who relies on subsidies to stay in business.

Small farmers may not produce much of our food, but they provide many other benefits for society. Among the more important is keeping rural communities alive. The National Farmers' Union frequently uses this argument in its justification of farm subsidies in general. However, it is not the subsidised farms which contribute most to the rural economy, it is the small farms, the farms that generally fall outside the support net.

The big specialist farms provide few jobs and spend little of their huge cash turnover locally. Many of the major field operations, like silaging and grain harvesting, are carried out by hired contractors, often from miles away. Most of the purchases made by large farms are from firms outside the locality, sometimes from outside the country. Major inputs like fertilisers, agrochemicals, seed and animal feed are supplied by multinational companies. Many of these products are manufactured abroad, as are most of the big machines. The robot milker that so impressed *Farmers Weekly* came from Holland; the big combine harvester launch of 1995 featured a £225,000 giant from Germany.

Small farming is, by definition, labour-intensive. In small farming areas there are simply more people around to spend money in local shops, garages and pubs, more users of threatened rural services. The economy of the family farm is intimately bound up with the local economy in a way that the large agribusiness holding can never be.

Small farmers are also better guardians of the environment. This does not necessarily mean they are any more interested in conservation than larger farmers.[15] It may be simply that they cannot generate the capital to invest in land 'improvement'. Small farms are more likely to be located on poor soils in difficult terrain. Farm development is largely financed out of retained profits, so the lower profitability of small units holds back the damaging changes that have impoverished the landscape elsewhere. Even if only by default, there is likely to be more wildlife than on the larger farm.

Some conservation groups now argue that farm support funds should be withheld from large farmers and targeted at small family farmers. Through a process known as modulation – rejected by John Gummer during his time as Minister of Agriculture – a ceiling is placed on the total support payment to any one individual farmer. In this way the subsidies going to large, intensive producers are capped and a higher proportion of the cash ends up in the pockets of family farmers.

Whether such a change would assist the small-farm sector in the long term is open to question. There is the risk that it would unleash the same disastrous drive to intensify, this time on a small acreage. A better solution might be to end all production subsidies to farming, for it is these that put the small farm at such a huge disadvantage. William Waldegrave's CAP Review Group concluded that the removal of support would create new opportunities for outsiders to get a start in farming. No longer would the mere ownership of land virtually guarantee an income from the state. Under a truly free market system all farmers, whether full-time, part-time or new entrants, would earn a living only by meeting the real needs of society.

77

6

THE VIEW FROM THE HILLS

The high uplands of Britain contain the last great areas of solitude left on these islands. From the grandeur of the north-west highlands and the plunging glacial valleys of the English Lakes to the granite tors of Dartmoor, these are landscapes to refresh the spirit. Their remoteness provides an antidote to crawling traffic queues and the tedium of supermarket check-outs. Their very emptiness lends them an air of permanence. Yet not even this wild and beautiful scenery escapes the deadly influence of the farm 'improvers'.

Up here the damage is done by livestock subsidies; headage payments on the animals that browse the fellside grazings and mountain sheep-walks. The government and the EU put a price on the back of every ewe and suckler cow grazing what they prosaically call the less favoured areas. Not surprisingly the upland farmers stock their pastures with as many sheep and cattle as they can get away with. Whatever may be happening in the meat market they are guaranteed an income just for owning ruminant animals and running them on the hillside.

The result has been a livestock population explosion throughout the wild uplands of Britain. Everywhere cattle and, more particularly, sheep munch their way across remote heather moors and high mountain heathland. The payments were designed to support farm incomes in areas where the traditional systems for rearing lambs and suckler calves had become uneconomic, but they have had the effect of wiping out thousands of acres of fragile upland habitats: moors of purple heather and bilberry, with birds like the golden plover, hen harrier and merlin; mountain heaths of dwarf shrub and moss, dotted with alpine ferns and flowers.

Nor have the payments succeeded in keeping farmers and their families in the hills. While a few have built great highland kingdoms

78

with the aid of subsidy cheques, the majority have watched their incomes slide, in part because of market saturation by heavily subsidised producers down on the lowland. Mountain communities which have held together through hardship and recession are breaking up at a time of unprecedented public support. Could this be coincidence? Or are these remote local economies as fragile and vulnerable to political interference as the shrubs and flowers of the upland sheep-walk?

From the first floor of the Royal Society for the Protection of Birds' mid-Wales headquarters at Newtown it is possible to get a good view of the surrounding hills as they rise steeply from the edge of town. At first glance the countryside looks in good shape. The fields are green; the hedges tall and vigorous, if a little gappy in places. And everywhere on these lower slopes and valley bottoms there is woodland, from the small isolated copse to long, dark forest stretches that clothe the valley sides. It is a landscape of slope and contrast, of order and natural beauty. Visually it is attractive, at least from a distance.

However, the picture is an illusion. Like the arable acres of the lowland, these fields are dying, victims of a million sets of chomping jaws and four times as many crushing hooves. Subsidised sheep have steadily stripped the living mantle from the hills and hillsides of upland Wales, leaving a barren, lifeless desert. And scarcely anyone has noticed it happening.

At the 1995 Royal Welsh Show in Builth Wells the RSPB launched a report on the status of farmland birds in Wales. They called it *Gwlad Tawel, Silent Fields*.[1] For the great and the good of the Welsh political establishment, hoping to enjoy a day in the country, not to mention a decent lunch, the report came as something of shock. Like the tens of thousands who holiday in the Welsh uplands every year, they had always associated the hill country with living nature, teeming and profuse. What they read was a catalogue of loss, damage and decay which had gone on for years under their very noses.

The facts are as sombre as they are indisputable. The lapwing, abundant in every Welsh county at the beginning of the century, is now in danger of extinction everywhere but on a few nature reserves. In the early part of the century the golden plover – an upland breeding species associated with blanket bogs on the high hills – bred widely on hilltops from Snowdonia to the Black Mountains. Now it is rare, at least as a breeding species. The curlew, a ground-nesting bird once common throughout Wales, is now reduced to just six pairs in the Preseli Mountains, with fewer than 20 pairs in the entire county of Gwent. The linnet, which used to nest in large numbers on rough commons and gorse brakes, is today largely confined to a narrow zone of rough vegetation found on clifftops at the coast. Other birds in 'significant decline' include the red grouse, black grouse, yellow wagtail, snipe, redshank, barn owl and yellowhammer.

It is not only birds that have vanished. The wild flowers have gone from hillside pastures, while the heather and bilberry have been stripped from the upland plateaux. Of the rarest invertebrates, 68 species on the Red Data List – a catalogue of species recognised by national or international authorities as being in danger of becoming extinct – are now thought to have gone from Wales. Another 70, for which there are no modern records, may well have met the same fate. The diversity of life that once clothed these solitary hills has been replaced with the gaudy bright green of a closely cropped grass monoculture, with all the natural life of a snooker table baize.

Even the wooded areas are dying. The sacred ovine, which now dominates this once-wild countryside, grazes the woodland floor so tightly that regeneration is impossible. There is no longer a 'woodland community' of shrubs and flowering plants with their associated invertebrates. Instead the gnarled birch and blackthorn must age and wither on barren, bare earth. Woodland ecosystems, like heather moorlands and the flower-rich meadows of the hillside, are victims of the killer sheep and of the even more deadly SAPS, the Sheep Annual Premium Scheme.

As Barbara Young writes in her foreword to the RSPB report: 'Wales still appears a fertile country of rolling hills and green valleys. However, in wildlife terms, this image is a sad illusion, for the veneer of wildlife that the countryside now supports is becoming paper-thin.' The comment could apply equally to almost all the upland areas of Britain. Hill-farming subsidies have dramatically altered the life and character of these remote regions.

At the end of World War Two 40 per cent of farmland in Wales was classified as rough grazing. A little more than 40 per cent was listed as improved grass – land which had been ploughed and reseeded with the more vigorous and productive perennial ryegrass – and, surprisingly, about 17 per cent of the farmland area was in tillage crops. In a land of hills and high rainfall this may seem odd. Wales is now overwhelmingly a grassland country. Yet for an earlier generation of livestock farmers tillage crops represented an important source of animal feed.

Even in hill areas the better land on the lower slopes would be used to grow root crops like turnips and swedes for feeding to cattle and sheep. Many farmers grew fields of barley and oats, not for selling as cash crops, but for use at home as livestock feed. Improved grassland for grazing or haymaking was chiefly confined to the lower slopes, while the bracken-clothed hillsides, or 'ffridd', together with the heather moorland and coarse mountain grassland made up the rough grazing area. Stocking rates were low – a ewe to two or three acres on farms with both hill and valley land – giving the overall system a high degree of sustainability.

The 1937 edition of Watson and More's classic farming textbook, *Agriculture,* describes a typical Welsh mountain sheep farm. With about half its land lying above the 1,000-foot contour, the farm had a few enclosed fields at the bottom, an intermediate pasture area – the ffridd – plus an expanse of open mountain grazings. In all 1,300 acres carried a breeding flock of 550 Welsh Mountain ewes together with a dozen or so cattle, a stocking density that maintained the diversity of moorland and mountain grazings.

Spending on purchased animal feeds and 'manures' was minimal, scarcely more than the cost of harness repairs. The major items of expenditure were rent – two shillings an acre – and labour. For even in the depths of an economic depression this mountain farm still managed to employ a shepherd and a labourer as well as providing casual work for the village at haymaking time. There was a reasonable income for the farmer, too, and all with barely a penny in public subsidy.

This basic pattern of farming had survived for centuries. It wasn't merely sustainable in its use of natural resources, it was economically sustainable, which was equally important. The contribution it made to village life was real and lasting. There were also substantial benefits for wildlife. The steep, unploughed ffridd with its bracken, gorse and hawthorn provided an ideal habitat for songbirds, while the rank shrubs of the moorland produced good cover for ground-nesting species like the plover, lapwing, black grouse and curlew.

With the coming of hill subsidies the traditional pattern began to break down. Hill farmers wanted to join the technical revolution now gathering pace in the lowlands. It wasn't simply that sheep populations soared, though this was startling enough (during the twenty years from the mid-1960s numbers increased by more than two-thirds in five of the old Welsh counties – Anglesey, Carmarthen, Cardigan, Denbigh and Montgomery), farmers also wanted to get more cash out of them.

The traditional crop of the upland farm had been draft ewes, those that had grown too old for the hill flock, along with ewe lambs for breeding and store lambs for fattening on the lowland. With the protection of subsidies hill farmers were keen to get into a new business – the production of fat lamb for slaughter. And this meant getting more out of their grasslands.

With revivalist zeal Welsh farmers began 'improving' their upland grazings, or at least the younger ones did. Improvement meant taking the plough and the fertiliser-spreader to every square yard of hill that could conceivably be reached by tractor. From the early 1970s the EU added to the crusading spirit with fresh injections of cash. Under new farm development schemes there were hefty grants for land improvement, including drainage, ploughing and reseeding.

Brussels was even prepared to make substantial contributions towards the construction of farm roads up mountain-sides providing tractor access to high moorlands. These grants were paid at a fixed rate per metre of road. The sums involved were so generous that many farmers opted to do the work themselves using farm machinery. They then pocketed the 'profit' which often amounted to many thousands of pounds. One hilltop in mid-Wales is currently served by no less than nine farm roads.

Nor were the steep valley sides safe from the enthusiastic improvers. For many young bucks the ploughing of upland pastures became something of a virility test. Who was prepared to tackle the most death-defying slope with nothing but a four-furrow plough to anchor him down? Welsh sales of large four-wheel drive tractors rose from fewer than 100 in 1977 to about 1,500 in 1992. And so the hills were 'greened', the bright green of artificial fertilisers. By 1992 two-thirds of all Welsh farmland was classified as improved grass, while less than one-third remained as rough grazing. The area remaining in tillage crops had fallen to just 4 per cent.

There is no better way to see the transforming effect of public money than to take the A470/A44 trunk roads through the Cambrian Mountains in west Wales. Heading towards Aberystwyth, the route follows the upper Wye valley through hill country as spectacular as any to be found in Wales. Yet apart from the forest plantations almost everything is green, often bright green, even in the depths of winter. On the high plateaux, the valley bottoms and all but the steepest slopes in between, the vegetation is the same – short-cropped grass. And everywhere there are sheep.

Out on these stunted swards there are few other life forms to be found. The insect population of this near monoculture is minimal.

Nor are there likely to be many birds around, except perhaps for crows. These and a few other carrion-eating species are currently thriving in the hill country. Because sheep numbers are high there are plenty of carcasses around most of the time. The scavengers do well out of the Common Agricultural Policy. Sadly you will seldom hear the call of the curlew in this 'improved' landscape.

To survive on open moorlands ground-nesting birds like the curlew, lapwing and skylark need the cover of heather and bilberry. On the overgrazed stubbles they are at the mercy of predators, the rooks, crows and foxes. Any chicks that do manage to hatch in this hostile terrain are likely to go short of food. The short-cropped vegetation allows the ground to dry out, thus further reducing the invertebrate population. The moorland acid bogs dry out, too, and with them go the wetland birds like snipe and redshank. In the kingdom of the mountain ewe nothing else can survive.

Seven miles west of Llangurig the A44 road turns briefly south to skirt brooding Plynlimon, source of five rivers. Here the roadside verge is wider, and here the purple heather grows thick and strong. The fence which keeps the sheep from the road also keeps them from the heather, preserving a tiny fragment of the moorland habitat that once clothed the hills as far as the eye could see. In a bizarre reversal of convention the benevolent road protects a shard of unspoilt countryside from an agriculture that would destroy it. Everything else is ryegrass.

A few miles to the south of Plynlimon lies a research farm known as Pwllpeiran, a name familiar to a generation of upland 'improvers'. Owned by the Welsh Office, Pwllpeiran is one of a string of experimental farms set up by the government in the 1950s to show farmers how to farm more intensively. While subsidies provided the inducements, the experimental husbandry farms promulgated the mission statement. 'Progressive' farmers flocked in their thousands to pick up the latest messages on how to boost barley yields or double the stocking capacity of their pastures.

The task of MAFF scientists at Pwllpeiran was to increase the productivity of hill farming. The new landscape of upland Wales shows just how successful they have been. Throughout the 1950s and 60s they pioneered new systems for improving grasslands, for breeding bigger mountain ewes and for increasing the output of fat lamb. Following Britain's Common Market accession in the early 1970s the Welsh farm researchers became even more ambitious, developing ingenious new ways of increasing the output of mountain grazings without recourse to the plough. The centuries-old plant communities were first broken up with cultivators, then modern ryegrass varieties were broadcast into the shattered turf.

Farmers copied the new methods with gusto. Bright new, green pastures became a badge of farming success. Those who retained their unimproved moorlands were regarded with pity and mild disdain, wedded as they were to outdated concepts of husbandry and sustainability.

Not that the country needed this extra output from the hills. The additional meat could have been produced far more cheaply on the lowlands. But political lobbying by the National Farmers' Union and their equivalents in other EU member states kept the hill sheep and cattle subsidies in place. And until the 1990s the civil servants of ADAS saw it as their mission to help farmers extract as much as possible from the public pot.

The whole process is now seen to have been a mistake. An estimated 436,000 acres of Welsh moorland have deteriorated to a severe degree as a result of agricultural improvement and the subsequent intensive grazing.[2] Predictably the government is offering farmers public money to maintain and restore the very habitats and landscape features they were so recently paid to destroy. Thus under the Cambrian Mountains Environmentally Sensitive Area scheme farmers can collect £22 an acre for conserving heather moorland, or £34 an acre for managing overgrazed hill areas in a way that brings back the heather. This means stocking the hill sheep-walks at no more than a ewe to 2 acres, and in the winter, a ewe to 4 acres.

Unfortunately the livestock subsidies look a far better bet to most farmers. The government and the EU between them continue to pay about £30 a head for the sheep that run on these sparse mountain grazings. About £25 of the headage subsidy comes through the EU-funded Sheep Annual Premium Scheme, while the remainder is paid through the largely UK government-funded Hill Livestock Compensatory Amounts (HLCAs). Thus the inducement to over-stock remains as powerful as ever, despite the conservation schemes. Many Welsh hill grazings carry stocking densities as high as a ewe per acre, three times the level recommended if environmental damage is to be avoided.

A five-year review of the ESA schemes showed that they had succeeded in reducing the entire Welsh flock of over 11 million animals by just 1,500 sheep. The cost to the taxpayer was £3 million, or £2,000 per sheep removed.[3] Other evidence suggests that the designation of ESAs in Wales merely intensifies grazing pressure on the surrounding land. The wild Welsh hills continue to resemble billiard tables.

This needless destruction of fragile upland ecosystems goes far beyond Wales. Throughout Britain's remote and beautiful hill areas heather moorland is under constant assault from subsidised sheep. From the Cairngorms to the Pennines; from the lonely fells of Lakeland to the moorlands of the Staffordshire Peaks; everywhere the country of the heather is under threat. Headage payments on sheep and cattle were worth £655 million to UK hill farmers in 1996.[4] As a result the sheep population in the UK is fast catching up with the human population. Between 1981 and 1993 it rose by 37 per cent to reach nearly 44 million.

A new study has examined the impact of subsidised sheep-keeping on a typical farm of the central Lake District, an area of poor grazing, extreme weather and considerable tourist appeal.[5] The flock of Herdwick sheep is likely to be the farm's most important enterprise. But while the Herdwick is well adapted to the harsh climate, its productivity is low. Only two lambs are weaned for every three ewes put to the ram, while a fourth, shearling ewe must be kept as a replacement. Thus the crop from every four adult ewes amounts to just two lambs reared.

Assuming equal numbers of males and females, the female gimmer is retained as a future replacement ewe while the wether lamb is sold to the store trade or onto the European market. The sale value of this lamb is £25, but it will have cost taxpayers £130 in sheep annual premium and HLCA payments. For the typical Lakeland flock of 1,000 ewes, the charge to the public purse adds up to £30,000 for producing a crop of just 250 lambs plus a few old draft ewes of little value.

Under the subsidy system the Lakeland farmers are paid for each breeding ewe they run on the fellside, no matter what its performance. There is no incentive to farm efficiently. So it is hardly surprising that they appear more concerned with flock size than with the number of lambs they sell each year. Most are in business to farm the subsidies, using the profits to expand their holdings, drive up land values and increase their eligibility for even more public support. In the process they destroy the very landscapes that subsidies are claimed to protect.

Some of the worst environmental damage is done to common land. Common grazings make up a large proportion of Britain's upland pastures. In Wales, for example, one-third of all semi-natural rough grazings are made up of commons, while in the Lake District a high proportion of remaining heather moorland is common land. As freehold rough grazings disappear through 'improvement', the remaining common grazings are increasingly important for wildlife, particularly birds. Unfortunately the farmers with rights to these crucial areas are as eager to maximise their subsidy income as farmers everywhere else. As a result many commons have become severely overgrazed. And since there is no legal way of preventing commoners from exercising their rights, the devastation of Britain's heather moorlands continues unabated.

Typical is the damage caused to Crosby Ravensworth Fell, on the edge of the Lake District Environmentally Sensitive Area. The fell, part of which is a designated SSSI, has been badly overgrazed for years. Yet the graziers resisted English Nature's proposals for a management agreement that would have reduced the numbers of sheep and allowed the heather to regenerate, at least on the SSSI. In 1996 MAFF belatedly began pressing the farmers to cut their stocking rates,[6] but it remains doubtful whether the heather will ever return to other parts of the fell. In many areas the damage is probably irreversible. Nor is Crosby Ravensworth atypical of the Lakeland landscape. Everywhere the fellsides are draped in bare, matted grass where once the purple heather grew thick and strong.

A few miles to the east of Crosby Ravensworth Fell, below the limestone outcrop of Grange Scar, lies a stretch of open water known as Sunbiggin Tarn. Each spring this remote upland lake becomes the nesting site for thousands of Blackheaded gulls. The annual spectacle of this screaming mass of seabirds soaring and wheeling across the lonely heather moors has become a local attraction for walkers and birdwatchers.

Cumbria Wildlife Trust conservation manager David Harpley recalls a family day out here as a small child. His chief memory is of the difficulty he experienced in running from the road down to the tarn through tall and tangled heather. There is no such difficulty for today's youngsters. The heather has virtually gone from the land at the northern end of the lake.

Pass Sunbiggin Tarn by the road leading up to the limestone scar and you cross a cattle grid. To the south of this grid the moorland is still thick with heather. On the northern side the heather stops abruptly. Overgrazing has wiped it out completely, perhaps beyond recovery. The generations of gulls that soar across this remote country will in future look down not on heather moorland, but on scrubby, drought-stricken grassland.

A hundred miles south the Shropshire hills, those 'blue remembered hills' of A. E. Housman, rise majestically from the sea of arable that now engulfs the plain. Noblest of all is the Long Mynd, a great brooding ridge of high plateaux and deep, ice-scoured hollows or batches. This is a land of tumuli and hill forts, of Bronze Age trade routes and high drover roads. Most is common land, its character formed by the generations of commoners who have run their sheep and occcasionally their cattle on these steep hillsides and high plains.

For centuries the activities of the commoners draped the Mynd with heather. Protected by the thick, purple canopy, meadow pipits, skylarks, ouzels and red grouse built nests on the damp peaty soils, while buzzards and merlin hung on summer thermals. All depended on the time-honoured skills of the commoners and their small flocks of the diminutive and hardy Long Mynd sheep. Controlled burning encouraged heather regeneration and kept the canopy young and vigorous. Low stocking rates allowed the young seedlings time to mature. The rules governing such things as stocking levels and the removal of animals in winter were strictly enforced.[7]

But the management system that had sustained the heather moorland over generations failed to survive the coming of subsidies. The Long Mynd breed gave way to bigger sheep, stocking rates multiplied. No longer were the animals taken off the hill in winter. As a result the heather has largely disappeared from the valley sides and is fast retreating from the plateaux. Each year winter feeding areas grow bigger and grassy areas are grazed tighter. Yet the sheep that scour the hill in such numbers are there only because Brussels pays for their keep.

No one now practises the traditional methods for regenerating heather through controlled burning and cutting. They are no longer worth the effort. The dense army of sheep would strip away any regrowth almost as soon as it appeared. Thus the ancient moorland habitat of the Long Mynd seems destined for senility and final extinction like the sheep breed it gave rise to.

The very vegetation of the hill chronicles the ravages of state-controlled agriculture. Many of the steeper valley sides carry hawthorn and mountain ash trees, the result of natural regeneration from scrub. Yet none are less than half a century old. The introduction of hill sheep subsidies in the 1940s put paid to any such natural regeneration. Thirty years later the coming of the CAP with its less-favoured area payments sealed the fate of the Shropshire hill.

Ever since the 1980s surveys have recorded a steady decline in the heather moorland of the Long Mynd, part of the Shropshire Hills ESA. For years the common has been overgrazed by the commoners, with stocking densities as high as 2 ewes or more to the acre. Only in 1995 did MAFF begin putting pressure on the graziers to reduce the damage, introducing an upper stocking limit of 1.4 ewes an acre. Yet even this tardy action falls well short of what is needed to restore the heather. To allow regeneration the stocking rate would need to come down to just 1 ewe to three acres, a level that would provoke howls of outrage from upland farmers.

The collapse of Shropshire's red grouse population has accompanied the destruction of heather moorland. There are now estimated to be fewer breeding birds in the entire county than might have been shot on the Long Mynd in a single day a century ago.[8] Without radical measures to restore heather cover on the 'improved' uplands there is now a real danger of the species becoming extinct in the county.

Habitat destruction like that of the Long Mynd is taking place on both freehold moor and moorland commons throughout the length of Britain. Independent research carried out by the Institute of Terrestrial Ecology and English Nature concluded that 24 per cent of heather moorland in England was chronically overgrazed.[9] Earlier evidence from the 1980s suggested that as much as 71 per cent of English ericaceous moorland was overgrazed.[10] Since 1993 MAFF has had the power to withhold livestock subsidies from farmers found to be overgrazing their land. But having espoused the sacred 'voluntary principle' during the passage of the 1981 Wildlife and Countryside Act, the Ministry clearly has no intention of brandishing the big stick at its time-honoured clients, the farmers.

In 1994/95 the grand total of four English farmers had their hill livestock subsidies withheld as a result of overgrazing.[11] In answer to a House of Commons Written Question, Welsh Secretary William Hague said the Welsh Office Agriculture Department had investigated nine cases of overgrazing during the previous five years. The investigations were still in progress, but where overgrazing was proven farmers would be encouraged to change their management practices or reduce stocking levels to prevent further damage. In no cases had hill livestock subsidies actually had been reduced.

In a new guide outlining the environmental obligations of livestock farmers MAFF reiterates its powers to withhold subsidies when land is so heavily grazed that the vegetation is adversely affected.[12] However, these powers are only to be used where the overgrazed area is of environmental importance, says MAFF. Since most upland grazing has already been 'improved' and is presumably no longer considered important, those farmers who have now destroyed their heather moorland will clearly receive favoured treatment under the subsidy system. The Wildlife Trusts, who have mounted a long campaign against upland overgrazing, want to see the sanction applied to all land eligible for subsidies,[13] but MAFF refused to entertain the idea. As always, there must be no conditions on the farmer's absolute entitlement to subsidies.

Hardly a muscular response, particularly at a time when the wholesale destruction of heather moorland is apparent to every upland walker. Instead the government chooses to rely on its traditional method for ensuring compliance from farmers – the offering of sweeteners. Thus through a battery of designated Environmentally Sensitive Areas schemes across the country hill farmers are offered special payments for limiting the numbers of cattle and sheep on heather moors. But as on the Cambrian Mountains, the farmers are finding the lure of livestock subsidies rather more appealing.

The uptake of many moorland protection schemes has been dismal. In the Lake District ESA, for example, farmers entering agreements to restrict grazing in both summer and winter account for less than 2 per cent of the land area. Most of those joining the voluntary scheme opt for the less rigorous management prescription and the lower levels of compensation that go with it. The farmer with a 1,000-ewe flock will collect £20,000 a year or so for changing his farming scarcely at all.[14] He undertakes only to maintain his standing walls and to limit his farming at its present level.

Some of the larger Lakeland farmers pick up £40,000 a year or more in ESA payments. As with other subsidy schemes the largest pay-outs go to the biggest farmers, many of whom use the cash to buy up the remaining small farms. This does not stop them complaining that the environmental payments are too low when compared with the rewards from sheep-keeping. In the Pennine Dales ESA a survey by the National Farmers' Union showed that half the farmers who had entered the scheme were considering leaving it because the payments were not high enough.[15] As on the lowlands, farm subsidies are bidding up the cost of conservation.

Among the most recent measures for buying off the upland improvers are payments made under the new Moorland Scheme introduced in early 1995. Its aim is to 'encourage the conservation and enhancement of semi-natural heather and shrubby vegetation to the benefit of wildlife and landscape'. Farmers are offered an annual payment of £30 a head for every ewe they remove from moorland grazing in line with specific stocking targets. Thus the subsidies for running sheep on heather moors are counter-balanced by subsidies for taking them off again.

However, in its first year of operation the new scheme proved a dismal failure. The cash on offer for taking sheep off the hills was no match for the money on offer for putting them there in the first place. MAFF Rural Affairs Minister Tim Boswell was obliged to tell the House of Commons that during the scheme's first year a mere thirteen English farmers had been signed up, thus safeguarding 10,000 acres of heather moorland for the nation. Only another half a million acres to go.

Not that this apparent contempt for conservation schemes should be taken as a general satisfaction with the level of livestock subsidies. Far from it. Despite their rejection of de-stocking incentives on the grounds that they fail to match headage payments, hill farmers miss no opportunity to complain that such payments are far too low. No matter that 40 million sheep and lambs are busy reducing exquisite upland areas to a wasteland, their owners think they should be getting more for keeping them there. In the run-up to the government's annual review of the UK-funded HLCA subsidy, the farming lobby swings into one of its well-rehearsed campaigns for prising more money from the Treasury.

'No help for the hard-pressed hills', complained the *Farmers Weekly* leader following a MAFF announcement that the subsidy was to be pegged in 1995. Inside the paper a spokesman for the lobby group Hill Farming Initiative forecast that the decision could leave 70 per cent of the nation's 60,000 hill farmers facing bankruptcy. In a Commons adjournment debate North Cornwall MP Paul Tyler reproached the government for failing to tackle what he described as a 'collapse in farm incomes in less-favoured areas'. Reading from NFU briefing notes he complained bitterly that while four out of ten farmers in Less Favoured Areas received incomes of less than £10,000 a year their 'pleas for help had been roundly rejected'.[16] It was down to Minister Tim Boswell to put the more meaningful figure of average net income on livestock farms in the English uplands. For the year 1993/94 it came to £18,000.

However hard done by hill farmers may feel, they are entirely dependent on the taxpayer for their very existence. The UK taxpayer's contribution to hill farmers' incomes works out at around 140 per cent, a far higher proportion than the cost of set-aside and other payments to lowland farmers.[17] In some parts of the country the level of hill farm support may be even higher. In a speech to European agricultural economists, Scottish Farm Minister Lord

Lindsay reported that in Scotland aggregate farm income amounted to £612 million in 1995, of which no less than £400 million came as direct subsidy from the taxpayer.[18] On the specialist Scottish sheep farms direct subsidies represented more than 200 per cent of income.

Every mountain ewe that munches its way across a heather-rich moorland represents not a public asset but a national liability. Livestock farming in the uplands makes no contribution to the UK economy. Indeed it acts as a drain on GNP. So if hill subsidies are failing to protect the environment or to satisfy farmers, why do we continue to pay them?

The roots of the present subsidy system for the hills and uplands lie in the Hill Farming Act of 1946. This provided grants for farm 'improvements' while continuing the wartime headage payments for cattle and sheep. The aim of this early legislation was to boost the supply of food from hill farms. It was more concerned with production than securing an economic future for struggling farming families.

With Britain's accession to the Common Market in the 1970s these national support schemes were brought under the Less Favoured Areas Directive of the EEC, a piece of legislation with a very different purpose.[19] The Directive had clear social and environmental aims. It was intended to 'ensure the continuation of farming, thereby maintaining a minimum population level or conserving the countryside'. This wider purpose has been consistently ignored by UK governments so that, far from protecting the communities and landscapes of the hills, farm subsidies have wrecked them.

Headage payments on cattle and sheep represent the scatter-gun approach to helping fragile rural economies. Much of the money ends up with the 'improvers' and 'expanders', those who are prepared to stock sheep 'wall-to-wall' across a heather moorland. As a means of injecting public money into remote hill communities hill sheep subsidies are about as effective as scattering £10 notes from a mountain rescue helicopter.

In his pivotal report *The Upland Landscapes Study* Geoffrey Sinclair showed that state support to agriculture benefits mainly the most prosperous farmers on the best land.[20] Smaller family farms, by contrast, are 'passive', they are slower to change. This does not mean they are less productive, merely less able to exploit a system of public subsidy.

Farm support has been terminally damaging to the traditional hill farm. In encouraging the process of industrialisation in lowland agriculture – a process which led inexorably to the beef and butter mountains of the late 1970s and 80s – it destroyed the hill farmer's chief outlets. As markets became awash with the products of intensive lowland farms, the more 'natural' beef and lamb from the hills was made uncompetitive. Increasingly, hill farmers came to rely on their own subsidies, skewed though these were towards the easier land and the bigger producers. The traditional hill farmer found himself trapped between the big industrial-scale producer on the lowland and his neighbour lower down the hillside who was busy re-seeding old pastures and pushing up stock numbers.

Hill-farming subsidies made sustainable agriculture impossible. They squeezed out tens of thousands of small traditional farms and forced many more on to the same treadmill of intensification that had so damaged lowland Britain. Under the Less Favoured Areas scheme the farms collecting the most public money are not those making the greatest contribution to the environment. On the contrary, they are likely to be doing the least. With the biggest part of the subsidy paid per animal, many of the highest pay-outs go to the very farms where there is overgrazing.[21] As a way of safeguarding some of Britain's most prized landscapes the system scarcely seems credible. However, it has some powerful advocates.

Those who have prospered in an era of hill subsidies are those who now campaign vigorously for their retention. They warn of depopulation and dereliction if subsidies are withdrawn, ignoring the fact that the support system itself has contributed in no small measure to decline. For the upland improvers the remedy to environmental and social decay is an increase in subsidies, not a cut. But the landscape they seek to create is worlds away from that of the traditional hill farmer. A hilltop clothed in tightly grazed ryegrass is, for them, a far more pleasing sight than an unkempt heather moor.

Contributing to a history of the Somerset National Farmers' Union branch, hill farmer John Edwards tells of the transformation of an Exmoor farm between 1939 and 1989.[22] Immediately before the war the farm had no stock-proof hedges or gates, and practically no buildings. It carried a total of 140 sheep and lambs along with 25 cattle. Fifty years later the same farm carried no less than 2,250 sheep as well as 160 cattle, a transformation John Edwards clearly welcomes.

This is the kind of agriculture most hill farmers like to see: an intensive agriculture with high stock numbers and the heavily fertilised ryegrass swards needed to support them. Nature is tamed. Everywhere there is tidiness and order. Lush green fields and large, modern stock buildings are things to be celebrated, so long as the taxpayer foots the bill, of course. Yet it is the very wildness of these high places that so many people value. And this is what the upland improvers would take away.

Most of the sheep and cattle currently grazing hill pastures should be down on the lowlands, bringing fertility back to worked-out arable soils. Instead they make deserts of the high moors. The original justification for hill livestock subsidies was to compensate for the natural disadvantages of farming in an upland environment. One might equally well argue that Scottish fruit growers should be compensated for having less sunshine than the Isle of Wight.

The hills and uplands are remote and difficult places to farm. In a subsidy-free world the price of land would reflect such geophysical realities. There will always be farming on the hills, but left to the market it will be farming of the extensive kind, as it was in the 1920s and 30s. Equally, there will always be tough, independent-minded people who want to farm these areas. They are never going to match the returns of a fertile lowland farm. The attempt to turn the hill country into an imitation of rural Northamptonshire has been a recipe for destruction.

In the Cambrian Mountains, close to the MAFF experimental farm at Pwllpeiran, the overgrazed slopes are dotted with isolated cottages. Many of them are now holiday homes. But a century or so ago these were the cottages of workers in the local lead mines. As in much of upland Britain, mineral workings and quarries contributed substantially to the local economy of these remote areas. The miners and quarrymen were often part-time farmers, keeping a few cattle on their smallholdings and running sheep on the common.

They and their small farms are now long gone, but their history provides a pointer to a more sustainable future for the uplands. There is another way to support farming in the hills, the sort of farming that will protect the environment and the character of the landscape. It is to encourage complementary economic activities in these remote areas: tourism and leisure enterprises, for example, or small-scale food processing. Activities that will provide new opportunities for farming families to earn additional incomes.

For fifty years policy-makers have attempted to provide that income on the backs of sheep and cattle. It is now clear that the policy has failed. Subsidies on livestock have protected neither farmers nor the wild upland landscape. Instead they have spread a dereliction of tidiness and the ruin of abundance.

7

THE BIG WINNERS

'Tell them all loud and clear just how good British farmers are.' So ran the headline over an impassioned *Farmers Weekly* leader proclaiming the achievements of British agriculture.[1] The paper was responding to a wave of criticism of the industry, notably on the subject of calf exports. Now was the time to set the record straight, thundered the paper, time to beat the drum for UK farming.

The agricultural press has good reason to bang a drum for the industry. A substantial part of its revenue comes from advertisers, the manufacturers of fertilisers, pesticides, animal feeds, tractors, veterinary products and all the other inputs farmers are so heavily dependent on. Many of the top farming titles are controlled circulation publications. That means they rely entirely on advertising to stay in business. The last thing they are going to tell their readers is that there may be something fundamentally wrong with the industry. Any move to a more rational agriculture would be certain to cut the profits of their biggest advertisers.

If anyone has prospered from the great post-war transformation of farming it has been the agricultural supply industry, and in particular the pesticide companies. They have seen UK sales grow from a near zero base to almost £0.5 billion annually. Together with exports, UK sales were worth a total of £1.3 billion in 1994. During that same year eleven agrochemical companies each achieved world sales in excess of a billion dollars.[2] It is hardly surprising that they and the trade papers they advertise with should together put over the idea that all is well within UK Agriculture PLC. It is, after all, a creature of their own making.

Before the coming of capital-intensive agriculture, farmers were largely self-sufficient in the materials they needed to keep going from year to year. They retained their own seeds for sowing next season;

they grew crops that provided the feed for their livestock; they recycled dung as the main fertiliser input. Ploughs and other small items of equipment were often bought from the local blacksmith. But with the arrival of industrial agriculture farmers have come to rely on outside suppliers for almost everything they need to continue in business: seed, animal drugs, livestock feeds and, above all, chemicals – fertilisers and pesticides. They have swapped rugged self-reliance for almost complete subservience to an industrial process devised, supplied and driven from the boardrooms of big corporations.

As Professor Howard Newby has pointed out, the post-war agricultural revolution has been first and foremost a technological revolution.[3] Productivity gains, like the doubling of wheat yields in just thirty years, could not have taken place without the thousands of scientists who beavered away in government and company research laboratories around the country. It was they who developed the crop varieties, the machinery, the fertilisers and the agrochemicals which now underpin the food production process. It was they who transformed a largely self-sufficient agriculture into one wholly dependent on purchased inputs.

The agrochemical companies have good reason to be grateful to the agricultural policy-makers. That they now share a multi-million-pound market is thanks, in part, to government intervention. Without public subsidies that market could not have developed to anything like its present scale. Despite the popular perception of science as value-free it is almost always socially directed. Plant pathologists are not paid to sit around studying the fungal diseases of alpine toadflax, but there are plenty of jobs for those interested in septoria disease on winter wheat. Thus the scientists worked on the development of new production methods while the big corporations set about turning the emerging technologies into saleable products.

Farm subsidies were pivotal to the process. Public support gave farmers the confidence to take up the new products with minimum risk. Without support they would have been far less willing to abandon husbandry methods developed and tested over generations. State support provided both the motive power and the lubricant of revolution. Equally important was the form of the subsidies. Public funds might just as easily have been used to support jobs in the countryside. Instead governments have chosen to attach it firmly to output, a policy guaranteed to produce rich pickings for the supply industry.

The more the farmer can produce, the more subsidy he will collect from the state. Therefore a chemical company has only to show that the new wonder product will yield more than its own value in extra output to be assured of a market. Not surprisingly, the main thrust of agricultural research and development goes into the creation of just such products, the fertilisers and pesticides. Happily for the chemical industry these two product groups are synergistic. High levels of nitrogen fertiliser render crop plants more susceptible to disease. So if farmers can be persuaded to push up their nitrogen inputs in pursuit of yields, they are, at the same time, increasing their dependence on fungicides.

During the 1980s a number of chemical companies – including Shell, ICI and Ciba-Geigy – created new opportunities for expanding sales by buying into the seeds business. In this way they were able to breed crop varieties which, while being of high yield potential, were heavily dependent on inputs. With the European grain mountains costing a small fortune to store and dispose of it was a practice that had few benefits for the nation. A rational farm policy might have encouraged the development of lower-yielding varieties requiring fewer chemical inputs. There would have been real environmental gains. But with price signals distorted by output subsidies the development of high-yielding, high-input varieties has continued largely unabated.

The chemical roundabout is neatly summarised by Jim Orson of ADAS.[4] Herbicides minimise weed competition, making it possible to drill wheat earlier and use non-plough methods of cultivation. This means a bigger area can be devoted to the crop. Fungicides protect it from leaf disease and eyespot, while insecticides prevent damage by aphids and the viruses they carry. Finally the expensively protected new variety needs a high level of nitrogen to exploit fully its yield potential.

Orson believes the chemical approach to wheat growing to have been beneficial, enhancing as it has the yield and competitiveness of the north European crop. Indeed he considers the wider exploitation of this technology essential if cereal farmers are to thrive in a new, more open trading environment. All of which is great news for the chemical industry. Competitiveness is a euphemism for yet bigger acreages, for fewer farms and less labour, for the further concentration of cereal-growing into the hands of large-scale specialists. And these are structural changes the large corporations would love to see.

Fewer farms mean reduced marketing costs. The total acreage in wheat is not likely to change much. But when that acreage is controlled by a handful of specialists rather than tens of thousands of smaller growers there are fewer people to sell to, fewer to deliver to, fewer to invoice and generally communicate with. But there is another, more cogent reason for wishing to see a further 'rationalisation' of farming: because the big farmers employ less labour they have little flexibility in the farming systems they adopt. Not for them the complexity of rotations and mixed farming. They would not have the staff to manage them. Instead they must adopt simplified cropping patterns, even monocultures, and invariably this means more chemicals.

Thus the large specialist growers are 'locked' into high-input, industrial patterns of farming. The agrochemical manufacturers recognise this. While paying lip-service to the diversity of British farming they do not doubt that their future profits are bound up with the success of strong, industrial-scale producers – the corporate farming companies and the big-business operators who together make up farming's key decision-makers. This is the farm structure the pesticide manufacturers want to see across lowland Britain. And in this they see eye-to-eye with the government.

For decades Britain's farm policy has rested on the principle that large, 'efficient' farmers should be helped to expand while small inefficient ones should leave the industry. The 1995 Rural White Paper sets out government intentions succinctly – 'We want to see an efficient, prosperous and outward-looking agricultural industry, able to operate in increasingly open world markets.'[5] The word 'efficient' in this context refers to labour efficiency. The government's aim, as always, is to minimise the farm labour force, both in terms of farmers and paid staff. Thus its objectives are identical to those of the agrochemical industry.

During the post-war transformation of rural Britain, MAFF and its farm advisory section – then known as the National Agricultural Advisory Service (NAAS) – worked hand-in-glove with the chemical companies. Throughout the 1960s and 70s ADAS grassland and livestock advisers promulgated the simplistic message that the sure way to profit lay in piling on nitrogen fertiliser. Environmentally damaging practices like silage-making were given official backing in preference to the more benign process of hay-making, while research staff at MAFF experimental farms spent much of their time working out profitable fertiliser rates. The government-funded Grassland Research Institute even joined ICI Fertilisers to publish a joint advisory booklet for dairy farmers, with cover and illustrations printed in familiar 'ICI blue'.[6]

The same unhealthy alliance between government research and development and the chemical industry emerged in the arable sector.

MAFF experimental farms spent a large proportion of their arable budgets running pesticide trials. Research on the improvement of food quality or environmentally friendly cultivation techniques rated scarcely a mention in research programmes. Despite mounting surpluses the one thing ADAS scientists seemed interested in was the evaluation of the latest fungicide from Bayer or Ciba-Geigy. Such was the mind-set of state-managed agriculture. It was as if there were no alternative to a technology that had only existed for a decade or two.

This was the perfect technocracy: Whitehall and industry working as one to reshape the countryside. A symbiosis of public service and private capital, with the taxpayer picking up the bill while being excluded from the decision-making. The chemical industry provides the technology to get people off the land. In return the government delivers a form of subsidy that is guaranteed to lift returns to farm suppliers, particularly fertiliser and agrochemical suppliers. Measured by its own objectives of higher food output and rural change, the strategy has been extremely effective.

In the early 1990s the UK government had an opportunity to stem the flow of public funds into big-scale, industrial agriculture that has so despoiled the landscape. EU Farm Commissioner Ray Mac-Sharry's proposal to skew farm support in favour of small farmers would have severely cut the subsidies going to large producers, the heaviest users of agrochemicals. But the then Agriculture Minister John Gummer savaged the proposal on the grounds that it would discriminate against the UK with its larger farm structure.[7] The reform measures, when they were introduced, were much watered down so they no longer posed a threat to the big-scale producer. Though hailed as a victory for Britain, it might more aptly be described as a victory for 20,000 industrial farmers along with the shareholders of agrochemical companies. It was anything but a victory for the countryside or the majority of country people.

The 1992 CAP 'reforms' brought a collective sigh of relief to the company boardrooms of the farm supply industry. No doubt the champagne corks popped and glasses were raised to old chums in the Whitehall Place headquarters of MAFF. For a support system biased towards small farmers would have been the worst of all outcomes for the major agribusiness corporations. An across-the-board cut in support prices would have been preferable. Though it would undoubtedly have hit sales, their best customers, the large-scale specialist producers, would have remained firmly in the market.

In the event the supply companies got a better result than they can have hoped for. Support prices were to be reduced, but in return for putting land into set-aside farmers were to be substantially compensated under the Arable Area Payments Scheme. Although these area payments were to come direct from MAFF, they remained firmly linked to production. In reality the subsidies were to continue in a slightly different form. There remained every incentive for the arable farmer to continue pouring on the chemical inputs across his non set-aside acres.

Two years later the agrochemical giant Zeneca was able to reassure shareholders: 'There are welcome signs that the effects of the recent reform of the CAP, which depressed sales in past years, have levelled out.'[8] The company announced a 4 per cent rise in world agrochemical sales, with profits up 55 per cent. At the same time the British Agrochemicals Association, the industry's UK trade organisation, revealed a 2.4 per cent increase in its members' sales.[9] Despite the waste and crippling cost of EU overproduction, MAFF had stayed loyal to its allies in countryside industrialisation.

On a 1995 visit to a Somerset agricultural show, William Waldegrave, successor to John Gummer at MAFF, reminded his audience that the CAP was not all bad. Whatever its shortcomings as a means of supporting farm incomes, it did at least bring spin-off benefits for pesticide manufacturers and land agents. From a British minister this was an admission of rare candour. Agribusiness companies have long been beneficiaries of government enthusiasm for capital-intensive agriculture. But as a rural policy it is hardly likely to hold much appeal for the electorate. Few are likely to see pesticide manufacturers and land agents as among the groups most deserving of public support.

Following its unexpected reprieve over CAP reform, the agricultural supply industry has been busy trying to polish up the image of UK agriculture. Intensive farming is now more stoutly defended by feed and fertiliser companies than it is by farmers themselves. This should come as no surprise. If subsidies were to be withdrawn, it is the supply companies who would feel the loss most keenly, not the farmers, most of whom could switch to other, more sustainable ways of producing their crops. Hence the need for high-profile media campaigns to bang the drum for British farming.

It was one of Britain's leading seed-suppliers, Farmers Seeds Federal, which launched the 'British Farmers Feed Millions' campaign. A publicity newsletter, distributed in *Farmers Weekly,* issued the call to arms. It was a strident, if rather confused, piece. 'We have news for all those people who thought farmers did nothing for their money but collect subsidies, pour surplus milk down the drain and pollute UK water supplies with nitrates. Let alone rear animals just for export! In fact, what they did last year was to produce a staggering amount of food for consumption in this country alone. Anything wrong with that?'

Farmers Weekly thought not. It quickly responded to the call, mindful of its full-colour pages of pesticide adverts. 'For too long our industry has been content to sit back while a motley crew of individuals, united only in their opposition to everything which is good about UK agriculture, has indulged in one vitriolic attack after another. Enough is enough.'

The agrochemical industry's advocacy of British farming has been more circumspect and a good deal more influential. It is based on one simple and beguiling premise – that modern, chemical-based methods of food production are unavoidable if we are to feed a growing world population. The message is succinctly summed up in a pesticide fact-sheet prepared as part of a British Agrochemicals Association project pack for A-Level biology students. 'Pesticides have greatly increased crop production throughout the UK and saved many millions of people from starvation in Third World countries.'[10]

The argument is persuasive. At present rates of population increase, world agriculture will have to feed at least two billion more people by the year 2020. To achieve this farm production must grow by about 2 per cent annually.[11] The bulk of the increase will need to come in higher yields from existing farmland since to extend cultivation in tropical areas or on semi-arid range land would be to risk ecological disaster. Thus the world will need all available modern 'tools', including efficient pesticides.

The agrochemicals industry is busy promulgating this message to school pupils across the country. The BAA's resource pack *Good Enough To Eat* is now used by more than 20 per cent of UK primary schools.[12] Its secondary school resource *Feed the World* was used as the basis of a competition in which both pupils and teachers had the chance to win trips to Tanzania. A new generation of citizens is being taught that there is no realistic alternative to industrial agriculture. It is a notion that has some powerful advocates.

Dennis Avery, Director of Global Food Issues for the US Hudson Institute and a vehement critic of low-input farming, has put the case forcefully. He describes the environmentalist concept of sustainable agriculture as 'a sham'.[13] High-yield farming using hybrid seeds, chemical fertilisers, irrigation and pesticides is the only truly sustainable system for a world that will demand three times as much food output while still expecting to keep its wildlife. The alternative would be to plough up most of the world's 'wildlands', so destroying hundreds of thousands of wildlife species and rapidly eroding most of the world's topsoil.

Avery estimates that chemically supported high-yield agriculture is already saving about 10 million square miles of wildlife habitat from the plough, a figure enthusiastically publicised by the BAA.[14] For decades the pesticide industry has defended its products against environmentalist charges that they destroy wild species and habitats. Now at last there is an opportunity to go on the offensive. High-tech farming will not only feed a hungry world, it will safeguard the environment.

The fields and fellsides of the British rural landscape tell a rather different story. For most people on these islands the modern experience of countryside is overwhelmingly one of wildlife loss. If intensive agriculture is so good for wildlife how come the fields are silent? How come the meadows contain no wild flowers any longer? Rather than answer such fundamental questions, the pesticide companies have opted to green their corporate image.

During the 1980s when subsidised crop production was steaming ahead untroubled by thoughts of set-aside, the favoured product names for new pesticides were often terms denoting battle and conflict. Thus the pages of the farming press were full of adverts for products like Commando, Dagger, Avenge, Stomp, Kerb and Lancer. Farmers saw themselves as waging war against the forces of nature, and the manufacturers were happy to supply weapons for the arsenal.

However, in the 1990s the strategy has changed. In an age of environmental awareness the images of war are no longer acceptable. Now the pages of *Crops* and *Farming News* are filled with pictures of predators from the animal kingdom. Cheetahs, tigers and panthers stalk the wheat land; the cold eye of the eagle stares out across the arable fields. These days the farming press has some of the best animal photography outside the wildlife magazines.

The subjects are carefully chosen. The animals have to be predators. The marketing executives insist on it. There must be the same macho appeal to the man on the 100hp tractor. But who can object when the killers come straight from nature? The industry has a new image to build. It may not be possible any longer to justify public subsidies for food production. But when the money supports an environmentally responsible production system, the case becomes altogether easier to argue.

The agrochemical industry now supports a whole range of environmental initiatives from straight-forward research to farm conservation projects. The British Crop Protection Council's 1995 conference in Brighton included papers on sustainable agriculture and the potential for using herbicides in the conservation of farmland flowers. The BAA's booklet *Crop Protection: The Way Forward* carries on its front cover a picture of a crop sprayer with an inset photograph of a ladybird devouring an aphid. Bayer's crop protection magazine *Four Seasons* has a feature on hedgerow management tied in with a competition sponsored by the company through Suffolk Farming and Wildlife Advisory Group.[15] Cyanamid sponsors a wildlife conservation competition for arable farms.

At a time when most industries are busily acquiring green credentials none is working harder at it than the agrochemical manufacturers. However, behind the public relations little has really changed. In 1994 Zeneca Crop Protection was number two in the global agrochemicals market; in the same year it sponsored a field guide to rare arable flowers.[16]

Among the 16 species featured were corn marigold, said to have become much rarer over the entire country, and shepherd's needle, described as occurring in fewer than 25 ten-kilometre squares throughout Britain. The following year DuPont, third in the 1994 global agrochemicals market, continued advertising its cereal herbicide Ally for use against 'problem weeds like thistles, corn marigold, cranesbill, fool's parsley and shepherd's needle'. The industry's image may have become greener, but out in the fields its business remains the same – the reduction of biodiversity.

Currently the most trumpeted piece of green camouflage is the concept known as Integrated Crop Management, ICM. This requires farmers to consider more natural ways of controlling weeds, pests and diseases in addition to their usual reliance on pesticides. For example, they might choose a crop variety with a high degree of inbred resistance to a disease, or adopt a crop rotation that helps keep down the weeds. In practice the concept changes very little. Most farmers remain as dependent as ever on pesticides.

The ICM concept is promoted principally through an organisation known by the acronym LEAF, Linking Environment And Farming. The organisation was set up, largely with the aid of agrochemical industry money, to proclaim the caring side of intensive farming. A series of demonstration farms has been established across the country to show public and farmers alike how profitable farming can be combined with environmental responsibility. Participating farmers are required to carry out an environmental audit of their methods.

The appeal from the pesticide industry point of view is that LEAF, like Integrated Crop Management, changes little. Farmers undertake only that they will use no more pesticides than the crop requires for healthy growth. In practice this is no restriction at all. They remain free to continue drenching their land in agrochemicals so long as each additional spray provides a marginal increase in profit. And while subsidies remain this is likely to be the case. The important thing from the pesticide manufacturers' point of view is that LEAF provides them with the ideal vehicle to show publicly their concern for the environment. It puts them on the side of the angels.

The manufacturers know only too well that their products are unpopular with consumers. Their fear is that a government seeking electoral advantage will introduce statutory measures to curb pesticide use, as have a number of other EU member states. A pesticide minimisation conference, set up jointly by MAFF and the Department of the Environment, appeared to presage just such an outcome. In the event Integrated Crop Management was seen as the best way forward, much to the relief of the pesticide industry. The risk of a 'retrograde' step towards mandatory reduction policies had been averted, at least for the time being. But the industry needed to appear responsive to the public's concern.

LEAF and its activities to promote ICM are heavily supported by corporate farming and agribusiness. The chairman, farmer and broadcaster David Richardson, also chairs the contract farming company Sentry Farming. The 1995 executive committee included Windsor Griffiths of the agrochemical giant AgrEvo and Richard Trow-Smith, Communications Manager of the British Agrochemicals Association.[17] Also included was a senior MAFF civil servant. The pesticide industry's old Whitehall ally is equally concerned that the farming system it created should acquire a favourable public image. The LEAF organisation's environmental audit was itself launched by the then Agriculture Minister Gillian Shephard.

Among those making 'significant contributions' to LEAF were the British Agrochemicals Association and the European Crop Protection Association as well as individual agrochemical companies including AgrEvo, Ciba Agriculture, DowElanco, Rhone-Poulenc Agriculture and Zeneca. Contributors also included the Fertiliser Manufacturers' Association together with the fertiliser companies ICI, Kemira and Hydro Agri. It is no surprise that the list of LEAF demonstration farms contains not one organic farm.

Integrated Crop Management is essentially a public relations exercise. It will do little to reduce the 20,000 tons or so of active chemical ingredient poured on UK farmland each year in the form of pesticide. The agrochemical and fertiliser companies know full well that Britain could not easily go back to non-chemical methods of food production. We no longer have enough labour on our farms. The traditional farmworkers, the skilled men and women who knew how to control crop pests and weeds without recourse to pesticides, have now gone from the land.

Even so the agrochemical companies recognise that their own position remains vulnerable. A large percentage of their sales is dependent on public subsidies to farming. Yet it is evident that the public is growing increasingly uneasy about the effect of chemical fertilisers and pesticides on its food and environment. This is why the major companies are willing to put their money behind initiatives like ICM and LEAF. It is an attempt to allay public anxiety. But there is increasing evidence that the public has reason to be sceptical.

A pioneering experiment at a crops research centre near Bristol has indicated a wide-scale overuse of pesticides in British agriculture. A small team at Long Ashton Research Station is carrying out a field-scale investigation of crop production using substantially reduced chemical inputs.[18] Compared with conventional methods the low-input system produced lower yields, but the costs were also reduced. The conventional winter wheat crop is routinely treated with an autumn herbicide together with an insecticide. In spring it is sprayed with a plant growth regulator to keep it standing despite heavy applications of nitrogen fertiliser. After that it is routinely sprayed twice, perhaps three times, with fungicides to keep crop diseases at bay.

But with their less-intensive system the Long Ashton scientists have begun to rediscover the benefits of good husbandry. They found that by adopting sound cultural practices, for example, by following crop rotations and using cultivations to keep down weeds, many of the standard pesticide applications were no longer needed. Insecticides were abandoned altogether while fungicide sprays were reduced by almost two-thirds. As a result the low-input wheat crop made more money than conventional wheat crops. In the dry year of 1995 it even produced a higher yield.

The fact that leading crop scientists need to 'rediscover' the benefits of good husbandry shows how deeply the interests of the chemical industry have been allowed to undermine sound cultural practice. In the conventional wisdom of modern farming there is a chemical solution to every cultural problem. Crop growing is no longer a skill, a complex management task encompassing soil, plant and human ingenuity. It is reduced to a series of simple choices between competing chemical products. Such has been the influence of the chemical companies.

One crucial finding of the study is that many modern crop varieties are poorly suited to low-input farming systems. The key characteristics are a high level of resistance to pests and diseases combined with agronomic traits like the ability to stand straight without the aid of plant growth regulators. Most modern crop varieties have been bred for a high potential yield. Other characteristics like disease-resistance and standing ability were given a far lower priority by the breeders. Thus farmers choosing many modern varieties are compelled to apply a battery of chemical sprays to realise their potential. The agrochemical industry's past investment in plant breeding companies makes perfect commercial sense. They were merely creating their future markets.

The motive force powering all such developments is the subsidy system. No doubt the market mechanism would have placed some premium on high yield, but it is inconceivable that farmers would be spending £100 an acre or more on fertilisers and chemical sprays had there been no price guarantees. It is far more likely that they would be using low-input methods of the sort being developed at Long Ashton.

The government and the EU have offered large financial incentives to producers of wheat, barley and oilseeds, no matter what methods they use. The pesticide manufacturers have been sharp enough to step in and snatch a sizeable share for themselves. Meanwhile the public is rewarded with contaminated food, a devastated landscape and a countryside stripped of its working population.

The logical way to end the damage is to get rid of the subsidy, and with it the inducement to squeeze every last ounce of production from the land. As always government pursues the voluntary approach, pledging to work with farmers and retailers in encouraging 'pesticide minimisation techniques'.[19] The pesticide industry muddies the waters by promoting diversions like Integrated Crop Management and demonstration farms. Yet the simple, obvious remedy would be the rapid halt to production subsidies, a measure that would lead to an overall drop in agrochemical use, as the Minister of Agriculture's own review group has concluded.[20]

Even within the agrochemical industry there is now a widespread recognition that the rules of the game are changing. The days of creaming the fat from a bloated farm support system appear strictly limited. While the pesticide companies may be mounting a spirited rearguard action, they know the good times are over, at least as far as the CAP is concerned. Hence their attempt to shift attention to the food needs of a fast-growing world population.[21]

It has been called the 'industrialised world to the rescue' scenario;[22] the north coming to the aid of the south. Once more industrial-scale production from highly mechanised operations will push small 'inefficient' farmers out of business, but this time they will be in poor, Third World countries. Along will come the large, intensive producers of Europe and North America, ready to trade their food with those who can afford to pay for it and have it distributed as famine relief to those who cannot. It is a scenario that has obvious attractions for agrochemical manufacturers. It would, after all, extend their threatened markets. For the people of producer and recipient countries alike, the results would be catastrophic.

In the developing world many millions would be denied the security of their traditional lands. Instead they would be consigned to urban shanty towns with all their attendant social and environmental ills. In the west, where the same process of urbanisation took place one hundred years ago or more, the impact would be scarcely less damaging: more pollution, more degradation of the countryside, further loss of wildlife. While promising a solution to threatened environmental disaster the agrochemical industry would accelerate the desertification of rural Britain. Are we to be fooled again?

There is another possible response to the global challenge to farming and food production, one that could bring real benefits to both rich and poor countries. It would mean replacing a bankrupt industrial measure of farm efficiency with one that puts people back in touch with the land. For the bare-earth farmer in Africa there is the prospect of higher yields and a more secure future. For the citizen of overcrowded Britain there is the promise of a new and living countryside. But first the country must free itself from the stranglehold of the agrochemical business and the subsidies that sustain it.

8

THE RICHES WE SQUANDERED

Food analyst Dennis Avery accuses environmentalists of offering fantasies in place of food production.[1] The idea that organic farming can triple its yields after 10,000 years of failure is a fantasy. Only high-yield, intensive farming can feed a growing world population. This is what the agribusiness would have us believe. However, the recent history of agriculture tells a rather different story.

The fact is organic farming has the potential to be highly productive. Until the take-over of agriculture by the state, British farmers were feeding people successfully with scarcely any of the chemicals, fertilisers and veterinary drugs they now rely on. Free of political interference, they might have gone on increasing output by sustainable methods, their development matching the post-war rise in national prosperity. They would have produced for real markets and kept in closer touch with their customers. Britain would now have an agriculture tuned to the needs of its people. Tragically, governments had other ideas for the land.

The author H. J. Massingham, an astute commentator on rural affairs in the 1930s and 40s, warned frequently that the industrialisation of agriculture would lead to catastrophe. In his book *The Wisdom of the Fields* he tells of a wartime visit to a friend's farm in west Somerset, and of meeting 'peasants' farming small acreages on the foothills of those two 'great ranges' the Quantocks and the Brendons.[2] His use of the term 'peasant' implies no disdain. On the contrary, it is a mark of his respect. In Massingham's view country people, peasants in particular, were the repository of an ageless wisdom which the nation abandoned at its peril.

Among those he met in Somerset's 'hillock and dingle' country were a certain Mr Rowe and his wife – there is no further identification. On a little more than four acres of steeply sloping land this couple grew enough food to feed a small hamlet, all without the aid of chemicals. Their crops included strawberries – 120lbs produced in 1944 – early and maincrop potatoes, orchard fruits, plus a greater diversity of vegetables than many a grower 'with 400 acres of fat and level land'. In addition they grew enough grass, fodder crops and flowers to support a pony, 130 chicken including 30 pullets, goats, 6 ewes and a lamb, a breeding sow with a litter of 8, and 30 hives of bees.

Massingham comments that their crops were of superlative quality and their animals in perfect health. Husbandry such as this would save old England from starvation and feed a hundred million people when the edifice of super-industrialism, international trade and the exploitation of natural resources came 'tumbling down'.

Not far away Massingham met Mr Meade and his wife, who with the help of a land-girl farmed 75 acres of hillside. Not a yard of their land was neglected. They grew wheat, barley, oats, kale, mangolds and turnips; milked 11 cows, taking 35 gallons a day and carting the manure to the fields; and fattened 60 hoggets (yearling sheep) on the roots, stubbles and pastures. With the land-girl Mr Meade was known to have planted 12,000 cabbages by hand in just five days, with breaks only for milking. In six years the yields from the farm had doubled, as had the fertility of its soils.

The charge that such farms as these were incapable of feeding the population is clearly nonsensical. Labour-intensive they certainly were, but the people who ran them were more than happy to do the job. Indeed there was nothing else they wanted from life. It was their sheer zest for farming that kept them going through the dark days of the pre-war depression. At the start of the war there were 288,000 farmers in England and Wales alone, each with less than 100 acres. Virtually without subsidies they had survived the depression, and largely without chemical aids they went on to feed the nation through six years of conflict. They were, by any reckoning, a great national asset, one which the politicians contrived to squander.

Massingham put it bluntly. 'That it should ever have entered the heads of modern busybodies to dispossess such men as these and absorb their plots into larger units on the ground that they are 'uneconomic' is a measure of that peculiar lunacy afflicting nations that put the factory before the farm.'[3]

While state intervention in farming culminated in the 1947 Agriculture Act, governments had been actively involved since before the war. In the 1930s it was the politicians who took a lead in setting up marketing schemes for such products as milk, bacon, potatoes and hops. With world markets stagnant there was also legislation to provide limited financial assistance to wheat and sugar producers. Restrictions and tariffs were imposed on food imports, and there were subsidies to encourage the use of lime and basic slag on the land.[4] But with the declaration of war in 1939, government involvement became total. From now on agriculture was to be a publicly managed industry.

Policy was carried out on the ground by the 'War Ags'. Composed chiefly of farmers, farmworkers, landowners and agents, these committees had enormous power. They issued compulsory orders for cropping and the ploughing up of grassland. They rationed fertilisers and animal feeds, allocated farm machinery and deployed farm labour. They were also given authority to terminate farm tenancies and dispossess inefficient farmers when they considered this to be in the national interest.

In his analysis of 'The State and the Farmer', Professor Michael Winter discusses the wartime role of the National Farmers' Union in the implementation of agricultural policy.[5] War Ag chairmen were selected by the Minister of Agriculture, and together they appointed the committees. Most chairmen were either leading farmers or landowners, usually office holders in the NFU or the Country Landowners' Association. NFU activists became the single most important voice on many committees, especially those appointed at the district level.

Not surprisingly, there was a considerable amount of resentment from farmers at this bureaucratic interference in their businesses. At the same time most of them were happy to see agriculture put back on its feet after the long years of depression. The civilian population was also being fed better following an expansion in milk and vegetable production.[6] Despite firm state control of food distribution and pricing, farming's gross income doubled between 1938 and the end of the war. Farmers could see the advantages of the wartime organisation. They gradually came to rely on the War Ags for such things as labour, credit and technical advice.

Sadly state involvement did not end with the coming of peace. By 1945 something of a political consensus had emerged, with all the main parties in agreement. There must be no return to pre-war uncertainties. The War Ags would be continued, with price guarantees introduced for all the major products and strict regulations applied to food imports. In wartime the state management of agriculture had been undertaken to save the nation from starvation. Now it was deemed necessary as a means of reducing foreign exchange. Besides, it seemed only right to reward farmers for their sterling work towards the war effort. Who could possibly object?

The politicians were content to leave the policy details to the specialists, which basically meant a small cabal of MAFF civil servants and the larger farmers who ran the NFU. Michael Winter records the emergence of a 'coherent policy community', capable of defending the interests of farmers.[7] They shared a common belief that more resources ought to be devoted to their particular policy area. They also shared a common 'culture', a sense of where the priorities lay and how they should be tackled. It was a culture confined largely to MAFF and the NFU. Other interest groups were excluded.

According to Michael Winter this closure of the 'community' to wider interests was a key aspect of the development of post-war farming policy. 'Even Parliament may find itself substantially excluded from the details of policy making and, even more, from implementation. By the end of the war agriculture had become very much a technical matter in which the interests of consumers, for example, were largely excluded.'

The 1947 Agriculture Act was the crowning achievement of this wartime alliance between the larger farmers and MAFF. Labour Prime Minister Clement Attlee had presaged the new deal a year earlier. As guest of honour at the National Farmers' Union annual dinner he had spoken of the need for an all-out effort. The farmers could hardly believe their good fortune. Here was a socialist government offering the kind of security that until now had never been available except in wartime.

The Act, when it came, marked as on tablets of stone the new status of agriculture in society. Its declared purpose was to promote 'by the provision of guaranteed prices and assured markets ... a stable and efficient agricultural industry capable of producing such part of the nation's food and other agricultural products as in the national interest it is desirable to produce in the UK, and of producing it at minimum prices consistent with proper remuneration and living conditions for farmers and workers in agriculture and an adequate return on capital invested in the industry.'

The Act was quickly followed by measures to extend the ploughing-up subsidy and to provide capital grants for hill farmers. Later there were subsidies on fertiliser use and on beef calves. But the 1947 Act remains the great watershed, the instrument that provided farmers with an unprecedented degree of public protection and ultimately set them on the road to industrialisation. Writing a year after the Act, even the NFU's former head of economics Geoffrey

Browne wondered how long subsidies could be maintained at the then enormous level of £400 million a year.[8]

'Economic necessity, and the goodwill of the community towards farming, enabled the Government, without opposition, to provide financial incentives on a scale that would have been out of the question in different circumstances ... The present treatment of agriculture is scarcely a policy; it is little more than the continuation of wartime emergency methods.' Geoffrey Browne could hardly have imagined that comparable levels of public support would still remain in place almost fifty years later. Such was the influence of the NFU and the landowning lobby. For decades they were able to shape rural policy to suit their own interests.

One of the chief effects of the 1947 Act was to set up the mechanism for price fixing. This was the annual ritual of the spring farm price review, when agriculture ministers would sit down with the NFU to work out the new set of guaranteed prices covering all the major farm commodities. The NFU became the only representative industrial body in the country with which the government was bound by law to consult. This annual circus in which the agricultural establishment decided how much money they were going to take from the public purse continued until the UK joined the EEC in the early 1970s.

In his 1975 review of British agriculture, Tristram Beresford explores the wartime origins of the relationship between MAFF and the NFU.[9] It began as an *ad hoc* link between Whitehall Place and Bedford Square, providing the War Cabinet with a means of communicating with farmers. By the end of the war the union, with its 200,000 members, had become accepted by government as the representative voice of farming. With each successive farm price review the relationship grew more intimate. The union had become more than a pressure group, says Beresford. It was now 'the seat of the agricultural establishment'.

'It became a bureaucracy that anticipated, interpreted, co-ordinated and amplified the inarticulate aspirations of the majority of farmers ... It was too important to offend. The government hobnobbed with it. Placemen touched their cap to it.' In the post-war struggle for economic solvency, the NFU achieved the status of national hero. More than just 'the farmer's friend and protector', it was now an 'instrument of government policy whose decisions made news'.

In *Agriculture, the Countryside and Land Use*, John Bowers and Paul Cheshire describe how the union used this privileged status to imprint its own rural vision on emerging policy.[10] It was as if there were no other voice in the countryside worth listening to. The narrow ideology of intensive farming was accepted almost to the exclusion of all other influences. This ideology maintained food production as the only proper use of land, whether or not that food was needed by the people. It is a myopic view that persists to this day, and it has led to the destruction of much beautiful countryside and to the extinction of a generation of skilled small farmers.

The new agricultural 'improvers' were bent on demolition from the start. The 1947 Act with its price guarantees had two main objectives – to increase farmers' incomes and to expand food production. The target was a 60 per cent increase in output by 1956. But in its early years the Act looked like being a failure. Instead of investing in new tractors, farmers preferred to spend their unexpected riches on such things as cars, washing machines and carpets for the sitting room. This is why the government began introducing production grants covering such diverse items as artificial fertiliser, the ploughing up of old meadow, field drainage and the removal of hedgerows.

Subsidies were increasingly linked to production. The more environmental damage a farmer perpetrated on his farm, the more subsidy he could expect to pick up. Long before Britain entered the EEC, her countryside was being eroded by the power and influence of the agricultural lobby. In the mid-1950s the Conservative government pulled off a remarkable sleight of hand by appearing to introduce a free market while at the same time maintaining the inflated returns to farmers. The mechanism for this trick was known as the deficiency payment. Farmers were now to sell their products on the free market, with the taxpayer making up the difference between the average selling price and a guaranteed price. Of course the so-called 'free market' was really no such thing. There were too many restrictions on food imports, especially after world prices fell in the early 1960s. Deficiency payments were, in practice, an attempt to limit Exchequer spending while maintaining support for agriculture.

For farmers now had support in high places. The Minister of Agriculture had a seat in the Cabinet. And as Tristram Beresford has pointed out, the Ministry of Agriculture made scarcely a move without consulting the NFU.[11] 'All this, and the interminable subsidies, £60–70 million on cereals, £35 million on eggs, £30 million on fertilisers, £50 million on pigs and sheep, about twice the total yield of surtax.'

Even when world food supplies began to grow substantially, the

NFU succeeded in convincing ingenuous politicians that yet more subsidised home production was in the national interest. Once again the import-saving role of agriculture became the industry's trump card. Labour Prime Minister Harold Wilson was particularly susceptible to this argument because of his concerns over the balance of payments.[12] Following intense NFU campaigning, tighter import controls were introduced in 1963 and in the annual price review of 1964. Four years later the Economic Development Committee for Agriculture reported that expansion was desirable without even investigating the cost to the nation of achieving it, so pervasive was the 'output first' philosophy.[13]

The House of Commons Select Committee on Agriculture, with no fewer than ten farmers among its membership, was even more enthusiastic in its support of farm intensification. They were, according to Bowers and Cheshire, largely unconcerned with the cost of higher production or with the net effect on the balance of payments.[14] Once again expansion was considered 'desirable' in itself, so long as the government was prepared to provide 'adequate incentives', of course. There was no question of expansion through efficiency, only through subsidies. Not surprisingly, net farming income rose by 43 per cent during the 1960s. But it was not the small farmers who were benefiting. The lion's share of the profits went to the farming 'industrialisers' who dominated the NFU.

One of the reasons given by the Commons Select Committee for backing farm expansion was the desire to 'cut the rate of outflow of labour from agriculture'. This was the supreme irony, for the very process they advocated was pushing people from the land at an increasing rate. Subsidies inflate rents and land prices. They provide profits for those prepared to tear out hedges and pour on the agrochemicals. But they disadvantage the small farmer, the mixed farmer, the farmer who cares for the environment. By accepting the NFU's vision of the countryside the politicians were not protecting employment, they were destroying it.

In 1938, the last year in which farming was still free of government control, there were 226,000 small farmers in England and Wales, each with fewer than fifty acres. By 1968 nearly 64,000 of them had gone out of business. With virtually no government help they had survived the depression of the 1920s and 30s. With no agrochemicals they had fed the nation in time of war. But thirty years of unprecedented public support for agriculture had driven them to the wall, victims of a voracious agribusiness and inflated land values.

During the same thirty-year period the real price of farmland rose by 87 per cent.[15]

This was good news for the land speculators, of course, as it was for the large farmers who made up the most active and vociferous section of the farming lobby. The number of farmers with more than 300 acres rose by almost 40 per cent over the period. The 1947 Agriculture Act had set British agriculture firmly on the path of industrialisation. Today two-thirds of UK farmland is in holdings of 250 acres or more. We have become a nation of large farmers, and British agriculture ministers are able to rail against Brussels for coming up with measures that discriminate against 'efficient' UK farmers.

For fifty years successive governments have pursued policies which discriminate against small producers and in favour of the industrial-scale agribusiness. By 1960 it was estimated that just one hundred 1,000-acre holdings in the eastern counties of England collected more in subsidy than all 7,000 farms in the county of Carmarthen-shire.[16] Three-fifths by value of all deficiency payments were being drawn by one-fifth of farmers. Not that this was of any concern to the politicians. As now, they were content to see public money used to construct a rational, competitive agriculture, an industry of large, efficient farms. Whatever was in the interests of the NFU must be good for the nation, too.

In their classic review of the late 1960s, *Farming in Britain Today*, J. G. S. and Frances Donaldson sum up the conventional wisdom of the time.[17] Discussing the small farm 'problem' they suggest that a large number of small farms constitute a threat to the 'balance' of the industry. Since the small producer needs a greater return per acre to make a living, a guaranteed price which provides a good income for the farmer on 300 acres may well result in hardship for the farmer on fifty. Thus a government trying to maintain farm incomes by means of guaranteed prices must inevitably concern itself with rationalising the industry's structure.

This is the thinking that has taken British agriculture up its industrial blind alley. The attempt to formulate policies that will protect the incomes of all farmers has resulted in waste and rural destruction and has led ultimately to the absurdities of the Common Agricultural Policy. The question the Donaldsons failed to address was whether it is any business of government to be intervening in farm incomes in the first place. Surely it is for the farmer to decide whether his prices and his income are sufficient to make the effort worthwhile? When the Rowes turned their handful of Somerset acres into some of the most productive in the county, they had decided, presumably, that the return was enough. No doubt the freedom and independence of a rural smallholding were worth as much as the financial rewards. Yet the government with its subsidies and industrial view of efficiency turned the Rowes and their like into 'the small farm problem'.

One of the abiding myths of modern farming concerns the state of the industry during the depression of the 1920s and 30s. In the popular imagination the inter-war years were a time of decline and ruin, of mass bankruptcies and suicide. The stories of misery are passed on to each new generation: stories of families walking out on their farms in despair, stories of collapsed barns and weed-choked fields. There is scarcely a farmer today who is not convinced that the 20s and 30s were a period of unmitigated disaster for agriculture. It is an article of dogma learned at the kitchen Aga. And the cause of all that misery is equally clear. It was the workings of the free market.

In the popular imagination of farming, the pre-war depression came as the culmination of half a century of decline, beginning with a run of poor harvests in the 1870s and exacerbated by the propensity of the New World to ship its meat, grain and dairy products to Britain in exchange for industrial goods. British farmers were sacrificed at the altar of free trade; thus ran the rhetoric of the myth-makers. And the farming community accepted it *en masse*. Anyone now arguing for an end to subsidies and regulation is generally considered a dangerous heretic. The move to a free market would be a step towards ruin, or so it is claimed.

In 1944 George Henderson published an account of the pre-war farming experiences of himself and his brother Frank on a small farm at the edge of the Cotswolds.[18] Called *The Farming Ladder,* the book told the rather idiosyncratic tale of a man with a particular vision for farming the land. It was an unpretentious book, rich in practical advice and interspersed with a philosophy of good husbandry and permanence. It became an immediate best-seller, running to a fifth reprint before the year was out. For in those dark days this was a story of hope. It showed how even in a depression the small farm can yield a good living, but only when farmed in a way that safeguards the soil and the countryside.

When George and Frank Henderson rented Oathill Farm near Enstone in Oxfordshire in 1924, farm incomes were in steep decline. The 85 acres they had acquired was thin, Cotswold brash, not the most promising of soils. What's more it was already in poor heart: worked-out, weedy and overgrown. They themselves had limited capital. Stocking the farm fully was going to be a slow process. Yet they made it pay, following the time-honoured practice of mixed farming and returning all the muck and waste to build up soil fertility. Not for them the newly fashionable specialist unit concentrating on all-arable or all-milk production. On Oathill Farm there were dairy cattle, sheep, pigs, geese and outdoor chicken as well as wheat, oats and root crops. The Henderson brothers had returned to a traditional Cotswold five-course rotation, akin to the ancient Norfolk four-course. They were convinced of the need for a balanced system of crop and animal husbandry if they were to prosper. They wanted to work *with* nature, not in constant conflict with her.

Prosper they certainly did. Within a few years they had accumulated the capital to buy the freehold of their farm. By the beginning of the war it was carrying three times the cattle, four times the sheep, ten times the pigs and twenty-five times the poultry of the average Oxfordshire farm, calculated on a per-acre basis. The improvement in soil fertility had raised the gross output from £7 an acre in 1924 to £22 an acre in 1932, the lowest point in the pre-war depression. By 1942 output was up to £87 an acre, a twelve-fold improvement in eighteen years, and this was in a period when there were virtually no subsidies, and returns to farmers were considered 'calamitous'.

The truth is, the farming depression of the 1920s and 30s was far from being the universal calamity it is now remembered as. It was a crisis for cereal-growing rather than for farming in general. In 1929 the price of American wheat collapsed. British wheat prices followed, as did those of most foodstuffs and industrial raw materials. The slump was worldwide, affecting most industries and leading to wide-scale unemployment. In farming the worst effects were felt by the major food-exporting countries. Throughout the main wheat-growing areas of Canada, the USA and Australia thousands of farmers faced ruin.

The same crisis afflicted the specialist wheat-growing areas of Britain, particularly the eastern counties of England. Even in the 1920s many wheat growers had embarked on the process of industrialisation. In their 1932 study *Land and Life,* Viscount Astor and Keith Murray cite the case of a 1,100-acre farm which had employed 30 to 40 men when horse ploughs were in use.[19] Following the switch to mechanisation the farm was run as a 'wheat factory' with just four staff employed. These were the farms which suffered in the 'great depression'. Yet the episode has been absorbed into the stock of farming folklore, to be recycled regularly in support of government subsidies and as a counter to any proposal for a return to the free market.

In fact while all British farmers were affected to some degree, most were protected by the diversity of their production. For specialist cereal growers the fall was ruinous, but the majority of farmers had other crops to sell – milk and meat, fruit and vegetables. The tradition of mixed farming which had made British agriculture so prosperous and productive in the mid-nineteenth century saw the family farm through the worst of the pre-war depression. Thus George Henderson was able to amass substantial capital from a farming system based on fertility-building and a balance of crops and livestock.

The response of most British farmers to recession was the one they had always taken in hard times. They moved out of arable production into grass. Cattle, sheep and pig numbers rose dramatically during the early 1930s. Milk production increased, and a growing number of dairy farmers close to urban centres set themselves up as producer-retailers, supplying fresh milk to local communities. Improved road and rail transport allowed milk from the more remote areas to reach major urban areas in good condition. Whatever the popular mythology, this was not a time of unalloyed gloom, at least, not for the family farm.

Richard Body cites figures from the Oxford Agricultural Economic Research Institute to show that overall farm production rose by 20 per cent in the inter-war years.[20] This was at a time when British industry was deep in recession and unemployment levels were peaking at three million. Thus farming expanded by one-fifth at a time when the overall economy was ailing. Yet the period is presented as one of unmitigated crisis by today's farming establishment. It is a dangerous notion. The events that inspired it may be historical, but the mythology continues to underpin farming policy.

Today's farmers still cling to the belief that an end to subsidies will propel them into the abyss. In fact the opposite is the case. Those very subsidies have set them on the road to ruin. State control and price guarantees have persuaded them to adopt the industrial techniques that made the specialist arable farms so vulnerable to collapse in the 1930s. Under the regulation of government they have abandoned the mixed farming systems that protected their soils and provided space for wildlife. The small mixed farm was the nation's insurance against catastrophic change. The politicians have traded it for international competitiveness. The arable factories of eastern England have now spread across the length of lowland Britain.

In *The Faith of a Fieldsman*, H. J. Massingham writes angrily about a 1946 planning survey of Herefordshire, a county of small farms and smallholdings, many of whose occupiers worked part-time in the fruit orchards and hop fields.[21] The economy of the small farmer, 'keeping a few sheep, pigs, poultry and geese, cultivating a little arable in suitable areas and maintaining small orchards is of immemorial antiquity in the county', says Massingham. This is not out of 'obdurate conservatism', but because this border country has neither the climate nor the physical structure for large-scale farming.

The post-war planners, it seems, had other ideas for the county. Their recommendations were that farms of less than twenty acres – around 40 per cent of all Herefordshire farms at that time – should be eliminated as 'uneconomic units'. There was a need for farms to be more mechanised, or, as Massingham interpreted it, for the county to become more industrialised. 'It offends because it is too rural; it is reprehensible because its farms are not factories; its lands are backward because they are not conditioned to the machine.'

The planners had their way in rural Herefordshire as everywhere else in lowland Britain. The 'arable factories' of East Anglia in the 1930s are now well represented on the deep silt soils of Ledbury and Leominster. Along with them go the familiar trappings of industrial agriculture, the hedgeless monocultures, the eroded soils, the unpeopled landscape; brought here and promulgated by the county's own Ministry of Agriculture demonstration farm at Rosemaund near Hereford.

Massingham anticipated all this in his reply to the planners fifty years ago. 'In all its long history, even in the Border wars, even after the ravages of Owen Glendower, even in the darkest of the Dark Ages, even before the Roman conquest, never have the farms of Herefordshire been so depopulated as now. What greater insanity can there be for a nation to leave its lands emptier than in the most primitive ages and turn its cities into ant-heaps?' And this was before institutionalised price support had even begun its transformation of the lowland landscape.

What might have happened to Britain's small farmers had there been no take-over of agriculture by the MAFF/NFU cabal is impossible to say with certainty. Undoubtedly there would have been farm amalgamations. The structure of the industry was bound to change as the wider economy grew and national incomes rose. It is equally certain that without the disruptive intervention of the state, family farms would have retained stronger links with their customers, kept a wider variety of crops and livestock and resisted the blandishments of the agrochemical manufacturers.

Those small farms which governments have now obliterated were the only ones capable of operating intensive yet sustainable systems of agriculture; systems like that of Mr Rowe and his wife in Somerset and the Henderson brothers in Oxfordshire. They were capable of feeding the nation safely, and with high-quality products. At the same time they would have maintained the classic British landscapes, with their rich diversity and teeming wildlife. Their loss must be seen as a national disaster.

In their place the politicians have substituted an industrial system producing large quantities of edible raw materials, though only for as long as its subsidies remain, and it is allowed to continue polluting the environment. For, of course, the system is unsustainable. With their fixation on an industrial model, successive governments have led British farming into a pit. Sooner or later we will have to re-learn the old skills of biological food production.

George Henderson summed it up in his second book, *Farmer's Progress*.[22] 'The future of British farming lies with the small farm and intensive farming. If the standards of production maintained on our best small farms were common throughout the industry, Britain could be self supporting in food, except for citrus fruits and a few luxuries.'

In the same volume he writes of farming's 'crowning folly' in agreeing to the 1947 Agriculture Act, by which farmers accepted control of the industry by officials, bartering their rights to manage according to their own judgement in return for an ephemeral guarantee of prices and markets. 'To invoke Government assistance is like tying a brick to the cow's tail after she has flicked you in the face.'

In an interview in *Farmers Weekly* John Major revealed that his father had been a small farmer.[23] The Prime Minister recalled photos of his grandmother feeding the hens on the Shropshire family farm. Perhaps because of his rural origins he expressed a strong attachment to the land. 'Love of the land is essential to the wellbeing of a nation. I want to ensure that, by careful husbandry and commitment to our rural areas, we pass on that love, a fundamental part of British life, to our children and grandchildren.'

Whatever modern children find to love about the countryside today, it will be a meagre thing in comparison with the treasures now gone. Perhaps if John Major had learned more about small farms like the one his father grew up on, he would have done more to arrest their passing.

9

A FAMINE AT THE HEART OF THE FEAST

Beef fat in the chocolate digestives; gelatin in yogurt and vitamin tablets. The BSE crisis set half the nation scrutinising ingredient lists on food packaging, many for the first time. But it was no mere chance that cattle products had become so ubiquitous in the British diet. The crops and animals from our farms have long since ceased to be the unadulterated foods of the national diet. They are now no more than raw materials for a global manufacturing industry.

Alone in Europe Britain abandoned the very concept of a wholesome diet when it threw its peasantry off the land. The enclosures of the eighteenth century robbed rural labourers of their vegetable plots, and sent them, as paupers, to the towns and cities in search of work. Ironically it was the bread riots of the 'hungry forties' which led, in part, to the repeal of the Corn Laws, so ending the protection of the British landed class and allowing the urban poor access to wheat from the virgin soils of the American prairies. The dispossessed had extracted a kind of vengeance against their oppressors.

Elsewhere in Europe peasant farmers were protected by tariff barriers designed to keep out American wheat. It was this surviving peasantry which maintained a cuisine based on locally grown, natural foods. Indeed the peasants became a repository for the very notion of a natural, unadulterated diet. To this day the peoples of modern, industrial Europe retain a deep attachment to the fresh, unprocessed products of the countryside. In Britain the Enclosure Movement divorced the mass of people from the natural world. In doing so it made them uniquely vulnerable to the blandishments of the food fabricators.

Food manufacturers and processors have been the main beneficiaries of rural policies which separate farmers from their customers. It is they who have stepped into the divide, adding value in the form of convenience, flavour enhancement and pop packaging, and at the same time exploiting urban misconceptions about the nature of 'real' food. In this way they take the lion's share of consumer spending on food while driving down returns to farmers. A potato costing a penny or two at the farm gate is worth forty times more as a potato crisp. Yet nutritionally the crisp is worth far less.

Manufacturers add value, not by improving foods, but by reconstructing them, then performing a clever marketing trick. We are prepared to pay 16p per 100 grams for own-brand cornflakes in which maize flour is liberally spiked with sugar, salt and emulsifiers, together with a handful of vitamins and minerals to replace those processed out of the original grain. By contrast, a bag of unadulterated oat flakes with as much energy and protein – and twice the content of dietary fibre – commands a price of just 7.5p per 100 grams. In this way food processors raise the price of eating and reduce the standard of nutrition.

A visit to the average, edge-of-town superstore gives little indication of any such flaws in the food system. In the great temple of late twentieth-century consumerism the range of products seems vast. This is the place of final judgement on the fruits of rural enterprise. Here they are paraded, up to 20,000 individual lines, for the ultimate approval of consumers. Those which fail to make the grade may be gone from the shelves within a week. Consumers decide, and the aggregate effect of their individual decisions changes the way things are done on the farm. That, at least, is the theory.

In reality few of the food items in the store are even recognisable as farm products. The great majority are packaged, dried, canned, extruded, frozen, reconstituted, flavour-enhanced, tenderised or in some way or other processed. True there is a fresh produce section. It occupies about the same length of shelving as the combined biscuit and snack food areas. Overwhelmingly the British diet is the invention of manufacturing industry. So it is hardly surprising that the countryside which sources the raw materials should come to resemble an industrial site.

In a speech to the 1995 Oxford Farming Conference the then Agriculture Minister William Waldegrave outlined the strengths of UK farming, an industry in which 10 per cent of farms produced 50 per cent of the total output, or as he put it, the equivalent of the whole output of Denmark. The agricultural industry, he explained, produced the raw materials for 60 per cent of all the food we ate. At the same time it formed a home supply base for some 'formidable export industries in food and drink'. Thus the Minister's conception of food production was clear; an essentially industrial process, it differed in no qualitative sense from the manufacture of light bulbs or garden furniture. This is the perception that has underpinned fifty years of British farm policy. The interests of the food industry are seen as coincident with those of the consumer and the countryside. In fact the opposite is true.

Under the agricultural support system of the 1950s and 60s, farmers received a deficiency payment, the difference between the market price and the guaranteed price of each commodity. To this day the system is known in the industry as the 'cheap food policy', one that kept down shop prices to the detriment of farmers. In reality the policy was never particularly cheap to citizens. It obliged them to pay twice for their food, once at the till and again through their taxes. It might be described more aptly as a cheap raw material policy. For it allowed food manufacturers to buy their ingredients at a discount, with prices being set by the major exporters selling on to world markets. At their lowest these 'world prices' were little more than those of dumped surpluses, scarcely covering the costs of production. William Waldegrave's 'formidable export industries' were erected on the foundation of farm subsidies.

There were other advantages for the manufacturers. Along with price guarantees, farmers were provided with a battery of production grants and subsidies covering everything from fertilisers to diesel fuel, from land drainage to hedgerow removal: the very aids to intensification that were to transform the landscape of farming into one suited to raw material production. The Ministry of Agriculture seemed to be acting on behalf of the food manufacturers, virtually constructing their supply industry for them.

More damaging still was the impact of subsidies on the vital link between farmers and their customers. Despite the opening up of Britain's food markets to meat, grain and dairy products from the Empire, most towns and villages retained links with the countryside well into the twentieth century. High Street butchers still hung the prime beef of local farms. The daily pint of milk was usually the product of a local dairy, and every town and village had its outdoor market selling fresh fruit and vegetables from nearby market gardens.

Before the coming of subsidies farmers – small family farmers in particular – worked to strengthen links with their customers. During the lean years between the wars many were glad to plant an acre or two of vegetables for sale at the local market. On farms with a dairy herd there might be a slab of butter or a block of farmhouse cheese to go with it. Enterprising dairy farmers on the edge of the big conurbations even put in pasteurising plants and began operating their own milk rounds. A number of today's biggest food businesses owe their beginnings to those early farm entrepreneurs.

The arrival of subsidies killed such rural enterprise. With their prices guaranteed, dairy farmers were content to send milk away in the tanker and forget about it. Beef producers trucked their animals to the local cattle market concerned only that they satisfy the grader and so become eligible for subsidy. The interests of consumers no longer mattered. During the 1980s, under the inflated price regime of the Common Agricultural Policy, many large-scale farmers were producing not for people but for the EU Intervention store.

It was a rift that was to have disastrous consequences for consumers. In the early days of the BSE epidemic a farmer seeing the early symptoms would often send the suspect animal off to market before the disease became too obvious. In this way thousands of diseased cattle were dumped anonymously in the food chain. It is inconceivable that farmers would have behaved like this had they been feeding people rather than supplying a bureaucratic system. Nor would cereal growers have been so cavalier in their use of insecticide sprays had their wheat been destined for the High Street baker rather than the Government Intervention store. When the customer is a quango producers no longer feel the same responsibility.

Yet the neglect of consumers has proved equally damaging to farmers. For it has played directly into the hands of the manufacturers, allowing them to complete their take-over of food markets. Had farmers kept their links with consumers they might have helped maintain nutritional standards in Britain. Like their European counterparts they could have become a beacon for sound nutrition and safe, wholesome foods. Instead they have allowed their products to be degraded by the food industrialists. It is the manufacturers and City investors who now dictate the UK national diet.

Almost 80 per cent of food items in the UK diet are processed in some way. This is the value-added which allows the manufacturers to hang onto a substantial slice of a £50 billion household food market. It is a business dominated by a handful of big players. By the early 1990s almost all the major product sectors of European food were controlled by two or three companies. For example, the top three suppliers of breakfast cereals account for 64 per cent of the market, the top three biscuit suppliers for 70 per cent of the market and the top three manufacturers of snack foods for 91 per cent of the market.[1]

In 1994 just eight processors accounted for 60 per cent of the entire UK food market.[2] Shortly before stepping down as chief executive of the milk co-operative Milk Marque Andrew Dare told a Somerset farming audience that 50 per cent of UK milk was produced by only 6,000 farmers, handled by six processors and finally distributed by just three retailers.[3] The concentration of food processing in Britain has gone further than in most other countries of the world. This may give agriculture ministers cause for celebration, but out in the countryside there is precious little to cheer about.

Food processors bring the ethos of big business to farming. In *The Food System*, Geoff Tansey and Tony Worsley point out that many started as preservers of food, but increasingly they manufacture products from basic ingredients such as sugar, starch, fat and flavourings. Where once they used batch processes, they now employ continuous-flow production lines. These are the techniques they apply to the countryside in their bid to drive down ingredient costs. Farmers are required to meet ever tighter specifications; crops and animals must conform to rigid production standards. No longer is the variety of nature to be celebrated. The food crop of the 1990s must be consistent, bland and uniform. It has to fit the production line and the latest diktat of the marketing department.

So wheat grown for biscuits must have the right specific weight, protein content and dough characteristics. Potatoes bound for crisping must have the required moisture content and fat-absorbing characteristics. Processors specify the crop varieties to be grown. Increasingly they also lay down the cultivation methods to be used, the types and amounts of fertiliser and pesticides to be applied.[4] Animals, too, must be made to fit the mould. Breeds, growth rates, slaughter weights and depth of fat are set out in production 'blueprints' as if they were instructions for assembling an MFI wardrobe. Dairy processors have even begun specifying feed rations to regulate the fat and protein content of the milk.

This is the food culture that has homogenised the countryside. A process designed to deliver a standardised, consistent raw material is one which produces a bland and featureless landscape. The two are inextricably connected; the production of edible raw materials and an empty, lifeless landscape. It is a landscape designed not for feeding people but for feeding production lines. And consumers are as much the victims as the countryside.

In 1994 Somerset trading standards officers conducted a routine analysis of a box of economy burgers bought from a local supermarket. The product contained just 12 per cent lean meat, the rest was largely skin and gristle.[5] One-third was composed of chicken slurry, with scraps mechanically recovered from the bone, while 16 per cent comprised an emulsion of meat extracted from the heads of cattle. The manufacturers were prosecuted for labelling the burgers as a meat product. Had they chosen some other designation the product would have been perfectly legal.

Unprocessed foods are difficult to adulterate or degrade. A joint of beef is a joint of beef, a carrot is a carrot. But once the natural structure of a food has been lost; once it has been re-assembled from edible raw materials, it is hard, even for a trained food analyst, to be certain what the contents are. Economy burgers are made from mechanically recovered chicken scraps, frozen 'chicken breasts' from mashed skin and soya protein. Tinned ham is made from reformed muscle segments held together by emulsified chicken skins. Yogurts are thickened with gelatin or starch in place of milk protein. There seems no limit to the ingenuity of the food fabricators.

Partiality to processed foods makes the public hostages to a manufacturing industry more used to producing down to a price than up to a quality standard. In 1996 manufacturers at the economy end of the burger market were budgeting just 9p a pound for their meat. By choosing such products consumers hand over control of their diets, and ultimately of their health, to food technologists and finance directors.

Though processing may add the modern essential of 'convenience', it rarely does anything for nutritional quality. The vast range of convenience foods which line the shelves of the superstore frequently contain the same basic ingredients – refined flour, sugar, saturated fats and salt, with chemical additives supplying the colour and flavouring. The World Health Organisation has linked such products with the emergence of a range of chronic, non-infectious diseases, particularly coronary heart disease and various cancers.[6]

The nation with the 'formidable' food industry has one of the highest rates of diet-related illness in the world. The British eat fewer vegetables than any other European country, half the amounts eaten in France, Spain and Italy.[7] Vegetables and fruit contain many of the protective factors for coronary heart disease and some cancers, Britain's main causes of premature death. A government study of the Scottish diet, for example, showed that Scottish children's diets were 'the worst in the western world'.[8] A high proportion of children ate neither green vegetables nor fruit. These are the human costs of policies which induce farmers to give up growing for people and produce instead for manufacturing industry.

Where once they were linked to farmers through locally sourced shops and markets, consumers are now subject to a barrage of food information from manufacturers. By 1990 more than £500 million a year was being spent on food advertising in Britain. But while there is little or no advertising of fruit and vegetables, millions are spent persuading the British public to eat processed foods, usually of the fat and sugary variety. A fifth of the total 'adspend' goes on confectionery. Children are often the targets. A study of food advertising on television concluded that children received 'a grossly imbalanced nutritional message'.[9] This created a conflict between food advertising and dietary recommendations. The cumulative effect of food advertising is to undermine progress towards a healthy diet.

Sadly the British seem resigned to their junk food habit. In a survey of food attitudes in eight western countries, the British showed least respect for their own national cuisine.[10] While 95 per cent of French people and 93 per cent of Italians believed their own national dishes to be the best in the world, only one-third of Britons voted for their cuisine. Almost half specified burgers and sandwiches as everyday foods compared with only 4 per cent of French people.

Food companies are more than happy to exploit such dietary confusion. Each year they launch thousands of products in their attempt to win over bewildered consumers. Most of the new lines require the minimum of preparation and cooking. At the same time cooking skills have been effectively dropped from the schools' curriculum.[11] Under the new National Curriculum introduced in 1994, practical cooking skills taught as Home Economics were replaced instead by a more theoretical, technology-orientated approach.

Modern homes are now filled with equipment used chiefly for serving pre-processed meals over which the consumer has little nutritional control. While kitchens are packed with new gadgets, skill levels are lower than they were a century ago. The food industry has so successfully fostered a dependency culture that people now have almost no option but to rely on its products.

Such ethical dilemmas are of scant concern to food manufacturers. They are too busy taking their brands to every corner of the globe, and with them the philosophy that it is the giant corporations, not farmers, who feed people. It has been called 'McDonaldization',[12] the translation of aspirant lifestyles into dietary form. The selling of the western, principally American diet, to the world. Just as epidemiologists begin to expose the dangers of a highly processed diet, replete with saturated fats and deficient in essential anti-oxidants, the multinational corporations are busy exporting it to the world.

At the same time UK farmers are cajoled into joining in this global crusade by becoming raw material suppliers to the food giants. Politicians and farming leaders proclaim this as the only way to survive in the new, competitive world of free trading. Writing on the food industry's ceaseless search for ingredient sources, Chris Bourchier of ADAS warns that unless the UK delivers them, the markets will go to the competition.[13] His advice to farmers is to form robust trading partnerships with the food industry, 'working together to improve product quality and image'. So farmers shackle themselves to the prescriptive production regimes of the food companies. The countryside is further homogenised.

However, the food giants who sell their brands around the world are also sourcing their raw materials globally. Farmers and farming companies entering into contracts to supply the food corporations are just as easily dropped in favour of lower-cost producers elsewhere in the world. So the UK is drawn into a technology-driven race to intensify farming, to re-fashion nature into what has been called 'a global assembly line'.[14] At the end of the process the markets may have moved on. We shall have destroyed our countryside for no purpose.

Rather than source their own ingredients directly, the major food corporations are increasingly turning to transnational trading companies for their raw materials. These are the invisible players in the global food business, buying and selling commodities around the world, trading in fertilisers and pesticides, processing food products and speculating in 'futures' and 'derivatives'. Like the food manufacturing business, trading is dominated by a clutch of big players. And the biggest of them all is Cargill.

Privately owned and based in Minneapolis, Minnesota, Cargill achieved sales of US$47 billion in 1994. Operating in 60 countries, it is involved in nearly 50 lines of business including oilseed and corn processing, grain trading and transport, flour milling, the manufacture of feed supplements and the mining of rock salt. The company now sees itself as playing a major role in alleviating world hunger. In the words of David Nelson Smith, Vice President for European Public Affairs, they are 'agents of change' in the global economy.[15] 'We help trade happen, and trade is the engine of economic growth around the world. We take costs out of the food system. We spread technologies and best practices. Governments need multinationals to assist them in the effort to feed the world.'

Among new technologies currently being spread by the multinationals is the genetic manipulation of plants and animals. In autumn 1996 farmers in the United States and Canada harvested their first genetically engineered corn crops. Modified varieties of sugar beet, soyabean and oilseed rape were also close to the market. Given approval by EU regulatory authorities, maize flour and soya from genetically altered plants will begin to appear in UK snack foods and processed products. European farmers will then have little option but to adopt the new technology.

As always, the justification for such developments is the growing food demand of a hungry world. Biotechnology will help prevent future famines, or so it is claimed by the multinational chemical companies driving the development. Yet the more obvious beneficiaries are the companies themselves together with the global food manufacturers who buy the products of industrial agriculture. Market domination by a handful of yield enhanced varieties will further standardise the landscape and concentrate production in the hands of large farmers all of whom will rely on the chemical companies for their seed.

Many early products of the new technology are crop varieties 'engineered' for resistance to herbicides. The idea is that a farmer choosing one of the new varieties will be able to kill off every other plant species by using a single, linked herbicide. Weed control is likely to be cheaper and more effective. But farmers adopting the technology will become reliant on the chemical company for both seed and weedkiller.

For food manufacturers the benefits will be a general driving down of raw material costs. With higher yields and a greater concentration of crop production in the most intensively farmed regions, the manufacturers can expect substantial reductions in the costs of sourcing their global products. The group least likely to gain advantage from biotechnology are consumers.

Sponsors of the new 'engineered' crops claim they will offer real benefits to the public. They will help cut the cost of food. In reality the impact on retail prices is likely to be small. Raw material costs are but one component in the overall production cost of manufactured foods. Transport, processing and marketing costs take an increasing share of the end price. Moreover, the lesson of the breakfast cereal market is that brand image is a far more powerful determinant of price than nutritional value.

What the commodities derived from genetically altered crops will not do is improve the quality of the national diet. Soya protein is already used in many manufactured products; corn starch is the basis of a range of manufactured savouries and snack foods. These are the products whose ingredients will come from 'engineered' crops. They are also the products consumed most voraciously by the British public. An industry dedicated to feeding people might be expected to concern itself with ways of raising nutritional standards. But the chief interest of the industrialists who drive western agriculture is securing long-term dividends for their shareholders.

Whatever the shortcomings of the food industry, consumers have, at least in theory, a new and powerful champion in the market place – the supermarkets. Their expansion over the past thirty years has been staggering. Between 1961 and 1978 the proportion of independent grocers fell from just over half to one-third, while the number of shops owned by multiple retailers grew from a quarter to half.[16] By 1993 the multiples accounted for almost 80 per cent of the grocery market, with just five multiple retailers handling 65 per cent of the retail food trade.

With their enormous economic strength the supermarkets were uniquely placed to break the manufacturers' grip on the food system and to begin improving the national diet. Certainly they have made spectacular inroads into the power base of the food industry. In the early 1980s food manufacturers and processors between them took more than 70 per cent of the total UK 'profit pie'.[17] Eleven years later their profit share had slipped to less than 60 per cent, while the share of the multiples had doubled from 20 to 40 per cent. Here was a new power to challenge the interests of the food fabricators with their seemingly insatiable urge to industrialise food and agriculture.

The retailers quickly identified fresh produce as a potential profit earner. Out went the limp lettuces and the heap of unwashed King Edwards. The modern supermarket offers variety, freshness and consistency of quality. Today's lettuces are likely to come in a dozen different forms from oak-leaf to cos, while the pile of unwashed potatoes is now differentiated into everything from small roasters to bakers. There are exotic items too, sweet potatoes, celeriac, mooli, squashes, yams, the sort of items rarely found in the traditional greengrocer's shop.

In Food From Britain's report on the vegetable sector the multiples were said to have raised the overall standard of produce by their 'consistent demand for quality'.[18] Not that supermarket vegetables are particularly cheap. Prices are often lower at the High Street greengrocer, certainly at the market stall. However, the supermarkets claim to offer better value for money. Since the quality of their produce is consistently high there is a lot less waste in the home, so goes the argument. And it seems to have been generally accepted by consumers.

The multiples' share of the fresh produce market has risen dramatically. From a share of one quarter in 1983 they had broken the 50 per cent barrier by 1995, and are expected to have taken 70 per cent by the end of the decade.[19] The supermarkets now dominate the fresh produce market and effectively set quality standards. In raising the banner for fresh, unprocessed foods they are uniquely placed to influence the British diet for the better. Sadly they have chosen to sell their customers short by following the rest of the food sector down the path of industrialisation. The result has been a degrading of what ought to be the healthy option.

In 1983 the British Association of Public Analysts reported finding detectable pesticide residues in more than one-third of the fruit and vegetables they sampled.[20] Some were of chemicals already banned or severely restricted, while others appeared on crops for which there had been no official clearance for their use. Ten years later the government's own monitoring programme showed pesticide residues to be present in almost one-third of sampled foods.[21] Again in 1995 residues showed up in one-third of samples.[22] Thus over a period of unprecedented change in the fresh produce market the major multiples had done nothing to reduce levels of contamination.

The reasons are not hard to unravel. The standards pursued by the produce buyers have been those related to appearance and to a limited extent taste. The nutritional quality of their fruit and vegetables has concerned them barely at all. Far from encouraging growers to reduce their pesticide applications, the supermarkets have, in the past, penalised those whose crops bore even the merest hint of a blemish. A slug in a lettuce or a cabbage containing whitefly was enough to bring about rejection of the entire consignment. Not surprisingly, growers made sure that no such life forms survived.

In concentrating on the cosmetic appeal of fresh produce the multiples ignored the danger of contamination with pesticides. Indeed their very preoccupation with appearance has contributed directly to the wider use of chemicals. For years the supermarkets have fostered the expectation of flawless fruit and vegetables. Who will now accept a blemished apple or a lettuce with a slug in it?

For a generation of young shoppers with no memory of natural growing methods such imperfections are regarded with horror. Therefore they must be avoided at all costs. Even the government accepts that pesticide usage could be reduced if retailers and their customers were prepared to accept fruit and vegetables with a small amount of pest damage.[23]

The multiples are well aware of growing public concern over pesticide residues. Following the lead of Safeway in the early 1980s, many of the major chains began introducing organically grown produce into their stores. Given the culture of perfection so assiduously promulgated by the multiples themselves, it was hardly likely to be a great success. In a display cabinet stuffed with immaculate produce few but the totally convinced were likely to select an item bearing a blemish, particularly when it cost more than the chemically grown equivalent.

For shoppers pesticide residues were a matter of vague unease rather than certainty. Faced with a choice between the blemished and the apparently flawless most opted for the cheaper, more attractive item. They trusted their favourite stores not to sell them anything harmful. Thus organic sales seldom made up more than 3 per cent of total fresh produce sales, and the supermarkets were able to dismiss it as a 'niche market'. Marks and Spencer abandoned organic food altogether.

The major multiples had every reason to resist any popular move to organically grown produce. Their success is founded on centralised buying through large regional depots which feed into efficient distribution systems. They are constantly trying to reduce costs by minimising the number of suppliers they buy from. As a result they rely increasingly on large grower groups whose members account for thousands of acres of intensively managed vegetable crops.

Across large swathes of Lincolnshire and East Anglia the supermarkets have helped create an industrial landscape of vegetables, row after row of brassicas or leeks or carrots stretching away into the middle distance. Highly mechanised, these vegetable prairie lands rely heavily on the chemical sprayer to produce the identical, blemish-free crops demanded by the multiples. Produce buyers insist on uniformity. On the farm this leads to standardisation of variety and husbandry methods, putting crops at even greater risk of pest and disease damage. Thus the very buying practices of the multiples increase the pressure on growers to spray.

The supermarket culture presents particular difficulties to organic growers. Most operate on a far smaller scale than the conventional grower, and since they cannot rely on pesticides to 'control' the environment their crops are inevitably more variable. They must maintain rotations and use a range of crop varieties to minimise pest and disease damage. This means their produce, though safer, seldom matches the visual appearance and uniformity of chemically grown produce.

Supermarket buyers complain that organic produce is variable in quality and inconsistent in supply. They claim it leads to excessive wastage. The truth is that it fails to match their conception of what the ideal product ought to be, one which is consistent month after month, year after year. But this ideal is based on an industrial view of the world. The natural world is different. Nature produces variety and abhors uniformity.

The major retailers might have encouraged their customers to celebrate the diversity of fresh produce. Instead they have raised the expectation that cauliflowers and carrots should be as identical as chocolate biscuits. Organic produce will not easily fit the mould. It is awkward, untidy, more difficult to manage. This is why the multiples have been happy to relegate it to the status of 'niche market'. If it became too popular it might disrupt their trading arrangements. Unfortunately concerns about pesticides refuse to go away.

A battery of studies have shown pesticides to be the aspect of farming which causes the public most concern. In a telephone poll carried out by NOP for SAFE Alliance, more than two-thirds of respondents wanted greater controls on farming methods in order to protect food quality, animal welfare and the environment.[24] As many as 82 per cent favoured an increase in organic farming. In a survey for the BBC *CountryFile* television programme more than half the respondents called for some move towards organic farming methods.[25]

Far from being irrational, as such fears are generally portrayed by the agricultural establishment, they are underpinned by a growing weight of evidence. In the late 1980s the Ministry of Agriculture's specialist working party found pesticide residues in one-third of dietary staples – bread, milk, potatoes – and in 20 per cent of fruit and vegetables sampled.[26] As many as 6 per cent of fresh produce samples contained contaminants in excess of the government's official MRLs, the Maximum Residue Level. One of 16 lettuces sampled for residues of dithiocarbamate fungicides was found to be contaminated at 45 times the maximum limit.

In a subsequent report the working party drew attention to insecticide contamination of carrots. As many as one-third of 55 samples contained residues of the organophosphate triazophos above the MRL.[27] Five years later a change in sampling techniques revealed that a small percentage of carrots contained organophosphate contaminants at up to 25 times the expected level.[28] Although many would have been removed by peeling and topping, those from the systemic insecticide phorate would have been distributed throughout the vegetable.

Organophosphates are neurotoxic chemicals originally developed as nerve gases. Their use in sheep dips led the Institute of Occupational Health to link repeated exposure to impaired mental function.[29] The ability of some pesticides to penetrate into the flesh or pulp of fruit and vegetables was highlighted by a Ministry of Agriculture committee in the late 1980s.[30] They warned that residue analysis of skin or peel alone might seriously underestimate the amount of pesticide consumed by the public. 'Consumers may be exposed to higher dosages of these chemicals than had hitherto been suspected.'

In its 1995 report the government's Working Party on Pesticide Residues drew attention to the contamination of milk with the organochlorine insecticide lindane,[31] a compound that has been linked with breast cancer in American research. In nine samples tested, levels of the compound were found to exceed the recommended MRL. The inclusion in cattle feed of vegetables treated with lindane is thought to have been the most likely cause of contamination.

Almost everyone consumes pesticides, though there is no way of knowing how much. Under our farming system residues are ubiquitous. Estimates of the levels in foods and in the total diet are based on a relatively small number of samples. Governments claim the associated risks are low, and certainly cases of acute poisoning are rare. However, virtually nothing is known about the dangers of prolonged exposure to low doses of a cocktail of toxic chemicals over a long period of time. As with BSE science will inevitably take time to catch up.

In the meantime it might be considered prudent to err on the side of caution. Yet so far the supermarkets have shown themselves remarkably indifferent to the continued ingestion of agrochemicals by their customers. To date their chief response to growing consumer concern has been to support the development of Integrated Crop Management.

A number of the multiples, including Marks and Spencer, Safeway, Sainsbury's and Waitrose, have got together with the National Farmers' Union to develop a series of 'protocols' for growing individual crops according to ICM principles. Yet these blueprints for so-called environmentally friendly growing methods permit the use of some of the most pernicious pesticides currently marketed.

For example, under the fresh cauliflower protocol chemicals

allowed for the control of cabbage root fly include the soil-acting insecticide aldicarb, an anticholinesterase carbamate compound subject to the 1972 Poisons Act; the organophosphorus (OP) insecticide chlorfenvinphos, also subject to the Poisons Act; and the broad-spectrum organophosphate chlorpyrifos.[32] To control aphids growers are permitted to spray with the broad-spectrum systemic OP insecticide dimethoate, which is dangerous to wild birds and animals as well as to a wide range of beneficial insects.

Permitted insecticides for caterpillar control include the broad spectrum OP triazophos and the contact pyrethroid lambda-cyhalothrin, both of which are dangerous to bees and other beneficial insects. Consumers are likely to be far safer with an occasional caterpillar or aphid on their vegetables than with a trace of any of these chemicals. Yet all are approved by the major retailers under a programme designed to reduce pesticide use.

The NFU-retailer protocols claim as a principal objective the minimisation of pesticides. The aim is to control pests and diseases by cultural and biological methods where possible, and to replace blanket chemical applications with selective treatments. This is supposed to give consumers 'a product second to none'. However, none of the recommended ICM methods is obligatory, and according to the Soil Association this virtually means 'anything goes'.[33]

The guidelines make no firm commitment to preventive measures such as crop rotations or the use of resistant varieties, nor do they make the use of biological controls mandatory. Although selective rather than blanket chemical treatment is recommended, broad-spectrum pesticides are allowed, and there are no limits on the dosage or number of applications other than those laid down under statutory regulation. Artificial fertilisers can be applied without restriction.

It is hard to escape the conclusion that the retailers have seized on ICM as a low-cost alternative to genuine pesticide-free foods, a fig leaf to obscure its connection with a destructive system of industrial farming.

'The quiet revolution' is the term coined in Sainsbury's publicity hand-out.[34] 'There is no single magic formula for doing without pesticides – but an enormous amount is being achieved by a careful mix of new technology and tried and trusted methods.' The company is even encouraging its growers to dig ponds and plant up woodlands on their broad expanses of intensive vegetables. As in the arable areas, industrial food production is to be greened at the margins. But it will remain dependent on agrochemicals.

Marks and Spencer, in its advertisement for strawberries, speaks of making the ordinary extraordinary.[35] 'Because we want you to enjoy the best strawberries in the world, we go to extraordinary lengths.' But not so far, it seems, as to preclude the risk of pesticide contamination. The NFU-retailer protocol for strawberries permits the use of organophosphorus insecticides like chlorpyrifos and dimethoate against aphids, as well as the organochlorine insecticide gamma-HCH (lindane) against wireworms and leatherjackets. In addition approved fungicides may be used prophylactically against diseases like botrytis.

Under the 1990 Food Safety Act retailers have a duty to ensure the safety of the products they supply to the public. In any future legal challenge on food safety they would need to show that they had exercised 'due diligence' – they had taken all reasonable precautions to safeguard the public. Codes of practice such as the NFU-retailer protocols are being developed, not out of concern for customers, but as a way of demonstrating this 'due diligence'. The supermarkets intend to give themselves a defence in the courts. What they refuse to do is supply their customers with genuinely pesticide-free foods.

By stocking only organically grown produce the multiples could remove virtually all residue risks. Instead they remain wedded to their cherished axioms of product uniformity, centralised buying and country-wide distribution. They pin their hopes on the halfway house of ICM, though it seems unlikely to produce any significant fall in the amounts of pesticide consumed by their customers. But while the multiples baulk at reform, others are determined to bring about change.

In a small warehouse on a trading estate in the Hockley district of Birmingham members of the workers' co-operative Organic Roundabout pack vegetables into consumer bags. The produce has arrived at the warehouse that very morning. But unlike the produce sold in supermarkets, these vegetables have not travelled halfway across the country. All were supplied by local growers, members of the Herefordshire growers' co-operative the Organic Marketing Company. Within twenty-four hours of arrival at the Hockley warehouse they will be delivered to consumer pick-up points around the city.

Organic Roundabout plans to change the eating habits of a significant section of the Birmingham population. These vegetables are treated as a premium product; they are grown organically, marketed locally and distributed as fresh, perishable food, rather like milk. The scheme was launched in 1993 as a way of bringing safe, high-quality vegetables to city dwellers at realistic prices. Within three years more than 2,000 Birmingham families had signed up for the weekly 'veggie box'.

The scheme is part of a country-wide programme to bring consumers and organic growers together. Launched by the Soil Association, the Local Food Links project had reached an estimated 10,000 households by 1996. Follow-up surveys of regular customers show that the weekly box of fresh produce encourages families to eat more vegetables and fewer processed foods. By raising the status of vegetables the scheme is improving diets along the lines recommended in the government's Health of the Nation White Paper.[36]

The Soil Association, which leads the organic movement in Britain, currently works with community groups and local authorities up and down the country in building a network of food link projects. In addition to 'veggie box' schemes there is support for more radical developments like food co-ops, farmers' markets, city farms and community shops. The objective remains the same – to make locally grown 'ecological' food available at affordable prices throughout Britain. Where the supermarkets have failed, local activists are stepping in to answer consumer concerns.

The last great popular movement for dietary improvement took place during the war, though that one was government-led. The 'dig for victory' campaign had its roots in the work of Sir Robert McCarrisson who had studied the link between health and nutrition. At the outbreak of hostilities the government established a Ministry of Food with the task of promoting the production of fresh produce. Suddenly the entire nation was growing vegetables, in allotments, parks, flower gardens, even on roadside verges.

The result was a population healthier than at any time this century.[37] Chronic disease rates fell sharply, and mortality from heart disease dropped to an all-time low. After the war the government embarked on its disastrous 'cheap food policy', with a farm subsidy system based on output rather than quality. While the nutrient value of foods fell, dietary fat and energy intakes increased, leading to a rise in the incidence of nutrition-related conditions, from heart disease to colon cancer. Diet is now considered a matter of individual choice.

Thanks to the Local Food Links programme consumers are at least able to exercise that choice. Most supermarkets limit their range of organically grown vegetables to a few staples – carrots, cabbages, potatoes – that is if they stock them at all. The Food Links programme gives consumers access to a far wider range of pesticide-free produce. And the benefits go beyond the mere provision of safe food. Consumers are beginning to discover what truly *fresh* vegetables look like and taste like.

Box scheme customers eat vegetables grown in their own locality. They know the farms and smallholdings where the food is produced. Many of them visit those farms. They see the growing crops, the chemical-free methods that produce them and the wildlife that flourishes around them. The connection is made: contaminant-free food comes from a contaminant-free countryside. A living landscape produces healthy crops. The scheme has begun to restore the link between farmers and their customers, a link that was severed when the state took over the management of agriculture.

The growing popularity of vegetable box schemes has spurred some retailers into looking again at organically grown produce. At the 1996 Royal Show Sainsbury's announced that it was extending its 'Partnership in Produce' scheme to include organic suppliers, a move designed to improve the consistency and continuity of supplies. Later in the year Tesco announced that in some of its stores organic fruit and vegetables were to be sold at the same prices as conventionally grown produce even though this might mean substantially reduced margins. However, the company continued to promote fresh produce under its 'Nature's Choice' brand, a variation on the ICM theme. The supermarkets remain obdurately behind ICM, a system which will continue to expose their customers to pesticide residues.

Rather than invest in safe food the multiples strive for novelty, constantly searching for new, high-value products to add to their fresh produce range. The one, overriding criterion is that they meet the supermarkets' requirement for consistency and continuity of supply. It means, in effect, that they must be grown on the highly mechanised industrial pattern with its dependence on agrochemicals. Cherry tomatoes, sugar snap peas, baby potatoes, mixed leaf salads, the choice seems immense. Yet all come from the same intensive growers and the same bleak, industrial fieldscape.

In their effort to provide year-round availability the big retailers have also begun sourcing many of their most popular lines from around the world. Thus Kenyan green beans and Guatemalan mangetouts are now displayed alongside sprouts and winter cabbage on British supermarket shelves. To get them there the multiples export their industrial farming methods to the Third World.

It is a development of which they are proud, as is clear from a Marks and Spencer report.[38] 'Searching for suppliers able to fill the October to June out-of-season period, our buyers found perfect climatic and soil conditions for growing runner beans in Kenya.

There our supplier harvests the beans from daybreak; they are then chilled and graded, prepared and packed, before being taken to the airport for the 10-hour flight to London's Heathrow, where after a short stop for further quality checks, the beans start the final leg of their journey to our stores.'

Supermarkets go to extraordinary lengths to develop new products and steal a march over their competitors. But there is little competition to raise the purity of food or improve nutritional quality. Like the food manufacturers the multiples manipulate consumer demand in ways that benefit their businesses. It may appear that shoppers have a vast and expanding array of choices. In reality they choose from goods selected to serve the interests of the retailer. Though nobody 'chooses' to consume pesticides, supermarket sourcing practices give shoppers little option. The vast majority of fresh products are sprayed, and one-third of them will contain residues. Many are likely to be nutritionally inferior in other ways, too.

During the 1960s and 70s western industrial farming methods were applied throughout Asia, Africa and South America in what became known as the Green Revolution. New crop varieties supported by heavy inputs of fertilisers and pesticides condemned many developing countries to soil degradation and made them wholly dependent on the multinational agrochemical companies. Though calorie intakes may have improved, many people are now on diets which cause ill health.

According to health writer Jane Seymour, the change from locally produced fruits and vegetables to the new, industrially grown crops is thought to have contributed to an epidemic of diseases normally linked to mineral and vitamin deficiencies.[39] Many diets are dangerously low in iron, zinc, vitamin A and other micronutrients. 'This is threatening to lock parts of the Third World into an endless cycle of ill-health, low productivity and underdevelopment.'

There seems no reason why intensively grown crops in the West should not be equally deficient in essential nutrients. It is known, for example, that high levels of inorganic nitrogen in the soil can have a profound influence on mineral uptake by plant roots. The drive to industrialise vegetable production, fuelled largely by the demands of the multiple retailers, may well lead to the nutritional impoverishment of fresh foods. Micronutrient deficiencies are far from unknown in the UK population, although the incidence is masked by the growing use of vitamin supplements and the food industry practice of fortification – adding vitamins and minerals to products from which the natural nutrients have been processed out, as in breakfast cereals, for example.

For the consumer looking for a healthy, wholesome diet the prospects are bleak. A vast manufacturing industry earns its profits by degrading natural foods, then adding minerals and synthetic vitamins to help offset the damage. At the same time fresh fruit and vegetables, the so-called healthy option, though available in increasingly exotic forms, are almost universally treated with toxic chemicals. While earlier generations have suffered hunger borne of poverty, this is the first to inflict malnutrition upon itself.

With their domination of the fresh produce market the major multiples are uniquely placed to raise nutritional standards in Britain. Instead they have followed the manufacturers along the path of standardisation and uniformity; driving down their costs at the expense of safety and nutritional quality. They have joined in the general industrialisation of the countryside.

The urban supermarket seems a world away from rural Britain. Yet the choices shoppers make from the shelves determine the life and health of the countryside. Conversely the health and vigour of Britain's farmland has a profound effect on the quality of our food and ultimately on the health of the people. A farming system that produces a sick countryside will eventually produce a sick population. We remain as dependent on the earth for our wellbeing as when we tilled the ground ourselves. The beef crisis serves as a timely reminder of this enduring truth. A handful of 'veggie box' producers may be pointing the way back to sanity.

10

THE WASTING GROUND

Take the country road that runs beside the River Otter towards the picturesque village of Otterton and there can be no doubt you are in the county of Devon. The road slips between tall, flower-filled hedge banks as it follows the languid river on its final few miles to the sea. Climbing away to the left are the rolling Devon hills, long remembered as the source of thick, clotted cream and tender grass-fed beef. But as you approach Otterton the landscape begins to look different: the fields are bigger and more open, some of the hedge banks have been stripped bare. This is where you start to notice the sand, a fine, red sand along the road sides and lying thickly in some of the field gateways.

Though you are heading for the coast this sand is not from the sea shore. The nearest holiday beach, across the river estuary at Budleigh Salterton, is made up of pebbles. The sand that lines this Devon lane has come from the land, dumped here by the process of water erosion, the effect of heavy rain on soils rendered unstable by cultivation and cropping. For these rolling hills are no longer clothed with the fertile grassland that once made Devon dairy products the envy of the world. They have become just another site of intensive arable production. The light, sandy soils that were once held firmly in place by deep-rooting meadow grasses are now being swept down the hillsides and into the roads and ditches.

From the village of Otterton the river continues southwards to the estuary, from where the South-West Coast footpath climbs along the red, sandstone cliffs towards Sidmouth. On a sunny morning in late March there is little to see of the dense, flower-rich turf that once covered these coastal areas. This is an arable landscape now with broad, open fields of wheat and potatoes. An area of cultivated soil is fissured with gulleys gouged by the winter rains that have sent topsoil cascading down the hillside. A pond at the foot of the slope is dyed red-brown with silt. The lower rungs of a nearby field gate have disappeared under inches of sand.

In the heart of the livestock-rearing west country, a switch to intensive arable cropping is eroding away the topsoil, that precious resource on which all human life depends. It is being squandered, not to meet some dire need, but in response to the set of distorted price signals that currently drive industrial agriculture. No farmer is happy to see his future washed away. Yet the subsidy system almost makes it inevitable, driving up land prices and farm rents, forcing him to intensify to stay in the game. Then through a battery of quotas and restrictions he is prevented from ever switching back to a more sustainable livestock enterprise.

It is a problem that stretches far beyond Devon. Topsoils are disappearing from susceptible land throughout the length of Britain. The rush to intensive farming is robbing a future generation of its capacity to grow food. We are stripping away the nation's true wealth and dumping it in our rivers and streams. Not that soil erosion is new. The signs have been there for decades. But farm support policies that make intensive arable cropping profitable on marginal land have added enormously to the scale of loss.[1] Everywhere old grassland has been ploughed up, particularly on the marginal land of hill and chalk down. The shift to arable crops leaves the land bare or thinly covered in the autumn and winter, when most of the damaging rains are likely to fall.

Larger field sizes have played a part, too. In their hurry to cash in on the arable bonanza, farmers have been busily pulling out the hedges that helped keep soils in place. Many hedges were originally planted in the places most vulnerable to erosion: at points where there is a change to the slope, for example. By opening up the landscape farmers have virtually guaranteed that increasing amounts of irreplaceable topsoil will end up in river beds and estuaries.

Heavy farm machinery has made matters worse. The bigger machines are more difficult to operate along the contours of a slope than the smaller ones they replaced. Many fields are now worked up and down the slope instead, a practice which greatly increases water run-off and erosion. Heavy machinery also leads to soil compaction, once more increasing the risk of damage. Water flowing along 'tramlines' forms rills or shallow channels. Any increase in the flow will gouge deeper fissures, sweeping away the topsoil.

The light sandy soils are not the only ones at risk, though they are most prone to a sudden dramatic mud slide. There is another kind of water erosion: the slow, insidious loss of heavy clay soil during the winter, which may go largely unnoticed. Thus the heaps of mud and sand in the road give no indication of the true scale of the damage. Some estimates put the proportion of UK farmland at risk from erosion at more than one-third.[2] The switch to intensive arable cropping is one of the chief causes of loss.

To identify conditions that lead to water erosion, the Ministry of Agriculture commissioned a study of twelve susceptible catchments in England and Wales.[3] Over a period of five years erosion was recorded in 39 per cent of all the fields monitored. Of these, 79 per cent were sown to winter cereals. However, it would be a mistake to conclude that this kind of loss is limited solely to arable farms. Modern livestock practices can be equally damaging.

In the autumn of 1994 a fleet of lorries and diggers was sent to clear a landslip which had blocked the eastbound carriageway of the A30 trunk road between Yeovil and Sherborne. Heavy rain on a crop of forage maize had caused the slide. It resulted in 100 tons of soil being dumped on the highway. Since the early 1990s a spate of landslip incidents across southern England have been linked to the current explosion in maize growing.

Maize for silage is increasingly popular with livestock farmers, and dairy farmers in particular, since it yields a lot more energy per acre than grass. Around 280,000 acres of maize were planted in 1995, and the area is expected to double within a decade. On the farm the crop is treated more like an arable crop than a forage. It is routinely plastered with slurry and liberally sprayed with the herbicide atrazine. Harvesting takes place late in the autumn, and in a wet year a great deal of soil can end up in the road or, worse, in the river.

Though farmers and landowners may worry about the long-term effects of soil erosion, the immediate costs to themselves are usually slight, being limited to the loss of a small area of seed and fertiliser. Neighbours are likely to be less sanguine. One of the more distressing results can be the flooding of property by soil-bearing run-off. Such incidents are common, particularly on the southern English chalklands. Over a fifteen-year period, 60 were reported on the South Downs alone.[4] The cost of the damage in the suburbs of Brighton approached £1 million in October 1987.

The somewhat myopic view of farmers to the loss of their most basic resource reveals the extent of the cultural shift undergone by the farming community over half a century of protection. Before the war farmers suffering similar incidents would have felt the opprobrium of their neighbours. They would have been labelled incompetent, and during the war or immediately afterwards might well have found themselves in trouble with the 'War Ags'. But in an age when income and production are all that matters, the term 'good husbandry' has begun to sound as dated as the horse plough.

A few miles south of Shaftesbury, where the chalk hills climb from the fertile Blackmore Vale to the west, the effects of soil erosion have become particularly evident. This is Thomas Hardy country: a land of bleak hillsides, of wide, empty fields and of brooding beechwoods. It was in memory of Dorset's most celebrated writer that the National Trust launched a public appeal to buy the Fontmell Down estate with its magnificent chalk grassland containing 90 different plant species and up to 25 different butterflies. Sadly there is precious little chalk grassland left outside this small reserve.

As elsewhere, the chief aim of these chalkland farmers is to grow intensive arable crops. So eagerly have they set about the task that they have begun shifting their thin, chalkland soils from the top to the bottom of the slope. Drive round the area in winter and they are difficult to miss – bare hilltops almost white with the chalk, while lower down the earth is brown.

For the farmers involved there is no immediate penalty. Given sufficiently high inputs of fertiliser and agrochemicals they can go on producing profitable crops, even with half their topsoil missing. But the costs to the nation as a whole are considerable, both from an environmental point of view and in terms of wasted resources. According to Professor Peter Bullock, director of the Soil Survey, losses on sandy soils could be as high as 18 tons an acre in some years.[5] And losses on some silty soils could reach 6 tons an acre. This is the kind of farming that causes famine and desertification in sub-Saharan Africa. In Britain we not only tolerate it, we subsidise it.

In a review of soil erosion in England and Wales, the Friends of the Earth Trust estimates the total cost at between £24 million and £51 million a year.[6] The great majority were external, off-farm costs, including damage and disruption to roads and property, road accidents, the pollution of watercourses and reservoirs, and the sedimentation of streams.

In its Code of Good Agricultural Practice, the Ministry of Agriculture acknowledges that water erosion is on the increase. The chief causes are listed – a shift to arable cropping, the use of tramlines for spraying, the desire to achieve fine winter seedbeds and the removal of hedges.[7] The document adds piously: 'Consider the possibility of soil erosion before you carry out any of these operations, particularly the ploughing out of pasture on sloping land.' MAFF goes on to outline a number of voluntary measures for reducing erosion: the planting of hedges and the introduction of 'buffer strips' of grass and other vegetation. Sadly there is no evidence that farmers are rushing to take them up.

The chalk streams of southern Britain form a timeless landscape that is quintessentially English – a clear, languid river overhung with willows, silent but for the occasional splash of trout taking fly on a fine, spring evening. As an example of a managed ecosystem producing safe food and a rich, diverse environment it would be hard to improve on this. Yet in these quiet, clear waters the influence of rampaging agribusiness is making itself felt.

River bailiffs call it 'chalk stream malaise'. The scientists are less convinced, and as yet there are no firm data. But the fly fisherman understands well enough. Subtly and surely the ecology of some of England's finest angling rivers – the Hampshire Avon, the Wyle and the legendary Test – is changing. A number are in danger of losing their salmon fisheries altogether, even though pollution inspectors confirm that technically the water quality remains high. For this is a malaise not caused by toxins, but by the slow, insidious suffocation of a living ecosystem with silt.

To the untrained eye the River Wyle in Wiltshire looks clean enough as it meanders lazily through lush green meadows at the foot of the chalk downs. The clear water sparkles in the sunshine, the waving ranunculus weeds appear green and strong. But lifelong anglers complain the river is not what it used to be. It has a turbid look about it, a dullness it never had before. The brightness has gone from these waters. Imperceptibly the character of the river is changing.

This is the effect of the silt. Washed from the soils of exposed downland cereal fields, it is slowly carried downstream and deposited in a fine coating over the weeds and gravel of the river bed. Not only has it altered the look of these chalk streams, the thin, barely perceptible film has reduced the spawning of trout and salmon. Increasingly game fish have to be introduced as fry or smolts, even in the finest streams. Natural breeding is no longer enough. On many angling beats coarse species are becoming dominant.

The plant life of the streams is changing, too. The thin sediment favours the growth of algae rather than ranunculus weeds. Nutrient enrichment, particularly in the form of nitrates from fields, exacerbates the process. The farming of the chalkland determines the life and quality of the rivers it gives birth to. When the downs were clothed in thyme-rich grassland their chalk streams were pure, clear and vibrant with life. Now the downs are little more than chemical factories and so the streams are dying.

Silt is far from being the only pollutant to enter our rivers in eroded soil. In 1989 a particularly damaging incident resulted in up to eight tons of phosphorus fertiliser entering the Exe estuary in Devon from just four fields under winter wheat.[8] Phosphates, pesticides and other contaminants stick to soil particles. So when the soil is eroded, they get dumped into the river as well. In 1992 and 1993 the National Rivers Authority carried out a comprehensive monitoring of pesticide levels in surface waters and groundwaters. They found that the herbicide atrazine exceeded EU drinking water standards in 11 per cent of samples taken from 3,500 sites in England and Wales.[9]

Since 1993 the use of atrazine outside agriculture has been banned, and pollution inspectors with the NRA (now the Environment Agency) are hoping pollution levels will fall. But the chemical is still cleared for use by farmers growing maize. Given the current popularity of forage maize with dairy farmers, there seems little chance that this form of pollution will decline. Indeed, at the rate the maize acreage is increasing, there is every possibility that the risks will grow.

In 1993 pesticides accounted for three-quarters of breaches in drinking water quality standards.[10] The herbicides atrazine and simazine were the pesticides most commonly found, with levels up to four times higher than EU standards found in East Anglian chalk aquifers. However, it is likely that the weedkiller isoproturon (IPU) will have taken over the top spot by now. In 1995 it was sprayed on more than half the UK cereal area.

In March 1994, Southern Water was forced to close its Isle of Wight drinking water supply intake on the River Eastern Yar when levels of isoproturon exceeded the EU standard by more than 50 times. Investigations showed that twelve farmers had used the chemical in combination with the herbicide chlorotoluron on more than 1,000 acres. Normally they would have used the chemicals over the winter, but because the ground had been wet they delayed spraying until March. Unfortunately, over the three weeks in which they sprayed, the Isle of Wight received 3.5 inches of rain. Thus an estimated 2kg of active chemical ended up in the Eastern Yar.

Isoproturon was turning up so often in drinking water supplies that moves were made to restrict its use. Arable farmers were immediately up in arms. A ban on this good, cheap chemical would cause them much hardship, they claimed. IPU is chiefly used for the control of blackgrass, a grass weed that has become troublesome since farmers abandoned rotations and switched to intensive cereal growing. It can be controlled by cultivation but this would mean a return to rotations, a move few cereal growers would be willing to make. They prefer to rely on a cheap herbicide, even when it is environmentally damaging to do so.

So intense has been the chemical assault on arable weeds that some, like blackgrass, have developed strains resistant to the main herbicide groups. But rather than return to cultural methods to deal with the problem, farmers have reacted by stepping up their opposition to any new restrictions on chemical use.

Under pressure from the industry the government's Advisory Committee on Pesticides stepped back from the brink and declined to restrict the use of IPU. *Farmers Weekly* hailed the decision in terms reminiscent of Neville Chamberlain's 'peace-for-our-time' speech. 'Common sense has prevailed,' the leader article crowed.[11] 'Science has won over emotion. The future of one of the most popular autumn herbicide ingredients has been assured.'

Like the squandering of our soils, the chemical pollution of our environment is an integral part of the farming system we have chosen to adopt. It is what we buy with our subsidies and, as with soil erosion, the bill is rarely paid by farmers. One estimate has put the investment cost of bringing pesticide-polluted water up to EU standards at £800 million.[12] On top of this initial capital outlay the annual cost of regulation and removal of pesticides has been estimated at £121 million.[13] This is what we pay to clean up our drinking water. Needless to say we continue to consume small amounts of many other chemicals whose levels fall below the EU threshold.

The biggest chemical pollutant of Britain's water supply comes in the form of nitrates. Fertiliser nitrates have fuelled the post-war farming revolution. Biological farming systems are both sustained and limited by the rates at which nitrates are naturally produced in the soil through the process of mineralisation. Farmers by-pass these natural cycles by applying artificial nitrates which stimulate rapid and lush plant growth. They also contaminate our water supplies.

Since the early 1950s nitrogen applications to UK wheat crops have increased almost sixfold, while application rates to temporary grassland have gone up sevenfold.[14] Every year UK farmers apply 1.5–2 million tons of nitrogen to their land in the form of nitrates.[15] Up to 300,000 tons of nitrates are leached annually into rivers and onwards to the sea, where they can lead to massive algal blooms. In inland groundwaters fertilisers often produce nitrate levels well in excess of the EU statutory limit of 50mg per litre, particularly in the most intensively farmed areas of eastern England and the Midlands. A study of a chalk aquifer in the Isle of Thanet showed nitrate concentrations under fertilised arable land ten times higher than those under unfertilised pasture.[16]

Groundwaters are particularly vulnerable to diffuse sources of pollution, especially nitrates. The rate at which they leach from soil into aquifers is little understood. Nor do we know how much nitrate is present in the unsaturated soil zone above important aquifers, so the polluting potential of the huge amounts of fertilisers applied by farmers over the past forty years is unquantifiable. In the past high levels of nitrate have been linked to stomach cancer and an infant condition known as blue baby syndrome. Both assertions have since been challenged. Even so the EU has stuck to its strict upper limit on drinking water standards despite intensive lobbying from UK farmers and landowners.

In his perceptive analysis *Rural Politics*, Professor Michael Winter charts the influence of the rural lobby in delaying action on the nitrate issue.[17] In East Anglia, the region most severely affected, the water authority was refusing to consider a limit on fertiliser applications even as late as the early 1980s, such was the strength of the farming interest. The agricultural consultancy firm Lawrence Gould, contracted by the Department of the Environment to report on the issue, recommended remedial action at the water treatment works as a more cost-effective solution than the imposition of restrictions on fertiliser use.

In a parallel campaign key interest groups like the National Farmers' Union and the Fertiliser Manufacturers' Association attempted to undermine the medical basis for the EU quality standards. The DoE's own Nitrate Coordination Group discussed alternative standards. Even the 1992 Royal Commission on Environmental Pollution questioned whether the EU limits were needed to safeguard human health. The challenge from farming interests continues to this day. As recently as February 1996 the chairman of Britain's new Environment Agency, Lord De Ramsey, criticised the DoE for failing to oppose the European Legislation more rigorously when it was first published.[18] That the head of the country's leading environmental protection agency should himself be a large farmer is testimony to the continuing influence of landed interests. Lord De Ramsey farms 6,500 acres in Cambridgeshire.

The government's response to the wide-scale pollution of water sources is best described as laggardly. In the early 1980s its position was one of defending the farmer's right to unrestricted use of fertilisers. Like the DoE's consultants, the government favoured treatment of the polluted water rather than action to end the contamination. It pointed out the measures available to water authorities enabling them to comply with EU standards, such measures as blending, denitrification, even the tankering in of uncontaminated supplies from other areas.

In line with its voluntary approach, MAFF then launched its *Code of Good Agricultural Practice,* advising farmers on how to handle both organic and artificial fertilisers. As Michael Winter points out, the code had as much to do with protecting farmers as promoting good practice. Once more agricultural policy-makers had responded to an issue in a way designed to preserve the freedom of farmers. On the nitrate question MAFF was unable to retain the control it had exercised over other environmental issues. When it comes to matters of pollution more powerful agencies and interest groups become involved. Even so MAFF succeeded in salvaging important benefits for its client group.

Following a draft EU Nitrate Directive, a series of Nitrate Sensitive Areas were set up. Within them the government was free to impose mandatory restrictions on the use of fertilisers. Instead it chose to further its cherished voluntary principle: in effect paying farmers *not* to pollute the environment. Under special NSA agreements they accept restrictions on their use of both chemical fertilisers and organic manures. In return they receive special payments which may be as high as £240 an acre for those who switch from arable cropping to ungrazed grassland, that is grass solely used for cutting.[19]

However, following approval of the Nitrate Directive by the EU Environment Council, not even MAFF could avoid stronger measures to reduce this form of pollution. The directive required member states to designate Nitrate Vulnerable Zones where the chemical was likely to breach EU limits, and to establish 'action programmes' that would become compulsory by 1999. The government had little choice but to agree. While this may look like a rare victory for the 'polluter pays' principle, NSA payments to farmers will continue even though all lie within the proposed NVZs. There are also to be grants for farmers inside the NVZs to help them comply with the restrictions. Some polluters, it seems, will continue to be bought off rather than stopped.

Meanwhile, outside these special areas farmers are free to go on applying nitrates at levels which damage the environment. And not just nitrates – phosphorus, too, is emerging as a key element in the nutrient enrichment or eutrophication of Britain's inland watercourses. NSAs and NVZs may help reduce the nitrate load in potable water supplies, but they do nothing for the wider environment. All over the country wildlife habitats are being damaged and destroyed by fertiliser nutrients from farms.

In England more than 100 Sites of Special Scientific Interest are reported to be subject to eutrophication, including both lake and river sites.[20] In Wales 12 lake and river SSSIs are affected, while in Scotland more than 15 freshwater lochs are showing signs of nutrient enrichment. But it is not just designated wildlife sites that are being damaged. As Robert Irving points out, countless other areas of the countryside are suffering, though the pollution goes largely unnoticed. The ecosystems in thousands of ponds, small streams, ditches and wetland areas are being silently altered. Habitats and wildlife are gradually losing diversity and richness.

The group claiming to be the natural custodian of the countryside has for decades used it as a sink for misapplied chemical wastes. Not only does society provide a direct subsidy on farm products, it pays a hidden subsidy as the cost of cleaning up the environment. When farmers in the proposed NVZs learned they might need to put in additional slurry storage facilities they were horrified. The aggregate cost among 8,000 of them could be as much as £10 million. There were immediate demands for new government grants to cover it.[21] Yet in 1989 the water industry's capital cost alone for removing nitrates in compliance with EU drinking water standards was estimated at £90 million over six years.[22]

Since Prime Minister John Major signed the Biodiversity Convention at the 1992 Rio Earth Summit, the government has been at least nominally concerned with the sustainability of farming. Its objectives, set out in *Sustainable Development: The UK Strategy,* include the need to 'minimise consumption of non-renewable and other resources' and to 'safeguard the quality of soil, water and air'.[23] Against the background of MAFF's compliance in half a century of environmental degradation the words have a hollow ring. 'Landowners have a long-term interest in the productive capacity of their land and the sustainable use of natural resources,' says the 1995 Countryside White Paper. Yet those same caring landowners seem prepared to accept the continuing loss of topsoil at the rate of 18 tons an acre annually.

Britain's industrial agriculture will never be made sustainable. It cannot cease to squander the country's natural resources. It cannot avoid the chemical contamination of land and water. Such things are part of its very nature; they are designed into the system. Yet the government tries desperately to hide the shortcomings, to keep the juggernaut on the road. There is nothing fundamentally wrong, it says. All that is required is a little fine tuning to deal with the worst excesses. As always MAFF searches for a technical fix.

Precision farming is a promising candidate, much talked about at farming conferences and shows. A satellite-linked positioning system mounted on the combine harvester records the yield from each part of the field. In future seasons the field map can be linked to the control system on the fertiliser spreader, so that the application rate may be varied according to the yield potential of each field area. In the same way weed maps can be used to target herbicide sprays to those parts of the field that most need them.

MAFF has set up an industry-wide research team to look into yield mapping and the targeting of fertiliser inputs. It is part of a programme for developing what Whitehall chooses to call 'technologies for sustainable farming'. Working under the same programme another industry-linked team is looking at the concept of Integrated Crop Management. MAFF crop specialists and the agrochemical manufacturers are together developing strategies to minimise the use of pesticides. That, at least, is what the press releases say.

The truth is that the construction of a genuinely sustainable farming would require rather more drastic remedies than those proposed by MAFF. No amount of fine tuning and pesticide targeting will make industrial agriculture environmentally friendly. While cattle are concentrated on big, specialist units their waste products will always pose a pollution threat to rivers and streams. Arable crops grown in isolation from livestock will continue to need heavy inputs of chemical fertiliser, much of which will inevitably end up damaging the environment. It is the way farming is organised that makes it destructive, not its lack of satellite positioning technology.

Crops grown with heavy fertiliser inputs are more prone to disease, so they must be protected with ever more pesticide sprays. Soils depleted of organic matter by decades of industrial cropping are more likely to wash away into the rivers. The list seems almost endless. Far from being sustainable, our present methods for producing food are so shot through with inherent weaknesses as to make calamity ever more likely. We have entrusted our environment and our food security to a system that looks daily more dangerous. Yet rather than make the relatively simple political and economic changes needed to correct it, the government gambles on some high-tech solution arriving in the nick of time.

The reason for official inaction is all too apparent. The move to a rational agriculture would damage too many powerful interest groups – the chemical industry, the big farmers, the landowners whose investment plans are based on inflated farmland prices. The National Farmers' Union, which speaks for all three, makes no secret of its adherence to the present system. Like MAFF, the union believes any minor imperfections are easily remedied by greater investment in technology. In doing so it attempts to portray industrial farming as not only inevitable but desirable.

NFU deputy president Ben Gill claims that farmers and growers will need to adopt new technologies in order to meet the growing demand for safe and wholesome food.[24] This seemingly innocuous statement reveals the deep distortions running through the NFU's publicity campaign. The clear implication is that such technologies as global positioning and the genetic manipulation of plants and animals are the direct response to consumer demands for safe food. The fact is these developments are technology-led. They are there to meet the needs of industrial agriculture, not a worried public.

Understandably, people are concerned about the safety of their food. The beef crisis has shown they have every reason to be. But providing safe food will mean going back to an old and tested technology, not bolting new and untried technologies onto an already flawed system. Biological farming – farming based on natural cycles – is the only system which can provide safe, wholesome food. It is also the only system that can be genuinely sustainable and non-destructive of Britain's soils and watercourses.

An end to pollution and to the loss of our soils can only come about with a return to extensive mixed farming. This means an end to specialisation, an end to the separation of livestock and crops into large-scale, factory-type units. Animals and crops need to be brought together once more on farms which are both economically and environmentally sustainable. We also need to see a return to rotations as a way of limiting disease and maintaining soil fertility. Before the age of pesticides these were the methods that kept food crops healthy. They can do so again.

Above all we need to see a repopulation of the farmed landscape. The replacement of people by machines and chemicals is what has led to the poisoning of our environment, the loss of our wildlife and the destruction of our soils. The human brain is a better manager of ecosystems than the satellite-linked computer installed in the tractor cab. To restore a living landscape from the industrial wasteland that now covers much of lowland Britain we need to take the very step that Agriculture Minister John Gummer rejected in 1992. We need to create more small farms.

Such changes need not be hugely expensive. Indeed, taking full account of the environmental benefits, they may show a net saving over the present system, geared as it is toward short-term profit. But change would incur a political cost. It could mean challenging those entrenched interest groups which have controlled rural policies for half a century. First there needs to be an end to the production subsidies that have powered the process of farm intensification since the war. But that alone will not be enough. For the first time we have to charge the full cost of environmental damage to the agricultural system that causes it. We have to make the polluter pay.

Industrial agriculture flourishes only because successive governments have made the wider community pay to clean up its mess. Thus society gave an unfair advantage to the sprayers and the hedgerow grubbers, while discriminating against those farmers who tried to care for their land. In doing so we all shared responsibility for the degradation of our environment. Now we have to make sure that the agribusiness pays, not just for cleaning up our drinking water, but for all the ecologically damaged streams and ponds, and for every landslip that dumps a few more tons of irreplaceable topsoil into the ditch.

In his best-selling book *The Farming Ladder,* George Henderson maintained that for the farmer there was only one rule of good husbandry – to leave the land in better heart than he found it.[25] This was his sacred trust: to maintain the soil's fertility and pass it on unimpaired to the unborn generations to come. For nothing justified the exhaustion of a farm, he claimed, not even the 'narrow demands of national extremity'. A civilisation lasted but a thousand years, while in the farmers' hands lay the destiny of all mankind.

11

A PLACE IN THE COUNTRY

For the people of the Lincolnshire town of Spilsby the cluster of small grass fields beside the road to Partney were a favourite spot for walking. They covered the earthwork and buried remains of a deserted medieval settlement known as Old Spilsby, believed to have occupied the site since before the late eleventh century. All around the settlement were the ridge and furrow cultivations of an ancient field system, set out in rectangular blocks and bounded by hollow ways and ditches.

In a county of vast, regimented landscapes of winter wheat and sugar beet, the unimproved pastures of Old Spilsby were an echo of a more intimate countryside, an agriculture of human scale. The townspeople loved the place with its rambling hedges and old, flower-rich grassland strewn with ancient anthills. Here they could stroll on warm summer evenings while the sound of songbirds spilled from centuries-old field maple and ash trees, a small remnant of rural Lincolnshire where people could still feel they belonged.

In the culture of agribusiness such places are an anathema. In December 1995 the land was sold by tender. The advertisements described it as easily ploughable and suitable for early potatoes, a piece of land agents' vernacular which effectively sealed its fate. Within days the bulldozer was at work, obliterating the handiwork of ox-team ploughman and ancient hedge planter, felling trees and driving out wildlife. Soon after came the land drainage machines, preparing this quiet countryside for intensive arable production.

Spilsby residents were horrified. They appealed to their district council to intervene. In the local paper a distressed ten-year-old begged the town's mayor to stop the destruction of the wildlife. Belatedly East Lindsey District Council introduced an emergency protection order on the trees, though not before dozens had been

154

felled and more than a mile of hedgerow destroyed. Immediately before the sale English Heritage had succeeded in scheduling the remains of the settlement together with some of the ridge and furrow system adjoining it. But there was no such protection for most of the site.

This was no place of great scientific interest. There was nothing here to warrant the status of a nature reserve or special habitat site. It was the preserve of very ordinary creatures like hares and foxes and owls; its ancient pastures contained the sort of everyday herbs and flowers once found in grassland everywhere. It was special not to the experts, to the botanists or ecologists or ornithologists, but to the people of the town. And because of that it had no value. At a time when taxpayers were spending £200 million a year on set-aside to keep arable land out of production, this small remnant of pastoral Lincolnshire had to be mobilised for intensive arable cropping. One of the first acts of the new owner was to apply for a licence to abstract more water from the adjacent River Lymn. He needed irrigation for his high-input cash crops.

So the locals lost their treasured patch of real countryside, its flowers and its wildlife. In its place they got another intensive food factory of the sort that already covered much of the county. Where once butterflies flickered across old grassland there were now to be pesticide sprays splashing over hybrid wheats, nitrate fertilisers streaming into the quiet river. Not that many of the locals expressed their anger openly. What was the point? Who listens to the concerns of country people any more, unless, of course, they happen to be farmers? It was left to the few to voice the quiet outrage of many.

Decades of watching their local environment despoiled has bred a sort of confused resignation among country people. They see no logic to the degradation going on around them, but they know the landowning lobby holds most of the cards. Farmers and landowners hold sway on many rural councils and dominate the internal drainage boards. They run two of the country's most powerful lobby organisations, and in 1996 counted 32 Members of Parliament among their number, including Rural Affairs Minister Tim Boswell.[1] It is overwhelmingly landowners who dictate the shape of the rural landscape. Country people have learned to live with that fact.

When the new owner of the Old Spilsby pastures was criticised for removing trees and hedges, he defended himself in the local paper.[2] 'Our role is to farm the land using modern methods of farm management ... Modern day farming has many roles to fulfil, the primary role being that of food production in an economic and efficient manner.' This has been the justification of agribusiness for decades, the perpetual mantra of the National Farmers' Union: that 'production must come first'. At a time when there were more than a million acres in set-aside the argument was hard to swallow.

It certainly wasn't production the residents of Spilsby wanted to see. There is no evidence of a popular clamour for more acres of intensive early potatoes. What they wanted was their lumpy old grassland with its anthills and wild flowers and bright green woodpeckers. But their voice was not heard above the screech of short-term economics. Indeed they scarcely have a voice. The government's rural White Paper[3] may speak piously of the contribution rural residents can make to the environment, but the farm support system provides for only one outcome – a landscape created in the image of agribusiness.

Farmers and landowners make up less than 1 per cent of the population. Despite this their possession of land gives them the means and the freedom drastically to alter the landscape, largely without reference to the planning system. Even in urban Britain of the 1990s one-third of the population is described as 'predominantly rural' or 'significantly rural'. But because most of them are landless they have no control over their local environment, beyond complaining about mud in the road or the smell of pig slurry. They have no stake in the countryside; they are effectively excluded. They live on the periphery like temporary expatriates in some foreign land. It was not always so.

For much of our history almost everyone had a stake in the land. Village Britain was the Britain of the peasantry. The very term now has a comic ring about it, so widely has it been used as a form of abuse. Yet the collective memory of our link with the land explains both our sense of alienation from the countryside and the reasons for its current abuse. In his classic study of *The English Countryman*, H. J. Massingham described the peasant cultivator as 'the base of the pyramid which we call civilisation'.[4] With varying fortunes, the peasant remained in possession of the land until the General Enclosure Act of 1845 put an end to it.

However brutish and short the peasant existence, it represented a social order of remarkable durability. In the open field system each village or parish held two or three large fields of unfenced arable in conjunction with meadowland, common and waste. Private property in portions of land was inseparable from co-partnership in the whole. Each village was a single farm in which every member of the hierarchy was at once servant and master, owner and shareholder, a unique form of collective responsibility which lasted from prehistoric times to the Enclosures. Massingham describes it as neither socialism nor individualism, but a fusion of the two: a land-based 'co-operative commonwealth' as an alternative to state socialism and the industrial anarchy of *laissez faire*.

George Monbiot links the wide-scale dispossession of the peasantry with the rise of a new and ruthless landed class, which quickly realised the value of its assets by seizing the commons and evicting the commoners.[5] A landed people were consigned to the squalor and misery of eighteenth-century town life. Today 1 per cent of the population owns more than half the land in Britain; just 2 per cent own three-quarters of it.[6] Scottish land clearances were even more ruthless than the English enclosures. Half of Scotland is now owned by 600 individuals. A landscape of the people has become a landscape of exclusion.

What the early land enclosers began the Ministry of Agriculture appears determined to continue. Ever since the war government farm policies have been obsessed with promoting what farm ministers call efficiency. This invariably means efficiency as defined in the narrow industrial sense of output per labour unit. Using both subsidies and fiscal measures MAFF has pursued relentlessly the cause of mechanisation in British agriculture. Its sole purpose has been to clear people off the land and replace them with machines and agrochemicals.

Since the war the number of people working on UK farms, both full-time and part-time, has fallen from nearly a million to just a quarter of that. The government now claims that with less than 2 per cent of the workforce engaged in agriculture its farms are among the most productive in the world.

Some commodities are singled out for particularly high levels of support while others get little or nothing. Arable crops, beef and dairy farming receive half their output or more in the form of public support, while horticulture receives just 6 per cent and pig producers virtually nothing. Here the object is to encourage intensive specialist farms rather than the mixed farms that employ more labour.

Capital grants, too, have been heavily weighted in favour of big farmers. The huge, EU-funded capital development schemes of the 1970s and 80s specifically excluded small and part-time farms. Such units were inconsequential as far as MAFF was concerned. The government wanted efficiency and the large, highly mechanised farms were the ones that would deliver. The countryside was to be organised like a Honda car plant. The public were paying to have farmworkers and small farmers cleared from the countryside.

Government contempt for small farmers was clearly shown in the then Farm Minister John Gummer's response to the 1991 EC Commission reform proposals. As Michael Winter points out, Agriculture Commissioner Ray MacSharry was seen as sympathetic to Europe's small farmers, particularly those in his native Ireland.[7] In a Commons response redolent of Margaret Thatcher's famous 'triple no' speech Gummer declared: 'We start by saying that we oppose Mr MacSharry's proposals. We hate them. We condemn them.' By the time the reforms were finally agreed, all suggestion of bias towards small farmers had been removed.

The state has seldom if ever been as benevolent to farmers and landowners as it is today. Farmland is subject to no taxes or rates. It is exempt from Inheritance Tax and qualifies for all reliefs under the rules of Capital Gains Tax (CGT). On top of this, farm businesses are now eligible for Re-investment Relief. This means capital accrued in some other venture has only to be invested in some farming enterprise to escape CGT. This makes farming and farmland an attractive bolthole for investors. Indeed many analysts now consider the tax regime for farmers and landowners more favourable than at any time this century.

All of which might sound like good news for the countryside. Sound businesses need investment. However, the kind of speculative investment attracted by the current tax climate is anything but healthy. It further inflates land values and increases the intensity of farming. City investors farm the countryside for profit. This usually means further impoverishment of the landscape and more pesticide contaminants in crops. When fund managers add farmland to their investment portfolios they contribute indirectly to the malnutrition of the people.

'Large CGT Reinvestment Relief/Inheritance Tax Opportunity,' says the *Farmers Weekly* advertisement for a 2,650-acre Norfolk estate supplying vegetables to leading supermarkets.[8] The same issue of the magazine carries a report of vegetable land in Lincolnshire fetching £3,383 an acre at auction.[9] City investment fuels the intensification and concentration of agriculture.

Encouraged by generous fiscal treatment the process of amalgamation and farm enlargement has surged ahead, pushing ever more people off the land. The major City institutions have been investing in farmland since the early 1970s, when it became apparent that Common Market membership was about to inflate land values. In 1972 alone they increased their agricultural holdings by 40 per cent.[10] By 1978 it had gone up from 50,000 acres to more than half a million. Not that the investment companies had any interest in farming and rural communities. Their main concern was capital growth. Most brought in contract farming companies to run their holdings at minimal cost, a practice which often resulted in the laying off of farm staff and the 'rationalisation' of field structure.

However, in the mid-1990s it was farmers themselves who were driving people off the land. Buoyed up by high profits from milk and arable crops, many joined the scramble to buy extra acres, pushing up the average price of farmland by two-thirds.[11] A 1996 survey by land agents Brown and Company showed that on the back of higher profits four out of five farmers were planning major capital expenditure on land, buildings or machinery.[12] Of almost half who intended buying new tractors, the majority farmed between 500 and 1,000 acres and were considering a reduced labour force and a greater reliance on machinery. Farmers claim they need good profits to create jobs in the countryside. Yet when they make money they spend it on land and machinery.

Farmland may be the basis of human life and civilisation, but to the modern agribusiness it is just another commodity, simply a factor of production. Each week the major farming papers carry glossy adverts from land agents alongside supporting articles designed to create an appropriate 'editorial environment'. For many journalists and investment analysts there is a good living to be made from forecasting land price movements. *Farmers Weekly* is as likely to be found in the reception area of a City accountants as the *Investor's Chronicle*.

The biggest land deal of 1995 was a purely institutional affair. Four years earlier the Royal Life insurance group had bought 22,500 acres of prime farmland in eastern England from Guardian Royal Exchange. The deal included a contract farming company called British Field Products (BFP) based at Weasenham Manor near King's Lynn. Although no sale price was officially disclosed, press reports put the 1991 price at £34 million.[13] In 1995 an investment group called the Lands Improvement Holdings (LIH) bought the farming company along with 19,500 acres of the land for a price reported to be more than £55 million.[14]

Following the acquisition the group sold off the majority of BFP's assets, retaining ownership of the farming company itself along with 6,500 acres of top-grade land in Lincolnshire and Cambridgeshire. LIH also retained the farming on 4,600 acres of the land subsequently sold on. This land is farmed by BFP on a contract basis or under the new Farm Business Tenancy legislation. Introduced in

1995, the legislation was widely welcomed by farmers as a way of bringing new entrants into the industry.

At the time of the deal LIH managing director Peter Clery told *Farmers Weekly* that the group would not have been interested in BFP but for new farm tenancy legislation.[15] He expected the newly acquired company to be a strong contender for future tenancies. LIH planned to turn it into a major farming and management company to rival the present big players.

The farming press was fascinated. It was the land deal of 1995, the biggest block of vacant-possession land to come on to the market that year, a giant step for rational, scientific agriculture. Here were City investors taking over large areas of highly fertile farmland, then having them run by a large, efficient farming company. Just the kind of structural change necessary to build a competitive industry.

In June 1996 LIH was listed on the Stock Exchange. At the time the group – valued at £48 million – owned 27,000 acres of mostly tenanted farmland. Its BFP subsidiary farmed 6,500 acres of the group's land along with 8,500 acres owned by third parties. Among its principal activities LIH lists the acquisition and management of rural land for long-term investment and/or development, arable farming and trading in land.[16] 'Group strategy is to enhance value by improvements and by obtaining planning permissions for alternative uses. Land may be sold when development value can be realised or if no further enhancement is considered likely.'

In the Lincolnshire cottage she shares with her husband John, Barbara Sutton sits at the kitchen table looking through photos of her childhood. Those that interest her most are black-and-white shots taken in the late 1950s on the small Lincolnshire farm of her grandmother and step-grandfather. Though Barbara lived and grew up in Bolton, she and her brother spent every holiday on the farm near Skegness. There she helped milk the cows, feed the livestock and lead the carthorse up and down rows of potatoes beneath the towering hedgerows.

Barbara recalls that in the bungalow at Orby Ground Farm there were no modern facilities, no electric lights or bathroom, just an old-fashioned washstand and a candle to light the way to bed. Even so she loved it. For the miner's daughter who grew up in industrial Lancashire that little farm in Lincolnshire was a rural idyll. She remembers it with obvious delight and affection. 'I would go back tomorrow if I could.' However, this would be difficult. The farm no longer exists.

Take the road from Burgh le Marsh across Orby Marsh towards

Ingoldmells and the coast. This is a land of broad open fields and wide skies, just the sort of intensive arable country favoured by City investors and the big farming companies. Turn left by Teapot Hall and head along the lane towards Addlethorpe. This is the countryside Barbara Sutton visited in those far off days of the 1950s. But there is no sign of Orby Ground Farm any more. The bungalow, the buildings, the hedgerows – all have vanished. The land is now a giant field. A lone sycamore tree beside the lane is all that is left of the family farm.

Barbara remembers when there were five family farms in that one small locality. All have been amalgamated into bigger units; on three of them the houses have been bulldozed. This is the social revolution that has destroyed a rural culture across the length and breadth of Britain. It is the singular achievement of post-war farm policy and subsidies, its monument a stark and empty prairie.

If Barbara Sutton wanted to get into small farming today she would find her hopes dashed by the planning laws. These are designed to further the process of farm amalgamation and concentration and to prevent the less well-off gaining access to the land. For a start the unconditional right to put up a farm building is available only to those with twelve acres or more. Anyone wishing to grow organic vegetables on a six-acre plot may be refused permission to put up even an implement shed. If that same person wishes to live on their smallholding the planning obstacles would be greater still.

As Simon Fairlie has pointed out, even to live in a tent or caravan the applicant must first prove his or her 'viability' by the standards laid down by the Ministry of Agriculture.[17]

Three acres and a cow are not considered enough. The applicant must have more than 50 dairy cows or 160 beef cattle to qualify. By this means MAFF effectively controls the way the land is farmed. It compels every new entrant to adopt a high-capital, intensive form of farming, the kind of farming that stresses livestock and damages the environment. But if a new farmer is content with the income of six acres of vegetables or half a dozen cattle, why should the government deny him or her the opportunity?

The answer, of course, is the policy of 'zoning', the division of rural land into separate agricultural and development zones. The policy was intended to limit urban sprawl and prevent such pre-war horrors as ribbon development along rural roads. In meeting these limited objectives it has been moderately successful. However, the policy has also blocked the emergence of new rural communities; people wishing to develop sustainable farming systems based on good husbandry rather than chemicals. Zoning excludes such groups and restricts the countryside to intensive farmers, investment managers and the highly mechanised contract farming companies.

Simon Fairlie describes zoning as a kind of 'social apartheid', squeezing out people of low income and excluding would-be small farmers. It has given a scarcity value, or 'betterment', to land with full planning permission. Thus when development rights are granted on a piece of farmland its value may increase fiftyfold, providing a huge, unearned income for the owner, often a speculative property developer or a land investment company.

The policy of zoning is intricately bound up with exploitation of land, whether through industrial farming or speculative development. At the same time it operates against those whose interest is to farm the land in a sustainable way. Many retiring farmers maximise the sale value of their farms by selling their farmhouses to wealthy ex-townspeople, then disposing of the land separately. Thus land is available to would-be smallholders at the lower agricultural rate. But since the planning system denies them the chance of living on their holdings, they have to look for a home in the development zone where house prices are inflated by the cost of providing the speculator with his 'betterment' value.

Simon Fairlie describes one more turn of the screw for the would-be smallholder. Since the price of agricultural land is low in comparison with development land, so its products command a weak price in the market. Yet somehow the smallholder has to make those low-value products pay the price of housing in the high-priced development zone. It takes a lot of organic carrots and free-range eggs to cover the mortgage payments for a house on a new estate. So there is pressure to intensify farming.

George Monbiot speaks of the disastrous consequences of excluding ordinary people from the countryside.[18] 'Without a sense of belonging to the land, and of the land belonging to us, we are the citizens of nowhere. Our alienation from our surroundings rebounds in the apprehension that we no longer belong to ourselves. Without a stake in the land we feel, moreover, that we have no right to determine what happens there.'

On a wooded hillside in Somerset a dozen or so people have tried restoring their links with the land. The Tinkers' Bubble Trust have embarked on a 'low impact' development project on forty acres of woodland, pasture and orchard that they own. Living in timber and canvas houses entirely hidden in the woods, they have begun producing organic apples, honey, lamb, vegetables and herbs, together with craft goods from the woodlands they are restoring. Internal combustion engines are banned. Labour is supplied by muscle or by shire horse, while firewood and solar panels meet their energy needs.

The Tinkers' Bubble settlement flies in the face of the planning laws. It is located in an area zoned for agriculture. The nearest land zoned for human habitation is in Norton Sub Hamdon, a genteel village of expensive hamstone houses and cottages. When the settlers' planning application went to appeal, Environment Secretary John Gummer called it in. Then in August 1995, he overruled the inspector's recommendations and told the settlers they would have to go. It seems he accepted that the group would need to live on site to have any hope of achieving its aims, but to grant permission might encourage similar applications which would have a serious cumulative impact.

What the Environment Secretary sees as a threat many in society would view as a sign of hope. Tinkers' Bubble was producing safe food and a rich and diverse countryside. Not for them the spray can or the fertiliser bag. On their hillside at Little Norton the orchards and meadows are alive with butterflies and bees, while the valley echoes with the sound of songbirds. Yet society will not tolerate them. For their message is deemed subversive.

On the hilltop above the settlement stands an ancient Iron Age fort, now known as Ham Hill Country Park. To the west the site affords a breathtaking view across lowland Somerset to the distant Quantocks and Blackdown Hills. It also provides a view of some of the county's most intensively farmed countryside. This area west of Yeovil has some of the most fertile soils in the south-west. It is a land of soft fruit growing and intensive vegetable production. Beyond are the cereal fields with their characteristic 'tramlines' providing access for the chemical sprayer at ever more frequent intervals through the growth cycle.

This is the kind of farming we choose to support with our taxes and protect with our planning laws: a farming that has given us a dying landscape and pesticide-drenched soils. An attempt to find a safer, sustainable alternative is given short shrift. In a bizarre irony the Tinkers' Bubble Trust was officially notified that the spring providing its drinking water contained high levels of nitrate, probably as a result of farm pollution elsewhere.[19]

The exclusion of groups like the Ham Hill settlers denies people the chance to influence the way their food is produced and their countryside looked after. It leaves today's big farmers and landowners free to pursue their own interests without reference to the public good. They can adopt whatever technologies they choose regardless of what they do to the countryside or to our food. There is no one to provide an alternative, no one to do things in a different way.

Industrial farming thrives, in part, because there is no one to look too closely at what it does. It is a product of the culture that confines people to towns, to their semis and their flats. Theirs is the role of consumer, nothing more; to make their choices from the supermarket shelves, with no real knowledge of how that food is produced. Industrial agriculture must be secured from the public gaze, hedged about by planning and property law. The countryside must remain empty, the preserve of the landowning hegemony. They, after all, are the people who understand it.

Not surprisingly, the 'freedom to roam' campaign from the Ramblers' Association provokes strong opposition from the farming and landowning lobbies. Not that the Ramblers have ever proposed unrestricted access to all rural land: what they are calling for is the freedom to walk across land known as 'open country', and then subject to a whole range of restrictions and exceptions. However, landowners are appalled by the idea. They have railed against it in the press and at meetings up and down the country.

Their argument is that 'freedom to roam' would give *carte blanche* to the thief, the poacher and the animal rights activist looking for a barn to torch. Rural vandalism would soar, while the tramp of boots across valuable wildlife areas would do untold damage to conservation. When the proposal came up for debate in Parliament under a 10-Minute Rule Bill, Conservative MP Tim Yeo spoke for landowning interests. He made the risk of environmental damage one of his key objections. Since landowners would be obliged to provide access to the countryside, who is to say some troublesome local authority would not demand the removal of ancient hedgerows or stone walls?[20]

Given the post-war history of the British countryside it seems a curious line to take. In the absence of public intervention, farmers and landowners have waged an unending war on the British landscape and its wildlife. In the early 1990s they were still causing the loss of 11,000 miles of hedgerow each year, either through neglect or removal. Any damage resulting from the requirement to provide access to open country would be infinitesimal by comparison.

The response of the Country Landowners' Association to the

Ramblers' proposal was a little more circumspect: in a densely populated country the 'right to roam' was not a realistic option.[21] It assumed that walking should be given priority over such land uses as agriculture, forestry, game management and conservation. In fact the Ramblers' proposal assumed no such thing. There was no suggestion that the rights of walkers should interfere with other legitimate rural activities. On the contrary, these were to be specifically protected. What the Bill did assume was that the people of these islands had a natural right to enjoy their own countryside, just as they had for centuries until the Enclosures. It was this simple idea that so threatened landowners.

Exclusion – of small farmers, of the rural poor and of the public – lies at the heart of our national malaise. We have abandoned our countryside to the grubbers and sprayers, the exploiters and the profiteers. We have allowed them to assault our landscapes, wage war on our wildlife and abuse our farm livestock. They have poisoned our soils and dumped millions of tons of soil and silt into the rivers. They have demolished nine-tenths of our wildlife assets. Now, finally, they have corrupted the purity of our food. None of this could have happened but for exclusion, the exclusion of people from the countryside and the decision-making that affects it. In failing to exercise our 'right to roam' we have given the despoilers of our island the 'right to ruin'.

The landowners now want to see the concept of 'open access' to the countryside replaced by one of 'managed access'. And as in so many rural matters they are supported by the government. 'We believe that a general right to roam, conflicting with other uses of land, leading to damage to crops or causing danger to livestock or disturbance of wildlife, and denying the rights of landowners, is not acceptable. It would elevate one interest above all others and institutionalise rights without obligations.'[22] This is a strange observation. In the town one has both the right to walk down a street and the obligation not to hurl bricks through shop windows. It would be no different in the countryside.

What the landowners are seeking is an extension of the 'voluntary' approach to countryside management. Access should not be a public 'right'. It should instead be a matter for negotiation, with individual landowners free to enter into voluntary agreements allowing public access to their land. They would, of course, receive public money in recognition of their public spiritedness. But the law should play no part.

The landowners' present argument mirrors the view of the earlier

Enclosers – that the common people have no rights in the countryside. The title deeds to a piece of Britain gives the holder absolute power to decide who comes on to that land and what is done to it. No citizen can object to the way it is farmed. None may complain when a centuries-old woodland is bulldozed or an ancient flower-meadow put to the plough. The payment of tolls to enter parts of the countryside confirms the visitors' lack of status. They have no stake in the ground they walk on and whose products they must consume. They have no rights to their ancestral land, whose culture pervades their literature and their music. They are truly made citizens of nowhere.

12

BREAKING THE CHAINS

It seems an odd place to go for a piece of beef, the rough, jolting drive leading between the tall poplar trees; the farm buildings, slightly down-at-heel, dilapidated almost. You begin to wonder whether you've got the directions right. There is a noticeable absence of the hand-painted signs and self-conscious tidiness normally associated with farm shops. Then you glance up towards the steeply sloping meadow and you know at once you have come to the right place.

In the bright spring sunshine a bunch of cattle meander placidly past an ancient cherry tree, now in full blossom. Their colours range from rich chestnut brown to the hue of ripening wheat. They seem to be of all ages; among them are calves, young heifers and elderly cows of slow deliberate gait. Overwhelmingly their disposition is one of contentment. For Kite's Nest Farm on the northern scarp of the Cotswold Hills is no ordinary farm. Anywhere less like the chemical-drenched landscapes beloved of Whitehall Place would be hard to imagine. This is a countryside that lives.

To describe Mary Young and her grown-up children Richard and Rosamund as organic farmers would be like saying Shakespeare was a playwright. It is true, of course, but such a shallow version of truth as to be of little worth. For Kite's Nest is not merely a place to produce beef. It is a place to celebrate nature and diversity, from the owls and warblers that haunt the woodland glades to the cowslips, harebells and wild thyme of the meadows and the rooks squabbling in the treetops.

These are not pests and weeds to be controlled or sprayed out. They are part of the process that provides the Youngs with a product to sell. And not just a product, but food with a flavour, texture and nutritional quality to surpass anything from the conventional 'meat factory'. Far from being relegated to the margins, the wildlife here is encouraged. For it is the natural world that has made Kite's Nest Farm beef the highly sought-after product it is.

Many of the Youngs' regular customers come from far afield to the little shop in the mellow stone farmhouse near Broadway in Worcestershire. Some have travelled the thirty-five miles or so from Birmingham, driving across the fertile Vale of Evesham, the once-thriving land of small growers, now increasingly the domain of agribusiness and big cereal farmers. For the Kite's Hill customers it is a journey well worth making. They have discovered a food they can trust from a farming system they can believe in.

A score of food scares and animal welfare abuses have dented public confidence in Britain's farmers. Of course there are those for whom the way their food is produced is of little or no interest. But there are others, and an increasing number, for whom the image of a tethered sow or the calf pressed muzzle-first against the slats of an export lorry is profoundly disturbing. So, too, the sight of vast fields of regimented crops where the only moving thing is the pesticide sprayer. Always there is the unspoken question – since these compounds are designed to destroy life, may they not also damage the people who will eat the crops?

To such people bland statements from Agriculture Ministers about insignificant risks are of little comfort. It is empty rhetoric, an all-purpose palliative, aimed at protecting the reputations of politicians and the investments of the agrochemical industry. The Youngs have no need for public relations. They farm in the way they consider ethical, and they do it in full view of their neighbours and their customers. The living landscape and its teeming wildlife are all the publicity they need. For they and a handful like them have begun to heal the rift that has separated farmers and the community for too long.

Even by organic standards the system of cattle husbandry at Kite's Nest Farm is remarkable. Underlying it is the absolute principle that the animals must never be allowed to suffer. The aim is to interfere as little as possible in the way they spend their lives. As a result the sixty-strong herd of single-suckle cows and their calves live in family groups, some of which represent several generations.

No calf is ever taken forcibly from its mother. Instead the cow weans her calf naturally when her milk supply dries up, about a month before the next calf is due. When the new calf is born the cow transfers most of her affection to it. Even so the older calf remains with her, getting to know its younger sibling and remaining part of the family group. The entire herd is free to range over all the grassland – the gates at Kite's Nest Farm are seldom closed. Since the unfertilised pastures are full of flowers and herbs, the cattle have a great deal of choice over what they eat. They are able to select the plants which they know instinctively will provide the balance of nutrients they need.

It is a regime that combines freedom with care. And the care does not stop when the animals go to slaughter. The cattle are killed at between 24 and 30 months of age. When the time comes Richard himself takes them to the local abattoir where they are dispatched without delay. The animals always travel to slaughter in pairs to reduce the anxiety of this final journey. Afterwards the carcasses and edible offal are delivered by refrigerated lorry to the Kite's Nest Farm coldstore for hanging and butchering.

Thus when the Youngs sell a piece of meat they are able to assure the customer that they have known and cared for the animal from the day it was born until its last moments. Richard rejects the notion that having cared for it he and his family partners should not be part of its transformation into a food product. On the contrary, their involvement in the slaughtering process is part of the responsibility they owe to their customers as well as to their cattle.

Whatever diseases afflict the national herd it would be hard to imagine a safer food than the beef of Kite's Nest Farm. The herd has been 'self-contained' since 1977. No animals are brought in and all beef cattle are born on the farm. The Youngs buy in no feed either, apart from a little organically grown barley for feeding to cows with twins. The cattle are fed naturally on grass and home-produced hay and silage. Mary Young gave up using compound feeds in 1974 when she discovered they contained chicken carcasses. No case of BSE has ever occurred at Kite's Nest Farm, nor has any animal given a positive reaction to routine MAFF tests for tuberculosis or brucellosis.

It is their trust in the product that brings the customers jolting along the track between the poplar trees time and time again. Many have been buying Kite's Nest beef for years, happy to pay a premium price for a product they know to be safe. They are there to have their faith restored in farming, to play some part in constructing a kinder, more diverse countryside.

On a hillside at Kite's Nest Farm there is a piece of meadowland with an unusually rich community of wild flora. The most rare is a low, broom-like plant with yellow flowers, Dyer's greenweed. Around it, among the waving summer grasses, are others like lady's bedstraw, hawkbit and bird's-foot trefoil, while higher up on the escarpment the sward is festooned with pyramid orchids and clustered bellflower. Such species-rich meadows do not survive in spite of the farming, nor do the myriad butterflies and insects that inhabit them. They are there *because* of the farming, or that particular brand of farming practised by the Youngs.

When customers buy their beef in the Kite's Nest Farm shop they are paying not just for the meat but for hawkbit and bellflower in the meadow and the warblers and owls in the woods. They are also contributing to the contented, stress-free lives of Dizzie and Gillespie and Christmas Bonnet, the cattle in the pasture. All this and the finest beef in the land – it seems quite a bargain for a modest price premium on the meat. It is only possible because the Youngs are prepared to work tirelessly and live frugally.

Given the environmental and animal welfare benefits of their farming system, it might seem a likely candidate for any public support going. But such is the perverse nature of the subsidy system it actually discriminates against the Kite's Nest Farm methods and in favour of industrial agricultural systems.

Richard Young explains the process by reference to a 34-acre field at Kite's Nest. In 1991 it was growing an arable crop, so under the rules of the CAP reform package it became eligible for arable aid. If the Youngs had abandoned organic farming and gone on cropping the field year after year with the aid of agrochemicals they could have collected up to £7,000 each year in subsidies, depending on what crops they grew. But because they will not use chemicals, they returned the field to grass and clover so the fertility could begin to build up again.

However, the land was now registered as arable land so it was ineligible for livestock quotas. And as a result of the distortions introduced by the subsidy system, rearing livestock without quota was no longer economic. Thus mixed farming, with its promise of sustainable cropping and rich wildlife habitats, had been blocked by the support system; once more public money was being used to entrench the separation of crops and livestock which elsewhere had proved so damaging to the environment.

As a final irony the Youngs are now offered environmental payments for keeping their former cereal fields in grass. The farm lies in the officially designated Cotswolds Environmentally Sensitive Area, so it is eligible for payments of £120 an acre on registered cereal land put down permanently to grass. Once the thin Cotswold soils were covered in grassland – the traditional wealth of the area was founded on sheep – but under the influence of EU arable subsidies the Cotswolds are now clothed in intensive cereals and oilseed rape crops. The ESA payments were designed to lure a few of these industrial farmers back to grass and livestock.

It is not an option the Youngs would have chosen had the profitability of mixed farming not been undermined by the support system. Ultimately mixed farming is the only system that will reduce the damaging impact of agrochemicals on lowland Britain. But Kite's Nest Farm is burdened with heavy borrowings. The Youngs were in no position to turn down payments of £120 an acre. They want to survive.

Direct links with consumers have become a lifeline for many organic farmers. In the market place they cannot hope to compete with chemically grown crops. While industrial farmers continue to impoverish the landscape, pollute soils and watercourses, and market contaminated food all without penalty, those who refuse to do these things are placed at a disadvantage. By linking up with consumers who share their views on food quality and the environment, organic farmers cut out wholesalers and secure a return closer to the retail price. In this way they can stay in business despite their higher costs.

Their struggle to keep going highlights the absurdity of EU and national farm policies. Any subsidy might be expected to go to organic producers in return for the 'public goods' they deliver; the diversity of wildlife and the clean environment. Instead the taxpayer rewards the conventional farmer for output whatever the social and environmental cost. Public policy supports the polluter, while the environmentally responsible producer must rely on a distorted market for his survival.

Organic farmers in Britain plough a lonely furrow. The government shares the view of the multiple retailers: organic producers are suppliers to a niche market. Not so in the rest of the EU. Some countries – Sweden, Denmark, Austria and individual states in Germany – are officially committed to, or close to achieving, a target of 10 per cent of farmland under organic management by the end of the century.[1] Over the past decade the area of organically managed land in the EU has risen from 300,000 acres to almost 3 million acres, an annual increase of 25 per cent.

In Britain the area of organically farmed land remains at less than half of 1 per cent. At the same time the true costs of industrial agriculture are hidden from the average citizen and supermarket shopper. Until the facts are more widely known Britain's small band of organic farmers must use their husbandry and marketing skills to stay in business under a hostile subsidy regime.

On the flat, windswept landscape of the Fylde coast in Lancashire, Alan and Debra Schofield grow organic vegetables on their three-and-a-half acres at Pilling, just a mile and a half from the sea. They used to sell to a major supermarket chain, but grew increasingly disillusioned with the way their crops were handled. First the vegetables were trucked nearly 200 miles to the central packhouse, only to be redistributed to retail stores throughout the UK. It was up to a week before the produce actually went on sale to the public.

In 1992 the Schofields began marketing direct to consumers in the north-west, dropping off fixed-price vegetable bags at communal collection points. They called the enterprise *Growing With Nature*, and within four years they were selling 600 bags a week. Such was the demand that three other organic growers in Lancashire were brought in to help supply them. Like the Youngs, Alan Schofield has discovered that consumer support can be a catalyst for change in the countryside.

Unlike cereal farmers, vegetable growers get little direct support from the EU. However, conventional growers receive the same 'hidden' subsidy of being allowed to contaminate their soils with nitrates and pesticides almost without penalty. The supermarkets have created an expectation of perfection among their customers. No one will now buy an apple or carrot with even the slightest blemish. Yet to achieve these unnatural standards growers must drench their crops in a seemingly endless array of chemical sprays. As many as 80 per cent of pesticides applied to fruit and vegetable crops are used simply for cosmetic reasons.

Having worked in conventional agriculture and horticulture, Alan Schofield knew this was not the sort of husbandry he wanted to be part of. He had learned first-hand how on a big arable farm it was possible to spray 600 acres in a single day. He had also been part of a strawberry-growing enterprise where the sheer volume of chemical sprays resulted in a quarter of casual fruit pickers leaving within one week because of allergic reactions. At Bradshaw Lane Nursery things were going to be very different.

When Alan Schofield bought his three-and-a-half acres of exposed but fertile land it had one great advantage. The previous owner had planted five lines of grey alder trees to split up the block and provide shelter from the winds that come whistling in from the Irish Sea. Alan had another purpose in mind for the shelterbelts. They and the grassland beneath them were to be left uncultivated; they were to become small wildlife areas, harbouring the natural insect predators that would control pests in the adjoining vegetable crops.

The biological pest control clearly works. Pest damage is minimal at Bradshaw Lane Nursery. Grey alders are known to harbour some species of aphid, yet susceptible crops like lettuces are never infested, even when grown alongside. Ladybirds and other beetles control aphid numbers so there are never enough present to harm the crop.

The vegetables are grown on nine quarter-acre plots, each separated from the adjoining plot by the 'wildlife break'. Crop diseases are kept under control by a strict crop rotation, combined with scrupulous cultivations aimed at burying crop wastes. Soil nutrients are introduced in the form of composted stable manure or as 'green manures', crops like wheat or rye which are sown in the autumn, then ploughed in the following spring to add organic matter to the soil. No chemical fertilisers are ever used.

The Schofields have one other method of pest control – a small flock of bantam hens and muscovy ducks. In winter the fowl have the run of the plots, and also of the glasshouses. They are particularly adept at tracking down slugs. Up to a quarter of Little Gem lettuces grown under glass used to be subject to slug damage, but the bantam patrols have virtually eliminated it. Such methods hold little appeal for crop technologists, fixated as they are on high-tech solutions. Yet they are both effective and sustainable, for they recognise the reality of farming as a biological and not an industrial process.

With no chemicals used, the wildlife flourishes at Bradshaw Lane Nursery. In winter the alder breaks with their wild grasses around them provide seed for flocks of goldfinch. In summer they provide insects for the swallows and a perch for the marsh harrier. The holding is bordered on two sides with dykes, and each spring the banks blaze with the bright marsh marigold. In a landscape still dominated by intensive arable fields and ryegrass monoculture the Schofields' three-and-a-half acres stand out as a oasis of wildlife.

They are putting into effect a truth that seems all too apparent to them, but which continues to elude the politicians – a living countryside will provide both safe food and a rich environment. If properly looked after, the land will deliver everything we ask of it. However, the mind of Whitehall remains fixed on the industrial model of food production, despite its all too obvious failures. Increasingly, organic growers are turning their backs on the supermarkets with their insistence on central buying and a standard product. Instead they are selling direct to the public.

Vegetable box schemes like that developed by the Schofields are springing up all round Britain. By the end of 1995 more than seventy were in operation, together accounting for 35 per cent of UK-grown organic produce. They are receiving an enthusiastic reception from a growing army of consumers worried about the safety of the food in their local retail stores. The result is a new alliance between growers and consumers. It is an alliance which some believe has the power to restore the British countryside.

Held in the straitjacket of the CAP, governments seem powerless to halt the deadly advance of industrial agriculture. As a palliative they introduce hasty conservation schemes to recreate remnants of what has been lost. Most are destined to fail. At best they produce pale imitations of past glories, an ersatz countryside. However, organic farmers are developing their own, more radical solutions to the present political paralysis. They work at the local level and they are based on the spirit of entrepreneurial enterprise.

The quiet village of Godmanstone hugs the River Cerne as it meanders slowly through the rolling chalk hills of Dorset. Near the centre of the village stands the stone farmhouse of Manor Farm, home of farmers Will and Pam Best. Each year in early autumn their big, homely kitchen becomes the venue for an evening of feasting and laughter, the annual harvest supper. This is no imitation, no faked tradition laid on for the amusement of weekenders and retired bankers from the Home Counties. This is a genuine celebration of the earth's bounty by the people who helped to gather it in.

The village of Godmanstone is not an inappropriate place for an event so reminiscent of Thomas Hardy. It lies at the heart of Hardy's Wessex. Just north of here Tess of the D'Urbervilles passed by on her epic walk to Beaminster. A few miles along the road stands the village of Cerne Abbas, Hardy's 'Abbot's Cernel'. The fourteenth-century tithe barn at Cerne Abbas abbey was thought to have been the model for the great barn in *Far from the Madding Crowd*, the scene of much uninhibited revelry.

Were Hardy writing today he would find few such gatherings of rural working people. For as the sheep and the ancient grazings have gone from these sombre chalk downs, so have the village communities that peopled them. These empty hills are now clothed in mile upon mile of regimented cereals, grown for the subsidy. Hardly anyone works this land any more. There is no one left to throw a party for, except at Manor Farm, Godmanstone, that is.

When Will and Pam Best turned their backs on industrial farming they were casting a vote for rural communities as well as for the environment. Instead of continuous arable cropping they adopted a traditional mixed-farming system, with dairy cows and sheep as well as cereal crops. Most of their 270 acres of chalk downland are in a rotation with three-year clover leys as well as winter and spring-sown cereals. Fertility for growing the grain comes not from a bag of artificial fertiliser, but from the nitrogen-fixing properties of the clover and the manuring of cows and sheep.

Like most organic farmers the Bests are market orientated. They have to be. Since they are not using pesticides and fertilisers to extract every last pound of production from their soils, they have to make the most they can from their lower-yielding but high-value crops. So the wheat grains go for stone-grinding into premium quality flour; the straw is sold for thatching; and the milk is cartoned on the farm for marketing through a specialist co-op to supermarkets and wholefood shops. This is where the people come in.

Organic farming is intrinsically more labour-intensive than industrial farming. Pesticides and fertilisers replace staff that would otherwise be needed for rotations and the cultivations that support them. So by abandoning chemical farming the Bests were, in a single step, creating jobs. But by adding value to their products they were creating still more. Milk cartoning creates the equivalent of two full-time jobs. The harvesting of winter wheat with a traditional binder so as to recover the straw for thatching provides casual work for a whole team of students. So does the task of threshing the crop later in the year.

In total Manor Farm employs four full-time staff, two part-timers and a host of seasonal staff. That's what makes the annual harvest supper a genuine celebration. A return to real farming is helping to put life back into an ailing community. It is also putting life back into the fields and the hedgerows.

Walk across these gentle downland slopes on a bright spring morning and you will see a small fragment of a landscape that Hardy himself would have recognised. A bunch of ewes and lambs are folded on a clover-rich pasture. Alongside them drifts of flowering blackthorn dapple the unshorn hedge, while beyond the dairy herd grazes placidly across a meadow flecked with yellow flowering dandelions. This is no easy farming option. It demands an intimate knowledge of land and soil type, the skilled integration of growing crops and grazing livestock so that both will thrive. Success does not depend on a chemical 'fix' but on the husbanding of natural resources, the management of complex ecosystems.

For those with the necessary skills the rewards are not inconsiderable. Though yields are lower than on high-input systems the value of the products can be considerably higher. Thanks to thatching straw and a premium price for their milling wheat, Will and Pam Best can expect a gross return approaching £1,000 an acre for their winter cereal crops. This would be a match for any conventional grower. However, the risks are greater, too. When a husbandry error leads to a weed explosion in a crop there is no easy recourse to the spray can. Organic farmers must live with the consequences of their mistakes.

At Manor Farm a good harvest brings benefits for the entire village community. The Bests prefer to spend their money providing jobs for local people, not on swelling the profits of the agrochemical industry. They also produce a range of other 'goods' that don't show up on the balance sheet.

In the spring sunshine finches and yellowhammers fill the untrimmed hedgerows; skylarks climb in the clear air. Bluebells and primroses grow in profusion among the coppiced hazel of a steep ash hanger. This is a vibrant, living countryside, one that contrasts sharply with the ordered blocks of industrial wheat now covering so much of the chalk downland.

Will Best reflects wistfully on the transformation of the Dorset landscape. He recalls that as a Cambridge student reading agriculture in the 1960s he witnessed the early manifestations of farming's subsidy-driven industrialisation. He and fellow students were taken to see continuous cereal-growing on heavy Essex clays. This was to be the farming of the future. And now the future has come to Hardy's Wessex. Will Best views it not as progress, but as an aberration.

His wish is to see the entire country return to a sustainable, organic system of farming, providing safe food and a place in the countryside for both people and wildlife, but until the support system is demolished even a modest shift towards organic farming seems unlikely. While taxpayers continue to underwrite environmental pollution, job losses, habitat destruction and the chemical contamination of food crops, organic farmers will always be at a disadvantage to those who seek an easy life.

Why go to the trouble of mixed farming when all you have to do is sow the crops that carry most subsidy, spray whenever the crop consultant recommends it, then collect both a fat subsidy and a high price for selling onto a buoyant commodity market? Of course, if the true environmental and health costs were ever charged to the high-input farmer, organic producers would be revealed as the genuinely efficient farmers they are. Until that day their numbers will remain small.

On a breezy Cornish clifftop Charlotte and Mark Russell move a bunch of two-year-old South Devon bullocks across the tight, herb-rich sward. Beyond them the furze-topped headland of Pencarrow reaches into a shining blue ocean. For the Russells there is no time to admire the view. With a young family to support, getting started in farming was never going to be easy, not even on a conventional farm. But they have chosen to convert their first farm to an organic system, and in a world that loads the economic dice in favour of land exploiters, they knew they were setting themselves a tough challenge.

Since 1993 Charlotte and Mark have been the tenants of Churchtown Farm, Lanteglos, a 320-acre National Trust holding close to the Fowey estuary. It is an idyllic place, with a rambling Cornish stone farmhouse nestling under the hill that protects it from the Atlantic gales. But it is not well equipped for livestock – there are too few buildings and the fencing is inadequate. For new tenants with limited capital the obvious policy would have been to plough up a large part of the farm and sow it to the cash crops attracting the biggest subsidies. It is a guaranteed way to profit.

Standing on the Russells' high clifftop pasture it is easy to see many other farmers who have taken just that route. Industrial arable production has redrawn the rural landscape even in the far south-west. Everywhere grassland has gone from the traditional mixed farms. In its place grow cereal crops or the even more heavily subsidised oilseeds, flax and linseed. In Cornwall's warm, moist maritime climate arable crops are at greater risk from disease than those grown further east. Intensive cropping is sustainable only with the aid of heavy fungicide inputs. So the county's landscape and wildlife take a heavy battering from pesticides.

It is not a system the Russells would contemplate. Mark himself grew up on a conventional arable farm in Wiltshire. He has seen the damage wrought by industrial agriculture both to the landscape and the quality of food. This was enough to convince him that organic farming was the only system that would feed the nation safely while safeguarding what remained of its countryside. That's why, whatever the inducements of the subsidy system, Churchtown Farm now produces high-quality beef and lamb from its flower-rich pastures beside the sea.

To protect the clifftop landscape the Russells have returned half the land to permanent pasture. Though the taxpayer may offer cash to plant crops to the very cliff edge, they are convinced this dramatic and beautiful coast, the haunt of guillemots and the soaring peregrine, should be edged with species-rich grassland. The rest of the land is in a rotation with red clover leys and cereals like triticale and oats, the pattern of mixed farming that once gave the British countryside its rich wildlife heritage.

While the pesticide-ridden farms inland are rapidly driving out their birds, the corn stubbles and hedgerows at Churchtown are filled with linnets, yellowhammers and finches. Whitethroats and black-caps flit among the briars and brambles, while meadow pipits nest in the rough grazings. Barn owls hunt the twilight hedge banks.

There are no special subsidies on hedges that teem with finches or on skies filled with larksong. Most of the support goes to those who rob the countryside of such things. Under the government's Country-side Stewardship scheme Charlotte and Mark Russell are able to claim a subsidy for putting their coastal fields back to grassland. But it provides nothing like the income they could earn by growing arable crops from the list of those supported by the EU. Not that it matters much to them. They choose to farm organically because they have no wish to abuse the land, no matter what the financial inducement. Even so they are optimistic about the future.

Charlotte is convinced that consumer pressure will change the pattern of UK farming, bringing an end to the post-war period of damage and destruction. Though she does not expect to see a universal adoption of organic methods on UK farms, the more chemically intensive systems will be dismantled. Even conventional farmers will move to a more sustainable system, with a greater reliance on rotations and mixed farming, so reducing their depend-ence on chemical fertilisers and pesticides.

Lamb and beef from Churchtown Farm are currently sold through a farm shop near Totnes in Devon. When the farm becomes fully organic, a holder of the Soil Association symbol, its products will begin to command a full premium price. The Russells are counting on it being high enough to keep them economically viable, despite their lower output. Meanwhile their Vendeen ewes and rich red Devon and South Devon cattle will continue to graze their clifftop pastures. In a county fast converting to 'agribusiness' they stand out like a beacon to the yachts passing by on their way to Fowey and Falmouth. There is another way to farm this land.

13

A LIVING COUNTRYSIDE

Strange though it may seem, farmers rarely give a thought to the nutritional quality of the food they sell. It is not their concern. They choose to think of themselves as efficient commodity producers, searching out new ways of reducing costs and increasing margins, running tight businesses. The proposition that they should worry about how to produce healthier, more nutritious products would leave most of them somewhat bemused. This is, after all, a matter for government. The role of the farmer is to strive for maximum profit advantage within the rules laid down by the politicians, nothing more.

Arable growers attending the 1995 annual conference of *Crops* magazine had every reason to feel content with the world. They were reaching the end of another vintage season. With a bumper cereal crop safely in the barn, profits were up for the third year in a row, and world prices were powering ahead as if unstoppable. The prospects looked rosier than for years. A good moment, one might think, to reflect on the benefits, if any, to consumers. What was the quality of food they provided? What impact were their methods making on the British countryside and wildlife?

Yet scarcely once during the entire conference was there any mention of food, still less of the environment. For this was a gathering of business people. Their talk was of investment decisions, performance indices and competitive advantage. There was a junior minister from MAFF to warn of impending changes to the Common Agricultural Policy. An agrochemicals specialist told them how, by adjusting their inputs, they might swell the ranks of the prestigious 'top ten club' of high profit earners.

A leading grain trader outlined strategies for attacking world grain markets, while a scientist from ADAS provided a glimpse into the futuristic world of biotechnology. No one appeared remotely concerned with how to eliminate organophosphorus residues from wheat, or how to make their products safer. Nor was there any debate on how the countryside might be made a less polluted place. It was the kind of profit-focused conference that might have been held by any industry anywhere. Except that this one happened to be favoured with £10 billion a year in public support.

Public subsidies make farmers responsible for nothing. They may destroy the life of a stream with their nitrates and wipe out the song-bird population of a parish with insecticides, then afterwards claim it was not their fault. After all, it is the government which licenses such products for general use. Farmers cannot be blamed when they cause damage, any more than they can be blamed when their cattle feeds spark a disease epidemic. It is the responsibility of others, just as it will be if organophosphates on carrots or isoproturon in drinking water are one day discovered to be harmful.

In this way farmers behave no differently from those other businesses; they are motivated chiefly by profit. Public support does not make them socially responsive. On the contrary, it allows them to shrug off any responsibility for their actions. Society must guarantee their incomes yet not hold them accountable when things go wrong. This, more than anything, is why it is time to end the subsidies.

The usual response of the National Farmers' Union to any such proposal is to threaten dire consequences for the countryside. For half a century too many farmers have plundered the land in their bid to maximise subsidy income. Now they would have us believe that by scrapping such artificial incentives we would unleash a worse destruction. With the support taken away the urge to survive in a competitive market would drive them to pull out every last hedge, to spray right to the very edge of the field, so the argument goes. However, it has little basis in reason.

The evidence is that while some limited intensification might take place, the overall effect of a free market for food would be a reduction in farming pressure. This is not to say that every specialist arable farm on good land would abandon continuous cropping. Clearly it would not happen everywhere, particularly in eastern England. Even before the era of subsidies many farmers on the 'prairie' lands of East Anglia had tied their fortunes to the international wheat price. When the world trading climate was buoyant they prospered; when the global market foundered, as in the

1920s, they suffered the same fate as growers in Canada and the United States.

Even without public support these specialists are likely to continue in much the same way. Many have already reduced their costs to a level that would make them internationally competitive. In 1995 the contract farming company Sentry Farming claimed to have recorded its lowest ever cost for producing a ton of wheat.[1] Yet even in the intensive arable areas there would be environmental benefits. Without the safety net of subsidies farmers are likely to be far more frugal in their use of pesticides and fertilisers, particularly if the strong world prices of the mid-1990s are not sustained.

Elsewhere in the country, in those lowland areas where continuous arable production has always been a marginal occupation, the removal of public support would bring huge and immediate environmental gains. Without subsidies farmers would have no option but to return to grazing or to mixed farming systems, with crops and livestock rotating round the same land. Such a change would transform the countryside.

With fewer chemicals applied to the land, wildlife would begin to return. As invertebrate populations grew, so would the numbers of farmland birds – the lapwings, fieldfare and grey partridges. Once-familiar arable flowers would start to reappear in corn crops, while seed-eating finches would re-populate the hedgerows. Freed from the tyranny of intensification, the countryside could begin to breathe again.

Such environmental benefits were recognised by William Waldegrave's CAP review group.[2] They concluded that a cut in production-related support would reduce the overall use of agrochemical inputs and lead to 'some arable land reverting to extensive livestock grazing'. In hill areas there was likely to be a reduction in grazing intensity. But the group warned that there might be negative environmental effects, too. Their worry was that a fall in farm incomes combined with a reduced labour force might mean less care of hedges, stone walls and woods.

This latter view seems unduly pessimistic. The ending of subsidies would lead to a steep fall in land prices. Far from pushing people off the land, the result would be an opening up of the countryside to new small-scale and part-time land-using enterprises, particularly if they were allowed to compete on an equal footing with industrial-scale producers. As part of a comprehensive rural renewal package, reform of farm support might actually increase the population of the countryside. There could be more people, not less, to look after the hedges and woods.

What the Minister's review team looked at in theory one country has applied in practice. In 1984 the New Zealand government decided that its farm subsidies were unsustainable and announced a programme to end them.[3] In the following years fertiliser subsidies were abolished along with investment and land development concessions. All capital grants and input subsidies were removed, and interest concessions on farm loans and agricultural producer board accounts were phased out. By 1990 public support for farming had been virtually eliminated.

One of the principal results was a substantial fall in land prices. In 1995 the value of farmland stood at 78 per cent of its 1982 peak level. The price of land in New Zealand now reflects the market value of its output, not the capitalised value of public support programmes. As a result aspiring young New Zealand farmers have a realistic opportunity to get started in their chosen profession, an opportunity that has scarcely existed for decades. Yet despite the pain of readjustment few farmers were actually forced to leave the land. Lurid predictions of imminent rural collapse failed to materialise.

The reforms brought immediate and lasting benefits to the countryside. Lower returns encouraged farmers to adopt less intensive production methods. Fewer fertilisers and pesticides were applied and less fossil fuel used in the growing of farm crops. By the mid-1990s rising world prices had led to some recovery in pesticide use, but at least this was in response to market demand, not to the artificial stimulus of subsidies. Had the support system remained in place the levels used would have been still higher.

Overall there is now less specialisation in New Zealand agriculture, with a much-reduced area of monoculture. The landscape is more attractive, with a greater diversity of wildlife. Sheep numbers have fallen dramatically – from 70 million to 46 million – reducing the overgrazing of hill areas. Forestry planting has increased, and marginal land, together with the land most vulnerable to erosion, has been removed from production altogether. With the shackle of subsidies removed, the New Zealand landscape is beginning to live again.

Yet in Britain the farming and landowning lobbies continue to warn of environmental disaster should such policies be introduced here. From the Country Landowners' Association comes the threat that even a partial reduction in farm support would have 'a major negative impact on both the environment and economies of rural areas'.[4] Although the CLA accepts that EU agriculture should become more competitive on world markets, it wants all current production subsidies converted to acreage payments, as under the present Arable Area Scheme. Farmers would continue to be paid these 'decoupled' subsidies, at least until new schemes were in place to reward them for looking after the countryside or for producing industrial crops.

In other words, the bureaucratic stranglehold on rural Britain would be prolonged. Farmers would continue to be paid simply for being farmers. The very people who industrialised the British countryside would go on being rewarded from the public purse for no other reason than that they occupied it. Land prices would remain at inflated levels. The countryside would remain closed and barred at a time when the real need is for new blood and fresh thinking, for people untainted by the ideology of industrial agriculture.

More than anything else, farming now needs a new ethic, a new culture, or rather, a new *old* culture. It must rediscover systems of rotation and mixed farming, methods of producing food that no longer rely on chemical fertilisers and pesticides. Not a harking back to a dog-and-stick agriculture, but a looking forward to a tractor-powered, computer-controlled, twenty-first-century agriculture which recognises the simple scientific fact that biological processes, not industrial processes, are the only ones capable of delivering safe, wholesome food and a safe, living countryside.

An ending of price support would set agriculture back on the right track, unleashing a small army of rural entrepreneurs seeking low-cost, sustainable alternatives to wasteful and damaging chemical methods. Yet it would be naive to imagine that this alone will lead to a renewal of the British countryside. Specialist arable growers on fertile soils in East Anglia are likely to maintain their destructive systems. While the demand for grain from China and the Far East keeps world prices buoyant, the big cereal barons will not easily give up their monocultures. However, there is no reason why the rest of us should pay to clear up the mess.

Britain's intensive arable farmers have made themselves competitive by standardising the landscape so that it resembles the American prairies. They have reduced their costs by using the environment as a dumping ground for chemical residues. As a result the people of Britain are obliged to pay higher water charges to cover the cost of removing nitrates and pesticides from their drinking water supplies. This is an external cost of industrial agriculture.

Studies in the United States have begun to identify and unravel such costs. It has long been assumed, for example, that each dollar invested in pesticides returns four in crops saved. However, Professor David Pimentel has identified a further two dollars' worth of hidden environmental and socio-economic costs, including the treatment of pesticide-induced cancers, the loss of honeybees and wild birds, and the cost of monitoring for pesticide residues.[5]

At University College, London, Professor David Pearce has proposed environmental taxes to counter the damage caused by intensive farming.[6] Depending on the price elasticity of such inputs as pesticides and fertilisers, environmental taxes would be introduced to discourage their use. For pesticides the benefits would be immediate. For fertilisers they would be less so since nitrate pollution is more the result of past runoff than of current practices. Even so, environmental taxes would raise revenues which could then be used for environmental improvement. They would also encourage organic farming and other forms of low-input production.

In 1986 the Danish environmental protection agency embarked on an ambitious programme to reduce pesticide use by half, a target which it achieved within a decade. The chosen measures, intended both to safeguard public health and to protect the environment, included taxes on pesticide use by farmers.[7] In 1996 a second generation of taxes was introduced at the rates of 13 per cent for herbicides and fungicides, and 27 per cent for insecticides.[8] The more environmentally damaging the product, the higher the tax. It is a principle that ought now to be adopted in Britain. For too long taxpayers have subsidised large farmers and the agrochemical industry, at the expense of chemical-free organic production.

Arriving at a tax rate to cover the cost of cleaning up water supplies is a matter of simple arithmetic. However, there would need to be an additional component to allow for environmental degradation. When grassland farmers smother their fields in nitrate fertilisers they destroy most of the wild species that live there. Cereal growers who apply a late-season spray of organophosphorus insecticide may be eliminating a link in the wildlife food chain for years to come, as well as adding an unwelcome contaminant to a food crop.

Surely this kind of environmental damage should incur a charge? Until it does, organic farmers will continue to be disadvantaged. By allowing space for wild flowers and butterflies, birds and mammals, they provide a service to the community. They enrich our lives, not just aesthetically, but with clear water, clean air and uncontaminated soils. For too long we have penalised them for their custodianship of the countryside. Assigning monetary penalties for environmental damage may not be easy, but that is no reason for failing to try.

An end to subsidies, both overt and hidden, would breathe new life into the British countryside. Many environmentalists argue that the current production subsidies should be redirected into land management schemes which reward farmers for restoring and safeguarding the landscape. The EU Commission is considering making CAP support more dependent upon enrolment in 'voluntary' environmental schemes. Professor David Pearce has himself advocated direct payments for positive environmental outputs alongside his taxes on damaging 'negative outputs'.[9]

Clearly an end to subsidies for growing wheat or oilseed rape will not, in itself, make good a damaged hedge or create a wildflower meadow. But all forms of subsidy are eventually capitalised into land values. This is what would happen to new environmental subsidies, just as it has with existing conservation management schemes. Land prices are inflated, thereby adding to the production pressures on farms where there is no special wildlife protection. The deadly cycle of over-capitalisation is once more ratcheted up. The countryside remains clamped in its bureaucratic headlock.

While grants for the replacement of lost hedgerows can only benefit the countryside, the introduction of blanket subsidies for conservation management would do no more than protect the investment of today's landowners. At the same time they would stifle renewal and change. Agriculture badly needs new entrants to work alongside those who have spent their lives farming the subsidy system. New blood will supply the vigour and creative energy to reinstate biological farming in a modern form. But until the bloated capital base of today's chemical farming is reduced there will be no opportunity for new entrants to get started.

Landowning lobbyists have long argued that a free market would ruin agriculture. They raise the spectre of the depressed 1890s when railways and refrigerated transport brought cheap food flooding into Britain from New Zealand, Australia and the prairie lands of North America. But as Northern Foods chairman Christopher Haskins has argued, such a scenario is unlikely to be repeated today.[10] The world has become a very different place.

In the nineteenth century potential farm output, particularly in North America, far exceeded the demand from those who were in a position to pay. Many parts of the world suffered from hunger, but their governments could not afford to import food. Inevitably world prices were weak. However, in the twenty-first century the emerging nations of south-east Asia are likely to be both short of food and wealthy enough to pay for imports. While world grain prices may not remain at the high levels of the mid-1990s, there seems little prospect of a rapid return to global surplus.

Whatever happens on the world stage, UK farmers possess one priceless asset – a market of 55 million people within a few hours' driving time. For the overwhelming majority of British farmers long-term security will rest on their success in supplying the people of these islands with fresh, safe and nutritious food from a diverse and living countryside. World commodity markets are for a few large specialists. Most farmers have little to lose and everything to gain from helping their urban neighbours to rediscover the benefits and pleasures of 'real' food.

The change need not prevent them from earning a good living. The ground-breaking 'LIFE' research project, developed at Long Ashton near Bristol, has shown how pesticide inputs can be cut dramatically without loss of profit, so long as sound crop rotations are followed.[11] Research into organic farming systems is equally convincing. The Ministry of Agriculture's own organic farming unit suggests that, even under a subsidy system which favours chemical farming, some dairy and mixed farms would make more profit by switching to organic methods.[12] Given a free market and a taxation system that charged polluters the full cost of environmental damage, organic farming would thrive.

Freed from the strait-jacket of subsidies and state control, farmers would become entrepreneurs again. For the first time in half a century they might begin to take an interest in the national diet. No one is better placed than the farming community to break the British public of their dangerous predilection for processed foods. And no one has a greater incentive for doing so. A growing taste for fresh, unprocessed foods will cut the toll of degenerative diseases and return a bigger share of the 'profit pie' from a £50-billion food market to the primary producer.

Farmers and growers are in a position to transform the national diet. Collectively they could take on the food technologists: the starch extruders, the flavour enhancers and the fat hydrogenators. They might also persuade the supermarkets to begin selling pesticide-free foods, locally sourced. By trucking their produce halfway round the country and, worse, halfway round the world, the major multiples choke the life from the countryside and its communities. Should the supermarkets fail to respond, farmers could begin building new regional marketing structures to supply local shops and community groups.

Britain badly needs more local food processing enterprises: small, rurally based firms making cheeses, dairy products, speciality meats and the like. For too long food processing has been dominated by a handful of large multinationals whose global sourcing of agricultural raw materials has done much to impoverish the landscape as well as human diets. Food processing needs to return to where it started – on the farms, in the villages and in the market towns of a living British countryside; not for reasons of ideology, but for the sake of healthy diets and a healthy environment.

Ultimately the renewal of the landscape will be consumer-led. It will depend on a new appreciation of naturally produced foods, on a re-evaluation of the fresh and the locally grown or locally processed. It will mean shoppers making greater demands of supermarkets and, when they cannot find what they want, seeking out farm shops and wholefood outlets. It will require nothing less than a revolution in the way we think about food. No one has more to gain from helping to ignite such a revolution than farmers.

Thus the move to a safe, sustainable system of food production promises real benefits for the majority of producers. But what will be the gains for citizens at large? No doubt many would consider healthy food and a renewed, living countryside as goals worth pursuing in themselves. Yet if the abandonment of industrial agriculture were to place a crippling burden on consumers, some might consider the price too high. Fortunately evidence suggests that a move to a safer, more rational farming system would cost no more in the shops than the hazardous and damaging methods we practise today.

The New Zealand experience provides a pointer. When the country scrapped farm subsidies in the late 1980s there were immediate and lasting benefits for its citizens. By 1993 the price paid to dairy farmers was less than half the heavily subsidised EU milk price, while New Zealand beef farmers received a little more than one-third of the EU price. At a time when European taxpayers and consumers were paying every full-time farmer in the Community £10,000 in subsidy, New Zealand citizens were spending virtually nothing on farm support. Yet they enjoyed the benefits of higher-quality food and a safer, less polluted environment.

By happy coincidence a policy change to end the destruction of wildlife and the landscape will, at the same time, reduce food prices in the shops. Outside New Zealand, most countries continue to provide substantial levels of support for their farmers. In aggregate these have the effect of depressing world prices while keeping those to domestic consumers artificially high. In his European balance sheet Professor Patrick Minford estimates the consumer cost of the Common Agricultural Policy at about £6.5 billion.[13] This amounts to about 14 per cent of total consumer spending on food for home consumption. Clearly an end to farm price support would lead to a substantial reduction in food prices.

William Waldegrave's CAP Review Group tried to estimate exactly how far European food prices might fall following a world-wide axing of farm subsidies.[14] Based on OECD and other figures they suggest that farmgate prices for such products as sugar, butter and beef might go down by as much as 30 per cent, while those for cereals, sheepmeat and pigmeat could decline by 10 to 15 per cent. The unilateral ending of agricultural support by the EU alone could lead to even greater reductions.

The National Consumer Council is more cautious in its estimates. It assesses the overall impact of the CAP on food prices at between 5 and 10 per cent.[15] However, the impact on individual commodities may be far higher. For example, EU tariffs on imported foods effectively add a tax of 13p a kilo on sugar, 24p on a 250gm pack of butter, 60p a pound on beef and 48p a pound on tomatoes.[16]

How far the ending of farm support might reduce prices in the shops is more problematical. The cost of the basic raw materials is only one component in the retail price of processed foods. On average, processing, marketing and distribution costs now account for half the shop price.[17] What is unarguable is that the scrapping of farm subsidies will lead to smaller bills at the check-out. A policy to save the countryside will save money for shoppers, too.

The removal of price support is only part of the programme to detoxify food and restore the British countryside. Equally important is the introduction of a tax on environmental damage, the 'input tax'. While the ending of subsidies will have the effect of reducing prices, the application of the 'polluter pays' principle will tend to push them up. For the first time it will charge some of the real costs of industrial farming to the industrial farmer. So the prices of industrially produced foods will go up, while those of sustainably grown organic foods, which now seem expensive, will begin to seem more reasonable.

Even ignoring the distortions of the subsidy system, the current price of most food remains bogus. It reflects only the more visible production and marketing costs, taking no account of a wide range of social and environmental costs which are paid for by society at large. When the supermarket chains truck fresh produce halfway across the country from central buying depots to their retail stores, they are taking advantage of hidden transport subsidies underwritten by all of us.

When food retailers, manufacturers and marketing executives combine to give the British people the most unhealthy diet in the world, they rely on a publicly funded health service to clear up the mess. When dairy farmers turn flower-rich hay meadows into over-fertilised monocultures of ryegrass they expect the community at large to pay the 'cultural cost', to have their lives made poorer by the loss of a valued amenity. A mature economic system would encompass all such hidden costs. The imposition of an input tax on pesticides and fertilisers would fall far short of a complete solution, but it would at least make a start at addressing the problems.

In a food economy that takes no account of the true cost of industrial production, the price of organic food looks high. By the summer of 1996 there were just 860 organic producers in the UK. In part because of MAFF's dismissive view, the organic market has been under-supplied in almost every sector, particularly following the upsurge in demand which accompanied the BSE crisis. The supply shortfall exacerbated the price difference between organically produced and chemically produced foods, especially for some meats.

This is not to say that organic farming is in some way inherently inefficient. Rather the alternative industrial system of farming is permitted to offload many of its costs onto the wider community. In a real sense organic prices reflect the true cost of food production while those of conventional produce are discounted at the expense of wildlife, the countryside, animal welfare and food safety. This is the system of false accounting which input taxes, however falteringly, would begin to remedy.

Following a series of food scares, demand for organic produce is growing fast. Even after half a century of government neglect the potential market is far greater than could be supplied by today's handful of producers. Given a major expansion in organic production, prices and premiums should start to come down as processors and distributors take advantage of scale economies. Axing subsidies and making industrial farmers pay some of their own clean-up costs will narrow the price differential and encourage growing numbers of consumers to switch to organic produce.

Thus under a rational food system overall prices are likely to rise, though how fast and by how much is difficult to forecast. In June

1996 the average price premium on organically grown fruit and vegetables was estimated at 22 per cent.[18] Premiums on organically raised beef, lamb and pork averaged 10, 12 and 50 per cent at the farm gate,[19] while organically produced milk secured a premium of 11 per cent. These were price differentials ruling under a support system which severely disadvantaged organic farming. Price increases which result from industrial farmers being made to bear the full social and environmental costs of their activities are likely to be well below these figures.

In the shops differentials between organic and chemically produced foods are often higher than at the farm gate. On the small quantities of organic foods currently traded, processing and distribution costs are relatively high.

Against such higher prices must be set the gains resulting from the abandonment of farm subsidies. The CAP as currently structured costs UK consumers £6.5 billion a year. This would go a long way to offset the higher costs of a sustainable agriculture. In addition there is the £3.5 billion now paid direct to farmers by UK taxpayers. Some or all of this could be redirected to the less well-off in income support or even in food vouchers.

Any increase in food prices inevitably hurts the poorer members of society since they spend a higher proportion of their income at the check-out. Yet this is no justification for maintaining a hazardous and environmentally damaging agricultural system. No doubt there are many who would encounter real hardship in meeting the true cost of food. But to destroy the countryside in a bid to bring them some contaminated and nutritionally impoverished substitute is surely no answer. A more ethical solution would be to help them find the money to buy the real thing.

Given an economic framework flexible enough to encompass the full costs of industrial agriculture, there seems no reason why a safe, sustainable farming system should be any more expensive than the present destructive version. Our highly protected industrial agriculture gives an illusion of efficiency but fails to deliver real savings. It diverts and hides costs. It concentrates returns in the hands of a few. It manages in a unique way to be costly to almost everyone while satisfying almost no one.

Yet despite the mounting clamour for reform, nothing seems to change. At least as far as agriculture is concerned, Britain remains locked into a federal European state. Government repeats its familiar theme: there must be a more market-oriented, less bureaucratic Common Agricultural Policy. At the same time ministers claim there is no strong desire for change elsewhere in the Community. The government appears resigned to the CAP as the price Britain must pay for the benefits of a single market.

However, the stakes are far greater than £10 billion or so of misallocated resources. It is clear that the policy is costing us both our countryside and our health. A poisoned, lifeless landscape and a contaminated and ill-balanced diet – these are the true costs of the CAP as it is presently organised. The public may consider this price too high. At the time of writing there are those on both the political Right and the Left who would abandon the EU rather than accept monetary union. There must be many more who would rather abandon the CAP and repatriate British agriculture than consent to the final desolation of the nation's rural heartland.

Nevertheless some accommodation within the EU would be the best solution. Clearly, having dispensed with farm subsidies, Britain could no longer import food from those countries which continued to support their farmers. Nor, having rejected pesticides, could we import from countries which went on using them. Yet if Europe could be persuaded to move down a similar path there would be real advantages in making good the shortfall in domestic food production from across the Channel.

So how much of her own food could the UK produce by largely organic methods? If we were prepared to change to a more healthy diet, to eat more fruit and vegetables and view meat as a luxury food, we might, as now, produce three-quarters of it at home. But if we insist on meat at every main meal, then more of it will have to be imported. A free-trading, largely organically farmed Europe would be the favoured supplier. For the sake of global sustainability, for the sake of hungry nations whose land should be used to meet their own food needs, the objective should be to buy locally and, where this is not possible, to buy regionally.

For UK farmers the proportion of the home market supplied from domestic production is of no real consequence. What matters is the income they earn, not the volume of their output. Indeed, this has been one of the great deceits of modern, industrial farming: the idea that the well-being of farmers is somehow tied up with the amount they produce. UK farmers have doubled their output since the war, yet the profits have accrued to only a few. Most have been squeezed out of business, while those who remain are forced to run ever faster to stay in the race. The aim in future must be to produce nutritious, high-quality foods, then persuade consumers to pay the necessary price for them.

But can such radical changes really take place in an industry so innately conservative, one whose short-term interests are intimately bound up with the most powerful institutions of state? It is hard to guess. Certainly the BSE crisis has left much of the population in a state of bewilderment. There is a widespread sense that something is drastically wrong with the way we produce our food. On a more limited scale there is a feeling that the countryside is being severely damaged for no good reason. Yet the forces ranged against real reform are daunting.

First there is a general disbelief on the part of government that anything drastic needs to be done. The politicians make their ritual demands for reform, but what they have in mind is a tidying up at the edges, not the root and branch restructuring that is necessary. Since 1947 rural policy has been founded on the industrialisation of agriculture. The problems this has created cannot be remedied simply by fine tuning. The entire edifice is constructed upon a falsehood. The urban industrial model is simply an inadequate description of what is essentially a complex biological process. The post-war attempt to make farming fit the industrial mould was always doomed to fail.

Then there is the strength of the rural lobby to contend with. Though the NFU may not have the influence it enjoyed in the 1950s, the BSE crisis has shown that it remains a force to be reckoned with. When government ministers floundered in search of a beef policy following the collapse of the market in March 1996, it was the union that came up with the plan to remove cows over 30 months of age from the food chain, though the supermarkets subsequently insisted that the scheme be extended to beef cattle.

While the programme was being worked out it is widely held that Agriculture Minister Douglas Hogg maintained two open phone lines, one to the NFU and one to the Treasury. Following the EU summit in Florence in June 1996, there was a real possibility that serious farmer dissent over the agreed culling programme might bring down the government. In the event the NFU was surprisingly restrained in its criticism. The Conservatives remained in power and in the following weeks NFU president Sir David Naish was given unprecedented access to Prime Minister John Major. It seems likely that the union will continue to have the ear of government whatever the colour.

The CLA, too, remains a formidable obstacle to real reform in the countryside. At 50,000 its membership is tiny compared with those of other rural interest groups like the Ramblers, the Royal Society for the Protection of Birds and the National Trust. However, its members include some of the wealthiest and most powerful people in the land. For fifty years they have seen their assets inflated by income from the taxpayer. They will not stand quietly by as the support is withdrawn, although they are astute enough to recognise that it cannot continue to be tied to output.

Under its director-general, former MAFF Under Secretary Julian Anderson, the CLA has proved hugely influential in the shaping of rural policy. Conservative ministers are known to hold the organisation in high esteem. CLA lobbying is widely believed to have produced the government's 1995 Rural White Paper. Through the European Landowners' Organisation – in which it plays a leading role – the association is currently fighting proposals that would make farm support payments subject to environmental conditions and 'modulate' them in favour of small farms.

Further opposition to reform can also be expected from the food manufacturers. Though they would certainly welcome the ending of farm subsidies, a move which would reduce substantially their raw material costs, they would resist measures to reduce pesticide use and encourage the consumption of unprocessed foods. The leading players in the industry are the transnationals, many with incomes to match those of the smaller national economies. They have the resources to persuade governments through political lobbyists, and to persuade consumers through advertising. Having captivated consumers with the notion of food as show business, they will not willingly let them go.

Finally, farming politics are dominated by the agribusiness, an amorphous mass of companies big and small which somehow has managed to impose its industrial vision upon an activity fundamental to human life. The agri-technocrats deny the inviolability of biological cycles. For them all life processes can be reduced to simple, industrial models. Thus plant nutrition is nothing more than N, P and K, the three elements of compound fertiliser, with perhaps a little sulphur thrown in. All ecology is boiled down to a broad-spectrum organophosphate molecule.

They have convinced politicians that the yardsticks of business are the only useful measure of the worth of farming methods. Worse than this, they have convinced farmers that the earth will produce nothing unless it is constantly prodded and bombarded with an endless array of gadgets, machines and chemical compounds. They will not vacate their place of power without a fight.

During the past half century farm subsidies have nurtured a vast peripheral industry making everything from bale wrappers to silage additives. Any threat to support will be seen as a threat to them all. Any move towards a more sustainable biological system of agriculture will damage their sales. So they are certain to oppose it. The much-vaunted efficiency gains of industrial agriculture turn out to be nothing more than a sleight of hand. The people who have been removed from the land now work as fertiliser reps or assemblers in the factory making pesticide sprayers.

Though fewer than 2 per cent of the working population are employed in farming, as many as 14 per cent work in the peripheral industries and in food manufacturing. So every attack on industrial farming is portrayed in the media as an attack on jobs. Such are the sectional interests that would have to be overcome before farming could begin to meet the needs of the wider population.

Yet change it must. For too long it has been run largely on behalf of those interests. During the last war ICI convinced the Ministry of Agriculture that what suited the chemical industry was also in the interests of the British people. To this day farming has continued to operate on that same false assumption. It is in the thrall of an alien technology that will one day destroy it, perhaps sooner than we expect.

It remains the sobering fact that even in the age of global communications and the Internet, civilisation continues to depend on a few inches of topsoil for its very existence. The activity in and around that soil provides the material to sustain life and the environment to give it meaning. The earth is very forgiving of our abuse. But it will not forgive for ever.

There is another, more profound reason for reconstructing agriculture in the interests of the wider population. It is about giving the people of these islands a new sense of belonging, countering the mood of rootlessness, alienation and despair that pervades our city streets. Even for those of us who live in towns it is the land that sustains us, that makes us what we are. Equally it is our separation from the land, uniquely in Europe, which contributes so much to our feelings of isolation.

We need to re-establish our stake in the land, to renew our interest in our food, where it comes from and how it is produced. We need to rediscover our spiritual ownership of the countryside, its landscapes and wildlife. And through owning it we shall begin to understand once more what it means to be British. With the healing of the land will come our healing as a nation.

NOTES

1   THE GRIM REAPERS

1 Richard Jefferies, *The Story of My Heart: My Autobiography*, Longmans, 1883.
2 *Agricultural Policies, Markets and Trade: Monitoring and Outlook*, OECD, 1991.
3 Patrick Minford, *Britain and Europe: The Balance Sheet*, European *Business Review/New European*/Centre for European Studies, 1996.
4 Ibid.
5 *European Agriculture: The Case for Radical Reform: Conclusions*, Ministry of Agriculture, Fisheries and Food, 1995.
6 W. H. Hudson, *Nature in Downland*, Dent, 1932, p. 48.

2   THE DESERT IN OUR MIDST

1 Edith Holden, *The Country Diary of an Edwardian Lady*, Michael Joseph, 1977.
2 *Nature Conservation and Agriculture*, Nature Conservancy Council, 1977.
3 J. K. Bowers and Paul Cheshire, *Agriculture, the Countryside and Land Use: An Economic Critique*, Methuen, 1983, p. 100.
4 Sir E. John Russell, *English Farming*, Collins, 1941, p. 16.
5 Oliver Rackham, *The History of the Countryside*, Weidenfeld and Nicolson, 1995, p. 26.
6 H. P. Allen et al., 'Selective Herbicides', in F. C. Peacock (ed.), *Jealott's Hill: Fifty Years of Agricultural Research*, Imperial Chemical Industries Ltd, 1978.

7   Chris Rose, 'Pesticides: An Industry Out of Control', in *Green Britain or Industrial Wasteland?* Polity Press, 1986.

8   R. J. Fuller et al., 'Population Declines and Range Contractions among Lowland Farmland Birds in Britain', *Conservation Biology*, Vol. 9, No. 6, December 1995, pp. 1425–41.

9   Bob Press, *Field Guide to the Wild Flowers of Britain and Europe*, New Holland, 1993, p. 56.

10 N. W. Sotherton, 'Observations on the Biology and Ecology of the Chrysomelid Beetle *Gastrophysa polygoni* in Cereal Fields', in *Ecological Entomology*, Vol. 7, 1982, pp. 197–206.

11 G. R. Potts, *The Partridge: Pesticides, Predation and Conservation*, Collins, 1986.

12 Biodiversity: The UK Steering Group Report, Volume 1: 'Meeting the Rio Challenge', HMSO, 1995, p. 31.

13 W. H. Hudson, *Nature in Downland*, Dent, 1932, p. 22.

14 N. J. Aebischer, 'Twenty Years of Monitoring Invertebrates and Weeds in Cereal Fields in Sussex', in *The Ecology of Temperate Cereal Fields*, Blackwell Scientific Publications, 1991, pp. 305–31.

15 Miles R. Thomas, Central Science Laboratory, Pesticide Usage Survey, personal communication.

16 Biodiversity: The UK Steering Group Report, Volume 2: 'Action Plans', HMSO, 1995, p. 277.

17 A. Stewart et al. (eds), *Scarce Plants in Britain*, Peterborough: Joint Nature Conservation Committee, 1994.

18 A. Hopkins and J. J. Hopkins, 'UK Grasslands Now: Agricultural Production and Nature Conservation', in *Grassland Management and Nature Conservation*, British Grassland Society, 1993, pp. 10–19.

19 B. H. Green, 'The Impact of Agricultural Management Practices on the Ecology of Grasslands', in *Environmentally Responsible Grassland Management*, British Grassland Society, 1989, pp. 1.1–1.13.

20 D. Tilman et al., 'The Park Grass Experiment: Insights from the Most Long-term Ecological Study', in *Long-term Experiments in Agricultural and Ecological Sciences*, CAB International, 1994, pp. 287–303.

21 Jerry Tallowin, Owen Mountford and Francis Kirkham, 'Fertilisers on Haymeadows: A Compromise?' in *Enact: Managing Land for Wildlife*, Vol. 2. No. 3, Autumn 1994, pp. 15–17.

22 Charles Darwin, *On the Origin of Species by Means of Natural Selection*, John Murray, 1859, p. 85.

23 David Tilman, David Wedin and Johannes Knops, 'Productivity and Sustainability Influenced by Biodiversity in Grassland Ecosystems', in *Nature*, Vol. 379, 22 February 1996, pp. 718–20.

24 Neil M. Wyatt et al., *Wildlife Sites in Warwickshire*, Warwickshire Wildlife Trust, 1995.

3   THE NEW INHERITORS

1 *Real Choices*, discussion document of the National Farmers' Union, 1994, p. 38.
2 Farming Subsidies, *Hansard*, 21 June 1995, Column 239.
3 *European Agriculture: The Case for Radical Reform, Working Papers*, Ministry of Agriculture, Fisheries and Food, 1995, p. 37.
4 'A Record Year That May Not be Repeated', Deloitte and Touche Agriculture Press Release, 26 September 1996.
5 'Why Should Farmers Alone be Ashamed of Making Good Profits', *Farmers Weekly*, 11 August 1995, p. 5.
6 Jim Ward, 'Golden Acres', in *Savills Magazine*, Issue 41, Spring 1996.
7 Catherine Paice, 'BSE Crisis No Drag on a Super-buoyant Market', *Farmers Weekly*, 30 August 1996, p. 80.
8 Richard Body, *Farming in the Clouds*, Temple Smith, 1984, p. 40.
9 'Land Snapped Up by Farmers', Royal Institution of Chartered Surveyors Press Release, February 1996.
10 'Substantial Rise For Incomes Forecast', Smithfield Farmtech Daily, from *Farmers Weekly*, 26 November 1995, p. 1.
11 D. Gale Johnson, *Less than Meets the Eye*, Centre for Policy Studies, Rochester Paper 5, 1995.
12 Dick Potts, 'Cereal Farming, Pesticides and Grey Partridges', in *Farming Policies and Birds in Europe*, Academic Press, 1996.
13 '100hp-Plus Barrier Broken', Smithfield supplement in *Farmers Weekly*, 17 November 1995, p. S46.
14 Vincent Hedley Lewis, *Facing the Financial Facts*, Paper to the 49th Oxford Farming Conference, January 1995.
15 Sandy Mitchell, 'Are Contract Farmers Killing Rural Life', *Country Life*, 22 August 1996, p. 34.
16 K. R. Norman, *Arable Farming for Profit: 1994 Results*, Velcourt Group plc, Dorchester, 1994.
17 Vincent Hedley Lewis, op. cit.
18 Dr Julia Walsh, Chief Executive's Foreword, in *Agricultural Strategy*, ADAS, 1995.
19 'British Hedgerows Fall to Advance of Machines', *Daily Telegraph*, 30 December 1968, p. 15.
20 Bryn Green, 'Agricultural Overcapacity', in *The Non-Food Uses of Crops and Land*, National Farmers' Union/Friends of the Earth, 1993.

21 Jock Anderson, 'Food and Agriculture: A Global Perspective', CAS Paper 31, Reading University, 1995.

22 Lester Brown, *Who Will Feed China?: Wake-up Call for a Small Planet*, Earthscan Publications, 1995.

23 Chris Bourchier, 'European Agriculture – A Ten-Year Plan', in *Agricultural Strategy*, ADAS, 1995.

4 THE COUNTRYSIDE IN RANSOM

1 Ceri Evans et al., 'Water and Sward Management for Nature Conservation: A Case Study of the RSPB's West Sedgemoor Reserve', in *RSPB Conservation Review*, 1995.

2 Marion Shoard, *The Theft of the Countryside*, Temple Smith, 1980.

3 Chris Rose, 'Wildlife: The Battle for the British Countryside', in *The Environmental Crisis*, edited by Des Wilson, Heinemann Educational Books, 1984, pp. 22–55.

4 J. K. Bowers and Paul Cheshire, *Agriculture, the Countryside and Land Use*, Methuen, 1983, p. 13.

5 Oliver Rackham, *The History of the Countryside*, Weidenfeld and Nicolson, 1995, p. 28.

6 *Guidelines for Selection of Biological SSSIs*, Nature Conservancy Council, Peterborough, 1989.

7 T. A. Rowell, *SSSIs: A Health Check*, Report for Wildlife Link, 1991.

8 The Wildlife Trusts, Environmentally Sensitive Areas and other schemes under the Agri-Environment Regulation: Response to the House of Commons Agriculture Committee, May 1996.

9 M. Robins et al., *An Internationally Important Wetland in Crisis: The Somerset Levels and Moors: A Case History of Wetland Destruction*, Royal Society for the Protection of Birds, 1991.

10 J. Froud, 'The Impact of ESAs on Lowland Farming', *Land Use Policy 11* (2), 1994.

11 *European Agriculture: The Case for Radical Reform: Conclusions*, MAFF, 1995.

12 *Review of Arable Reversion Incentive Rates*, Countryside Commission, 1994.

13 C. Potter, 'Processes of Countryside Change in Lowland England', in *Journal of Rural Studies 2*, 1986.

14 R. Munton and T. Marsden, 'Occupancy Change and the Farmed Landscape: An Analysis of Farm-Level Trends 1970–85', *Environment and Planning*, 23, 1991.

15 Dick Potts, 'Extensification: Nearly Midnight', in *Review of 1995*, The Game Conservancy Trust, 1996, pp. 70–4.

5 NO FIGURES IN THE LANDSCAPE

1 *Agriculture in the United Kingdom: 1995*, HMSO, 1996.
2 *European Agriculture – The Case for Radical Reform: Working Papers*, MAFF, 1995, p. 37.
3 *Real Choices*, NFU, 1994, p. 38.
4 Cited in John Sumner, 'Dairy Strategy: Ensuring Business Viability', *Agricultural Strategy*, ADAS, 1995, p. 25.
5 'Rotary Brings a Revolution', *Farmers Weekly*, 3 November 1995, p. 66.
6 'Fewer Sites, All Updated, Money Saved', *Farmers Weekly*, 26 November 1993, p. 56.
7 'Dairy Producers' Dream Is Now a Reality', *Farmers Weekly*, 17 September 1993, p. 62.
8 Richard Body, *Agriculture: The Triumph and the Shame*, Temple Smith, 1982, p. 13.
9 Bruce Traill, 'The Effect of Price Support Policies on Agricultural Investment, Employment, Farm Incomes and Land Values in the UK', *Journal of Agricultural Economics*, Vol. 33 (3), 1982, pp. 369–85.
10 D. Gale Johnson, *Less than Meets the Eye. The Modest Impact of CAP Reform*, Centre for Policy Studies, 1995, p. 34.
11 D. J. Ansell and R. B. Tranter, *Set-aside: In Theory and in Practice*, Centre for Agricultural Strategy, 1992, p. 80.
12 *What Value Your Labour?*, Royal Agricultural Society of England/ Deloitte and Touche Agriculture, June 1996.
13 A. Errington, 'Developing Talents and Team Building', *Farm Management*, Volume 8 (3), Autumn 1992, pp. 101–10.
14 Andrew Errington and Ruth Gasson, 'The Increasing Flexibility of the Farm and Horticultural Workforce in England and Wales', *Journal of Rural Studies*, 1996.
15 Clive Potter and Matt Lobley, *Small Farming and the Environment*, RSPB, 1992, p. 19.

6 THE VIEW FROM THE HILLS

1 Roger Lovegrove, Michael Shrubb and Iolo Williams, *Silent Fields*, RSPB, 1995.

2   Oliver Tickell, 'Too Many Sheep Spoil the Heather', *New Scientist*, 10 February 1996, p. 9.

3   *Hansard*, 5 February 1996, Col. 57, cited in The Wildlife Trusts, Environmentally Sensitive Areas and Other Schemes Under the Agri-Environment Regulation: Response to the House of Commons Agriculture Committee, May 1996.

4   Tim Boswell, 'Farm Incomes', *Hansard*, 11 December 1995.

5   Richard Duffus, *Farmers as Park-Keepers*, paper to the Great North Meet Conference, 1996.

6   'Wildlife Consultant Backs Farmers in Fell Graze Row', *Farmers Weekly*, 18 October 1996, p. 16.

7   Kate Thorne, *The Story of the Long Mynd*, Kate Thorne, Churton House, Church Pulverbatch, Shropshire, 1994.

8   Tom Wall, 'The Red Grouse in Shropshire', *The Shropshire Naturalist*, Vol. 1:2, 1992.

9   The Wildlife Trusts, personal communication, February 1996.

10 M. Felton and J. Marsden, Heather Regeneration in England and Wales, Report to the Department of the Environment, English Nature, 1990.

11 *Hansard*, Vol. 268, Number 13, Column 56, 4 December 1995.

12 *Your Livestock and Your Landscape: A Guide to the Environmental Conditions Attached to Livestock Subsidy Schemes*, MAFF, 1996.

13 Response to *Your Livestock and Your Landscape*, The Wildlife Trusts, 1996.

14 Richard Duffus, op. cit.

15 Alan Barker, 'Dales ESA Scheme Faces 50 Per Cent Walkout', *Farmers Weekly*, 23 February 1996, p. 10.

16 *Hansard*, Column 810, 11 December 1995.

17 Professor Michael Haines, Director, Welsh Institute of Rural Studies, University of Wales, Aberystwyth, in *The Market for the Hills*, a paper to the Welsh Farming Conference, 1995.

18 Lord Lindsay, *The CAP and the Countryside: A Scottish Perspective*, speech to the 8th Congress of the European Association of Agricultural Economists, September 1996.

19 Geoffrey Sinclair, *Hill Livestock Compensatory Allowances in the Less-Favoured Areas of England and Wales*, research report to the RSPB, 1987.

20 Geoffrey Sinclair (ed.), *The Upland Landscapes Study*, Environment Information Services, 1983.

21 Guy Beaufoy et al., *The Nature of Farming*, Institute for European Environmental Policy, 1994, p. 60.

22 John Edwards, 'Exmoor Hill Farming', in Arthur Court (ed.), *The Wind of Change in Somerset*, Somerset NFU, 1990, pp. 203–11.

7   THE BIG WINNERS

1   'Tell Them All Loud and Clear Just How Good British Farmers Are', *Farmers Weekly*, 2 June 1995, p. 5.
2   A. T. Woodburn, 'The Market for Agrochemicals Past and Present', in *Proceedings of the Brighton Crop Protection Conference*, Vol. 1, pp. 121–8, British Crop Protection Council, 1995.
3   Howard Newby, 'The Social Shaping of Agriculture – Where Do We Go from Here?', the 3rd Annual Lecture of the Royal Agricultural Society of England, Stoneleigh, Warwickshire, 1993.
4   J. H. Orson, 'Crop Technology: A Flexible Friend for the Farmer and the Environment', in *Proceedings of the Brighton Crop Protection Conference*, Vol. 2, pp. 623–32, British Crop Protection Council, 1995.
5   *Rural England – A Nation Committed to a Living Countryside*, HMSO, 1995.
6   C. Thomas and J. W. O. Young, *Milk from Grass*, ICI Agricultural Division/Grassland Research Institute, undated.
7   *Hansard*, Vol. 185, No. 53, Col. 1019, 14 February 1991.
8   Zeneca Annual Report and Accounts, 1994.
9   British Agrochemicals Association, *Annual Review and Handbook*, 1995.
10 Peter Freeland, 'Safe and Effective Pesticides', in *Food For Life – Food Crops and Crop Protection*, British Agrochemicals Association, undated.
11 Kurt Kusgen, 'The Agrochemical Industry in 25 Years – Chances and Challenges', in *Proceedings of the Brighton Crop Protection Conference*, Vol. 1 pp. 137–41, British Crop Protection Council, 1995.
12 British Agrochemicals Association, *Annual Review and Handbook*, 1996, p. 10.
13 Dennis Avery, 'Sustainable Agriculture Won't Sustain People, Wildlife or Topsoil Warns Farming Expert', Press release on a speech to the American Association for the Advancement of Sciences, Hudson Institute, 10 February 1996.
14 British Agrochemicals Association, op. cit.
15 'Competition Highlights Hedge Husbandry Tips', in *Four Seasons*, Bayer, Vol. 17, No. 4, Winter 1996.
16 Philip Wilson and Nick Sotherton, *Field Guide to Rare Arable Flowers*, Game Conservancy Ltd, 1994.

17 LEAF – Linking Environment and Farming, Annual Review 1993/94, National Agricultural Centre, Stoneleigh, Warwickshire, 1995.

18 V. W. L. Jordan and J. A. Hutcheon, 'Economic Viability of Less-intensive Farming Systems Designed to Meet Current and Future Policy Requirements: 5-year Summary of the LIFE Project', in *Arable Farming under CAP reform: Aspects of Applied Biology* 40, Vol. 1, pp. 61–8, Association of Applied Biologists, 1994.

19 'Action Plan for Responsible Use of Pesticides', in *Rural England – A Nation Committed to a Living Countryside*, HMSO, 1995.

20 *European Agriculture – The Case for Radical Reform: Conclusions*, MAFF, 1995.

21 Kurt Kusgen, op. cit.

22 J. N. Pretty, 'Sustainable Agriculture in the 21st Century: Challenges, Contradictions and Opportunities', in *Proceedings of the Brighton Crop Protection Conference*, Vol. 1, pp. 111–20, British Crop Protection Council, 1995.

8   THE RICHES WE SQUANDERED

1 Dennis Avery, 'Sustainable Agriculture Won't Sustain People, Wildlife or Topsoil, Warns Farming Expert', press release on a speech to the American Association for the Advancement of Sciences, Hudson Institute, 10 February 1996.

2 H. J. Massingham, *The Wisdom of the Fields*, Collins, 1945, p. 138.

3 Ibid.

4 Susan Foreman, *Loaves and Fishes: An Illustrated History of the Ministry of Agriculture, Fisheries and Food 1889–1989*, MAFF, 1989.

5 Michael Winter, 'The State and the Farmer: Post-War Farm Policy', in *Rural Politics: Policies for Agriculture, Forestry and the Environment*, Routledge, 1996.

6 Geoffrey Browne, 'Economic Background', in *Progressive Farming Volume IV*, Caxton Publishing, 1949, pp. 171–207.

7 Michael Winter, op. cit.

8 Geoffrey Browne, op. cit.

9 Tristram Beresford, *We Plough the Fields*, Penguin, 1975, p. 46.

10 J. K. Bowers and Paul Cheshire, *Agriculture, the Countryside and Land Use*, Methuen, 1983, p. 116.

11 Tristram Beresford, op. cit., p. 46.

12 Michael Winter, op. cit.

13 Economic Development Committee for Agriculture (1968), *Agricul-*

ture's Import Saving Role, cited in J. K. Bowers and Paul Cheshire, op. cit., p. 77.

14 House of Commons Select Committee on Agriculture (1969), cited by J. K. Bowers and Paul Cheshire, op. cit., p. 77.

15 J. K. Bowers and Paul Cheshire, op. cit., p. 87.

16 Tristram Beresford, op. cit., p. 47.

17 J. G. S. and Frances Donaldson, *Farming in Britain Today*, Penguin, 1969, pp. 147–60.

18 George Henderson, *The Farming Ladder*, Faber and Faber, 1944.

19 Viscount Astor and Keith A. H. Murray, *Land and Life: The Economic National Policy for Agriculture,* Victor Gollancz, 1932, p. 77.

20 Richard Body, *Agriculture: The Triumph and the Shame*, Temple Smith, 1982, pp. 105–6.

21 H. J. Massingham, 'Planning Survey', in *The Faith of a Fieldsman*, Museum Press, 1951, pp. 143–5.

22 George Henderson, *Farmer's Progress*, Faber, 1950, p. 72.

23 'Prime Minister with a Link to the Land', *Farmers Weekly*, 20 May 1994.

9   A FAMINE AT THE HEART OF THE FEAST

1 Geoff Tansey and Tony Worsley, *The Food System*, Earthscan Publications, 1995, p. 112.

2 *Real Choices*, National Farmers' Union, 1994, p. 38.

3 Andrew Dare, speech to the conference 'Milk and the Market', Royal Bath and West of England Society, February 1996.

4 David C. Samworth, 'From Plough to Plate – Effective Manufacturing Links', paper given to the 49th Oxford Farming Conference, 1995.

5 'The Beefburger With No Meat', *Daily Star*, 16 April 1994.

6 'Diet, Nutrition and Chronic Disease', technical report of the World Health Organisation, 1991.

7 Tim Lang, 'The Public Health Impact of Globalisation of Food Trade', paper for the 6th Annual Public Health Forum: Diet, Nutrition and Chronic Disease: Lessons from Contrasting Worlds, London School of Hygiene and Tropical Medicine, 1996.

8 'The Scottish Diet', Report of the James Committee, Scottish Office Home and Health Department, Edinburgh: Scottish Office, 1993.

9 Sue Dibb and Andrea Castell, *Easy to Swallow, Hard to Stomach. The Results of a Survey of Food Advertising on Television*, National Food Alliance, 1995.

10 'Even Britons Do Not Like British Food, a Survey Finds', *Guardian*, 11 October 1996, p. 3.

11 Tim Lang, Martin Caraher, Paul Dixon and Roy Carr-Hill, 'Class, Income and Gender in Cooking: Results from an English Survey', paper for International Conference on Culinary Arts and Sciences, Bournemouth University, June 1996.

12 George Ritzer, *The McDonaldization of Society*, Thousand Oaks: Pine Forge Press (Sage), 1993.

13 Chris Bourchier, 'European Agriculture – A Ten Year Plan', in *Agricultural Strategy*, ADAS, 1995, pp. 4–12.

14 D. Goodman and M. Redclift, *Refashioning Nature: Food, Ecology and Culture*, Routledge, 1991.

15 David Nelson Smith, 'Food or Famine: Politics, Economics and Science in the World's Food Supply', *Proceedings of the Brighton Crop Protection Conference 1995*, Vol. 1, pp. 3–15, British Crop Protection Council, 1995.

16 Geoff Tansey and Tony Worsley, op. cit., pp. 124–6.

17 Andrew Wileman, 'The Shift in Balance of Power Between Retailers and Manufacturers', paper presented at Food Industry and Food Trade: Cooperation or Confrontation? Impact on All Levels of the Food Chain, The European Food Industry Conference Management Centre Europe, June 1992, cited by Geoff Tansey and Tony Worsley, op. cit., p. 125.

18 Food From Britain: Vegetable Sector Group Report, 1992, p. 8.

19 Hugh Raven and Tim Lang, *Off Our Trolleys: Food Retailing and the Hypermarket Economy*, Institute for Public Policy Research, 1995, p. 20.

20 'Surveys of Pesticide Residues in Food', Report by the British Association of Public Analysts, cited in Nigel Dudley, *This Poisoned Earth*, Piatkus, 1987.

21 Report of the Working Party on Pesticide Residues 1993, HMSO, 1994.

22 Report of the Working Party on Pesticide Residues 1995, HMSO, 1996.

23 *Rural England: A Nation Committed to a Living Countryside*, HMSO, 1995, p. 113.

24 SAFE Alliance, 1992, cited in Peter Beaumont, *Pesticides, Policies and People: A Guide to the Issues*, The Pesticides Trust, 1993.

25 BBC CountryFile, *The Great Debate*, 1995.

26 Report of the Working Party on Pesticide Residues 1988–89, HMSO, 1990.

27 Report of the Working Party on Pesticide Residues 1989–90, HMSO, 1991.

28 *Consumer Risk Assessment of Insecticide Residues in Carrots*, Pesticides Safety Directorate, 1995.

29 *Neuropsychological Effects of Long-term Exposure to Organophosphates in Sheep Dip*, Report from the Institute of Occupational Health, 1995.

30 Report of the Research Consultative Committee Residues Subgroup, HMSO, cited by Peter Beaumont, op. cit.

31 Report of the Working Party on Pesticide Residues 1995, op. cit.

32 *NFU/Retailer Integrated Crop Management Protocol – Fresh Cauliflower*, National Farmers' Union, June 1993.

33 *Green Tokenism: A Look Behind the Labels*, report of the Soil Association, 1996.

34 *The Quiet Revolution: A Customer Guide to Pesticide Reduction*, J. Sainsbury, 1996.

35 Marks and Spencer advertisement, in the *Independent*, 23 June 1996.

36 Emma Delow, 'Food For Thought', *Living Earth*, No. 189, January 1996.

37 Professor Michael Crawford, 'Too Much Fat in the Land', in *Living Earth*, No. 189, January 1996.

38 'Investing in Quality, Innovation, Freshness and Value', Marks and Spencer, Annual Report and Financial Statement, 1995, p. 14.

39 Jane Seymour, 'Hungry For a New Revolution', *New Scientist*, 30 March 1996, pp. 33–7.

10   THE WASTING GROUND

1 Down to Earth: Environmental Problems Associated with Soil Degradation in the English Landscape, CPRE, October 1994.

2 Edward Long, 'When Winter Rains Carry Off the Earth', *Farming News*, 25 August 1995.

3 Chambers and Garwood (1995), cited in Royal Commission on Environmental Pollution 19th Report: Sustainable Use of Soil, HMSO, 1996.

4 J. Boardman (1988, 1993), cited in Down To Earth: Environmental Problems Associated With Soil Degradation in the English Landscape, CPRE, October 1994.

5 Professor Peter Bullock, interview on 'The Farming Week', BBC Radio 4, 30 January 1993.

6   R. Evans, *Soil Erosion and its Impacts in England and Wales*, Friends of the Earth Trust, 1996.

7   *Code of Good Agricultural Practice for the Protection of Soil*, MAFF/Welsh Office, 1993.

8   T. W. Garwood et al., 'Phosphorus Losses from Eroded Arable Fields', *Journal of the Science of Food and Agriculture* (in press), cited in Royal Commission on Environmental Pollution 19th Report: Sustainable Use of Soil, HMSO, 1996.

9   National Rivers Authority, *Pesticides in the aquatic environment*, HMSO, 1995.

10 'Pesticide Use Controls Needed MAFF Pollution Study Shows', ENDS Report 243, April 1995, cited in *Sustainable Agriculture in the UK*, CPRE/WWF, 1996.

11 'Isoproturon All-clear Sets a Precedent for Other Vital Pesticides', *Farmers Weekly*, 8 September 1995.

12 'DoE Pesticide Study Supports Water Protection Zones', ENDS Report 242, March 1995, cited in *Sustainable Agriculture in the UK*, CPRE/WWF, 1996.

13 Mark Redman, *Industrial Agriculture: Counting the Costs*, Soil Association, September 1996.

14 Royal Commission on Environmental Pollution 19th Report: Sustainable Use of Soil, HMSO, 1996.

15 Professor John Krebs, 'Environmental Obligations', paper to the 50th Oxford Farming Conference, January 1996.

16 *The Influence of Agriculture on the Quality of Natural Waters in England and Wales*, NRA Water Quality Series No. 6, 1992.

17 Michael Winter, *Rural Politics: Policies for Agriculture, Forestry and the Environment*, Routledge, 1996.

18 'Environment Agency Attacks Government Laxity on Nitrates', *Farmers Weekly*, 9 February 1996, p. 15.

19 'Agriculture and England's Environment', MAFF News Release, 10 August 1993.

20 Robert Irving, *Too Much of a Good Thing: Nutrient Enrichment in the UK's Inland and Coastal Waters*, WWF (UK), October 1993.

21 'NVZ Men Face a £10m Tab for EC Compliance', *Farmers Weekly*, 8 December 1995, p. 8.

22 John Krebs, op. cit.

23 *Sustainable Development: The UK Strategy*, Command Paper 2426, HMSO, 1994.

24 'Biotechnology is the Key to a Competitive Future', NFU News Release, 26 February 1996.

25 G. Henderson, *The Farming Ladder*, Faber and Faber, 1944, p. 35.

11 A PLACE IN THE COUNTRY

1 David Hencke and Edward Pilkington, 'MPs Test Mood on Home Farms', *Guardian*, 22 March 1996.
2 'Farmer's Views on Land Controversy', *Target*, 24 January 1996.
3 *Rural England: A Nation Committed to a Living Countryside*, HMSO, 1995.
4 H. J. Massingham, *The English Countryman*, Batsford, 1942.
5 George Monbiot, 'Whose Land?', *Guardian*, 22 February, 1995.
6 Richard Norton-Taylor, *Whose Land is it Anyway*, Turnstone Press, 1982.
7 Michael Winter, *Rural Politics: Policies for Agriculture, Forestry and the Environment*, Routledge, 1996.
8 *Farmers Weekly*, 11 October 1996, p. 104.
9 Ibid. p. 99.
10 Richard Norton-Taylor, op. cit.
11 Savills Agricultural Research Briefing, No. 6, February 1996.
12 Brown and Co, *Landbrief*, Issue No. 5, Winter 1995/96.
13 'Royal Insurance Plans to Sell 22,500 Acres', *Farming News*, 16 June 1995.
14 'Royal Life Unit Goes to Grower in Private Deal', *Farmers Weekly*, 17 November 1995.
15 '£60 Million Record Deal Set', *Farmers Weekly*, 3 November 1995.
16 Lands Improvement Holdings PLC, official listing document, June 1996.
17 Simon Fairlie, 'Green and Peasant Land', *Guardian*, 22 March 1995.
18 George Monbiot, op. cit.
19 'Bubble Settlers Given Warning After Water Tests', *Western Gazette*, 27 July 1995.
20 *Hansard*, 30 January 1996, Column 781.
21 'MP's "Right to Roam" Bill Basically Flawed Claims CLA', Country Landowners' Association News Release, 26 January 1996.
22 *Rural England – A Nation Committed to a Living Countryside*, op. cit.

12 BREAKING THE CHAINS

1 Nicolas Lampkin, 'Impact of EC Regulation 2078/92 on the Development of Organic Farming in the European Union', paper to CEOFAR/IFOAM Seminar on Organic Agriculture, Vignola, Italy, June 1996.

13 A LIVING COUNTRYSIDE

1 'Sentry Cuts Costs to Record Low', *Farmers Weekly*, 22 March 1996.
2 *European Agriculture: The Case for Radical Reform. Conclusions*, MAFF, 1995.
3 Ronnie Horesh, *Farming for the Market: The New Zealand Experience*, MAF Policy, Wellington, New Zealand, February 1995.
4 Tony Bailey, *A Rural Policy for Europe*, speech to the European Parliament, Country Landowners' Association, April 1995.
5 D. Pimentel et al., 'Environmental and Economic Costs of Pesticide Use', *BioScience* 42 (10), 1992, pp. 750–60.
6 David Pearce, *The Environmental Consequences of CAP Reform*, Notes to the MAFF CAP Review Group, Centre for Social and Economic Research on the Global Environment, University College London, May 1995.
7 *Pesticides: Missing the Target*, a report by the Pesticides Trust for the World Wide Fund for Nature (UK), November 1992.
8 'Safe Spray or Danish Way', *Farmers Weekly*, 29 March 1996, p. 53.
9 David Pearce, op. cit.
10 Christopher Haskins, *Some Options for CAP Reform*, paper for the Liberal Democrat Forum for the Countryside, November 1995.
11 V. W. L. Jordan, J. A. Hutcheon, D. M. Glen and D. P. Farmer, *The Life Project*, IACR–Long Ashton Research Station, Bristol, 3rd edition, 1996.
12 Organic farming: Are you overlooking a profitable opportunity?, Notes from MAFF Organic Farming Unit, 1996.
13 Patrick Minford, *Britain and Europe: The Balance Sheet, European Business Review/New European/Centre* for European Studies, 1996.
14 *European Agriculture: The Case for Radical Reform. Working Papers*, MAFF, 1995.
15 K. J. Thomson, *Evaluation Studies of the Common Agricultural Policy*, background paper for the National Consumer Council, 1987.
16 *Agricultural Policy in the European Union: The Consumer Agenda for Reform*, National Consumer Council, 1995.
17 European Commission, *From the farmer... to the consumer*, Green Europe No. 1, Brussels, 1990.
18 Peter Segger, Managing Director, Organic Farm Foods, Lampeter, personal communication, 1996.
19 Tim Finney, Marketing Manager, Eastbrook Farm Meats, Swindon, personal communication, June 1996.

INDEX